Solve it!

Version 7.0

Management Problem Solving with Excel, Access, and the World Wide Web

Spreadsheet and Database Cases for Excel and Access with Internet Web Cases

Kenneth C. Laudon
New York University

Megan Miller
Azimuth Interactive, Inc.

Robin L. Pickering
Azimuth Interactive, Inc.

New Directions in Learning
Visit us online: www.MySolveIT.com

1

Introduction to *Solve it!*

Welcome to the challenge of *Solve it!*

Solve it! is a learning system that teaches management problem-solving skills through the use of spreadsheet and database software. *Solve it!* is designed for use by college and university students in schools of business and management.

The management cases in this *Solve it!* package will help you learn how to address management problems using contemporary spreadsheet and database software. The cases are all derived from actual business applications.

When you successfully complete these cases, you will have mastered the basics of the software and learned how to apply this knowledge in realistic settings.

Learn Through Discovery

Solve it! uses real world case studies to present students with problems and challenges. The cases range from small businesses on Main Street to banks and brokerage firms on Wall Street to government agencies. It's up to you to discover the answers.

For each case there is a corresponding data file that your instructor will provide to you. You will then be asked to enter new data, formulas, and data fields, and to create reports, queries, and lists in response to business problems posed in the cases.

In general, we have sought to keep the amount of elementary data entry to a bare minimum and to emphasize conceptual tasks. The cases do not require advanced financial analysis or accounting skills. Explanations are provided for all formulas and analytic tasks.

Industry Standard

Solve it! is widely used in Fortune 1000 training programs. It is designed to bring students and working professionals up to a common intermediate level of proficiency in Microsoft Excel and Access. Beyond this level, industry training programs and seminars are advised for more advanced training.

Many universities and businesses use one of several powerful alternatives to Excel and Access. *Solve it!* works well with Access work-alikes and Linux-based databases. *Solve it!* also works with most known spreadsheet programs.

You may also use the data files included with *Solve it!* on Macintosh computers using software such as Microsoft Excel. You can use the *Solve it!* data files with any Macintosh software that can read .XLS, .DBF, and/or ASCII files. Ask your instructor for more information.

You may wish to keep both the book and the completed and graded exercises to show potential employers precisely what skills you have learned. You should also place this information on your resume.

Classic Business Problems

Solve it! uses cases that illustrate classic business problems typically encountered in the real world, such as net present value analysis, payroll accounting, inventory management, break-even analysis, accounts receivable aging reports, pro forma financial statements, quality assurance, production planning, marketing database management, sales management systems, and personnel tracking.

When you complete the cases in *Solve it!*, you will be well prepared to work effectively in a contemporary business environment.

Web Exercises and Cases

The Web is a major source of information and analysis for business professionals. It is very important that business students learn how to integrate this information into desktop spreadsheet and database programs, and how to analyze Web-based data for management purposes.

Solve it! includes a new chapter of exercises and case studies that explore the use of the Web in business problem solving. The Web has proved itself to be a valuable research tool for business. On the Web, you can discover industry trends, statistics, growth patterns, markets, and resources—in short, all the ingredients needed to make a well-informed business plan. The Web cases in Chapter 6 will show you how to use the Web to build a business plan and also help you explore other features of the Web.

Documentation Included

Solve it! contains all the documentation you will need on how to use Office 2010 spreadsheet software like Excel and database software like Access. The documentation is provided in the form of hands-on tutorials that show you how to use the software skills required by each of the cases. The cases and documentation were written using Microsoft Excel 2010 and Access 2010 for Windows. You will find the spreadsheet data files in *Solve it!* are compatible with all versions of the software. In general, the documentation instructions work equally well for clone software with only minor changes.

If you are using earlier versions of Excel or Access (as opposed to Excel or Access 2010), be sure to check the Web site and download the Excel 97- 2003 student data files and Access 2003–2007 files. In general, Access is downwardly compatible (newer versions will open older version files) but not upwardly compatible.

Students may wish to consult the original documentation for the software being used or any one of several large reference manuals. These are generally available in your computer lab or your corporate or college library.

Solve it! assumes students have a basic familiarity with the Windows operating system. If this is not the case, you should read through an introductory text on Windows or the Windows Users Guide.

The Skills Matrix

In order to select and develop cases, we created a Skills Matrix to identify both the software and management skills we sought to teach.

The Skills Matrix for spreadsheet software is shown on the following page (see Figure 1-1). A similar matrix is used for database problems.

Solve it! is designed to teach the management skills that allow you to organize, plan, coordinate, decide, and control. The software skills we will teach are basic (set-up and editing), intermediate (data analysis and organization), and advanced (database management, programming, and interfaces).

4   Solve it!

Each *Solve it!* package contains a mix of skill levels and skill areas. Approximately one-third of the problems involve basic software skills and elementary management skills of organization and planning. The remaining cases develop intermediate and advanced software skills along with more advanced management skills.

Figure 1-1

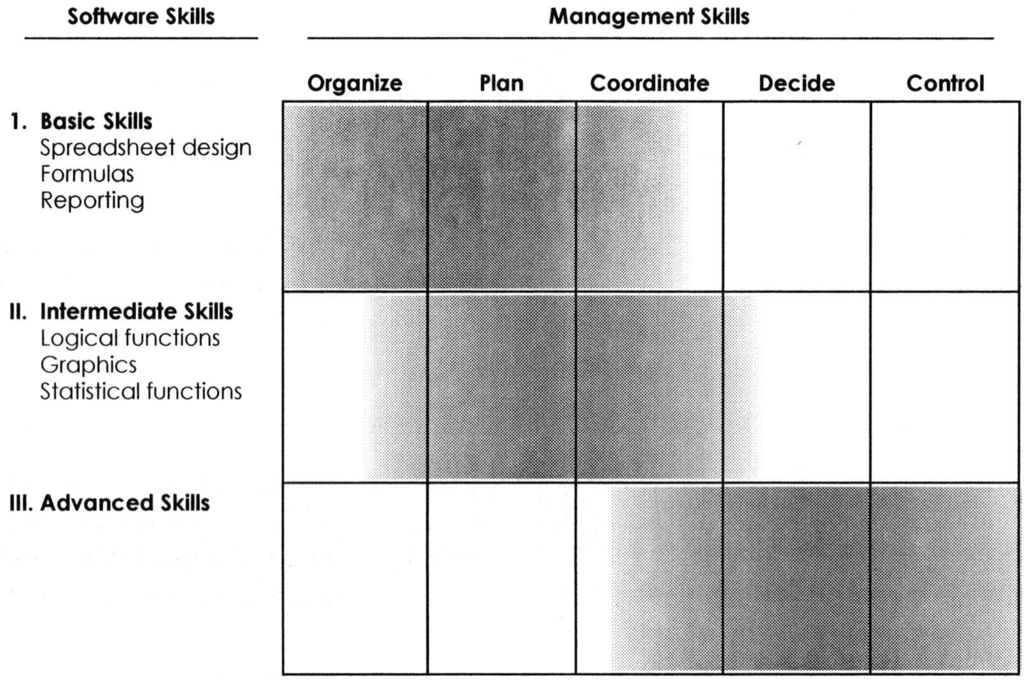

Software Skills	Management Skills				
	Organize	Plan	Coordinate	Decide	Control
1. Basic Skills Spreadsheet design Formulas Reporting	▓	▓	▓		
II. Intermediate Skills Logical functions Graphics Statistical functions		▓	▓		
III. Advanced Skills			▓	▓	▓

As you proceed from beginning to more advanced cases, the problems become less structured and more analytic. More advanced cases require a written summary.

In the beginning, each *Solve it!* case identifies the specific skills involved in the case. Also included are the approximate completion times for persons at different skill levels. These estimated times are based on our experience in university classrooms and industry settings.

How to Use *Solve it!*

There are 13 spreadsheet cases, 11 database cases, and 9 Web cases in each *Solve it!* package. The cases are graduated in difficulty, both in terms of software skills and management skills. The cases are short enough to be answered in one computer session lasting no more than 2 to 3 hours for a novice.

Each case has an estimated completion time. Students are strongly advised not to skip early problems. If you skip early problems, you will not learn the software skills required in later cases. This will, in turn, lengthen the time required to answer later cases by several hours.

A Tutorial Documentation section that carefully describes the software skills needed to solve each case follows the case. The software skills are demonstrated using a sample spreadsheet file (Course.xlsx) and a sample database file (Friends.accdb) that you will create in the tutorial sections.

You should first read the case to understand the nature of the problem. You should then study the Tutorial carefully to be sure you understand how the software works. Finally, you should begin work on the case itself.

How to Cope With Ambiguity in Cases

Because *Solve it!* cases are derived from real world events and circumstances, they often contain ambiguities—just like the real world itself. In advanced cases, you will typically find more than one way to solve a problem, and you will find that certain assumptions and value judgments must be made to arrive at any solution.

You should first clearly identify the nature of the ambiguity. Then consider the alternative solutions. Choose the solution you prefer and specifically state the assumptions and value judgments you are making. Be prepared to defend these assumptions, as well as to learn from others who made different assumptions.

System Requirements

Solve it! assumes that you have some basic computer knowledge, including the operating system. *Solve it!* provides specific instructions on how to start up the software in the special **Getting Started** sections of Chapters 2 and 4.

Solve it! assumes you are using a PC with at least 256 megabytes of RAM and sufficient hard disk capacity to run the application software. You must also be connected a printer with graphics capabilities.

General Instructions for Working With Student Data Files

1. Ask your instructor to provide you with a copy of the Solve it! student data files. Student data files contain the required case data and sample tutorial files for the exercises in this book.

2. Read the appropriate case study in the case book to identify the specific data file used in the case. This will also provide an overview of the case's basic issues. On the first page of each case, the appropriate student data file is identified.

3. Start Excel (or Access) and then open the case study data file required by the case.

You are now ready to begin. Chapter 2 introduces you to spreadsheet software in general, and specifically guides you through the basics of Microsoft Excel. This is followed by 13 spreadsheet business cases in Chapter 3. Chapter 4 introduces you to database concepts and Microsoft Access. This is followed by Chapter 5, which contains 11 database business cases. Chapter 6 describes the Web and provides 9 cases for you to solve.

2

Introduction to Spreadsheet Software

An *electronic spreadsheet* is the computerized version of traditional financial modeling tools—the accountant's columnar pad, pencil, and calculator. It is organized into a grid of rows and columns. When you change values on an electronic spreadsheet, all other related values on that spreadsheet will be recomputed automatically.

Spreadsheets are especially well suited for business applications that involve numerous calculations involving interrelated pieces of data. The power of spreadsheet software is the ease with which modeling and "what if" analysis can be performed. After a set of mathematical relationships has been constructed, the spreadsheet can be immediately recalculated using a different set of assumptions. As models become more complex, this capability for instant "what-if" analysis becomes even more valuable.

An Excel file is a workbook containing one or more sheets. These worksheets are considered part of the workbook, similar to the pages in a spiral notebook.

This chapter will focus on the basic spreadsheet skills you will need to start solving the spreadsheet cases in Chapter 3.

Introduction to Microsoft Excel

An Excel spreadsheet is divided into rows and columns, with each row and each column uniquely labeled. A sample spreadsheet is shown in Figure 2-1.

Rows are identified numerically, with values ranging from 1 to a maximum of 1,048,576 in Excel 2010. Columns are identified alphabetically, with letters ranging from A to Z and then from AA to AZ, BA to BZ, and so on. Excel 2010 (and its predecessor, Excel 2007) can accommodate a maximum of 16,384 columns. Earlier versions of Excel can handle a maximum of 256 columns and 65,536 rows.

Cells

The intersection of every column and row is called a *cell*. Each cell represents a unique location on the spreadsheet for storing a piece of data. Cells are identified by their column and row coordinates. For example, the cell located at the intersection of column B and row 8 is called B8. The maximum number of cells on the spreadsheet is equal to the number of rows times the number of columns. In Excel 2010, this amounts to over 175 billion cells.

Ranges

A rectangular block of cells is termed a *range*. A range can be a single cell, a row, a column, or several rows and columns. Many Excel commands are based on ranges. Ranges are identified by naming the cells that bound their diagonally opposite corners, thus the data in the columns FIRST NAME, LAST NAME, QUIZ, MIDTERM, and FINAL in Figure 2-1 would be identified as the range A1:E1. Range naming conventions require that you separate the cell addresses that specify the boundaries of the range by a colon, e.g., A1:E5. Ranges may also consist of nonadjacent cells and groups of nonadjacent blocks of cells that are selected by holding down the control key while highlighting them.

Another way to specify a range is to use a *range name*. Naming a range can make selecting and using ranges easier, especially if you need to select the same range frequently for different tasks or if the range is very large. For instance, we could name the range E2:E5, which contains the final grades, FINAL. You will learn how to name ranges later on in this book.

When you work with your spreadsheet, your cursor will always be positioned on one of its cells. The cell where the cursor is presently located is termed the *active cell*. The cell pointer—the thick border that appears on the active cell—identifies the current cell. You can move the cell pointer from one cell to another by clicking the mouse pointer on another cell, or by pressing the arrow keys or other keys defined for movement such as [TAB] or [CTRL]+[Home]. Pressing the [CTRL]+[Home] keys together will move the cell pointer to the upper left-most corner of the spreadsheet, cell A1.

The Excel 2010 Window

Across the top of the Excel window is the **Ribbon**, a central part of the new Office interface introduced with Excel 2007. The Ribbon replaces the Menu bar and

Standard Toolbar of previous editions and contains buttons and drop-down lists for almost all of the Excel commands, grouped into separate tabs according to the general category of task being performed. For example, you make an entry bold by selecting the entry and then clicking the *Bold* button on the Home tab. When you point to a button on the Ribbon, a ScreenTip appears that explains the function of the button and gives a keyboard shortcut, if available. You can also customize the Ribbon completely, from rearranging commands on tabs to creating your own custom tabs of commands. To do so, right-click the Ribbon and select *Customize the Ribbon*, or click the File tab, then *Options*, and then *Customize the Ribbon*.

Above the Ribbon is the **Title bar**, which displays the program name (Microsoft Excel) and the active file name in the center. At the far right of the Title bar, at the top, are the three Excel window controls. These are, in order from leftmost, the *Minimize*, Restore Down/Maximize, and *Close* buttons. You can also control the Excel window by clicking the logo at the far left of the Title bar, which opens a menu with the same commands to restore, move, size, minimize, maximize, and close the Excel window.

Just below the Excel window controls on the right are the three workbook window controls, which allow you to minimize, restore down or maximize, and close just the workbook, without affecting the application window.

To the left of the three workbook window controls are the *Microsoft Excel Help* button and the *Minimize the Ribbon* button. The Help button opens a separate Help window which you can use to browse topics or search for help with Excel. The Minimize the Ribbon button hides and shows the Ribbon.

At the far left of the Title bar is the **Quick Access toolbar**, which contains by default the *Save*, *Undo*, and *Redo* buttons. The Undo and Redo buttons undo (or redo) your last action. For example, if you delete a range of cells by mistake and you want to undo your action, you can click the Undo button to restore these cells. You can specify which buttons are included on the Quick Access toolbar by clicking the down arrow to the right of the toolbar. This opens the Customize Quick Access Toolbar menu with a list of commonly used commands you can add to the toolbar. You can also click *More Commands* and select any Excel command to add to the Quick Access toolbar.

Below the Ribbon, at the far left of the window, is the **Name box**, which displays the name or address of the current selection. To its right is the **Formula bar**, which displays the label, number, formula, or function in the active cell.

Clicking on the **File tab** opens a view similar to the File menu in previous versions of Excel or the Microsoft Office menu of Excel 2007. This view contains commands

10   *Solve it!*

used for working with the current Office document as a whole: for opening, closing, saving, printing, finalizing, publishing, and e-mailing a file, as well as viewing and editing file properties.

Figure 2-1 shows an Excel worksheet screen for a course roster with data entered in the range A1:E5.

Figure 2-1

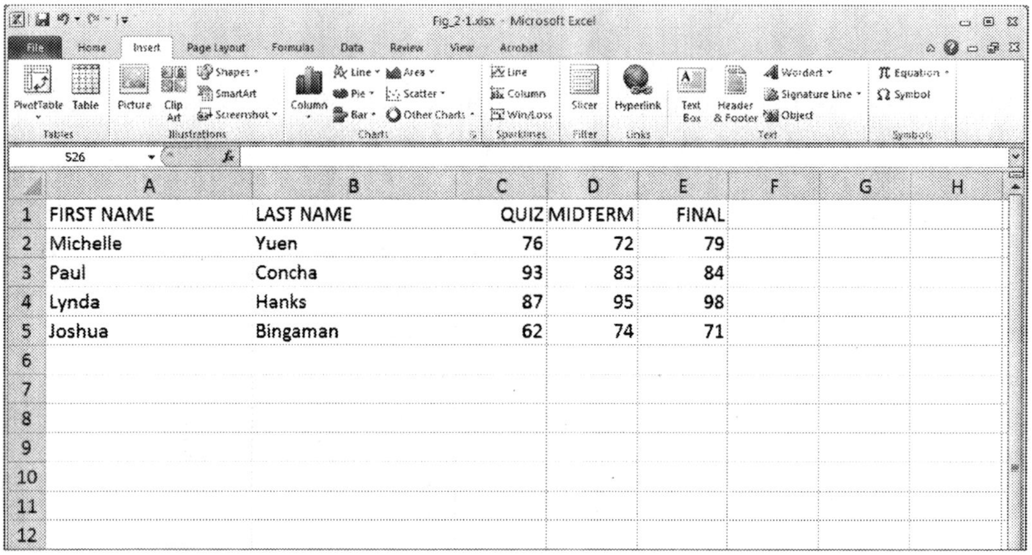

	A	B	C	D	E
1	FIRST NAME	LAST NAME	QUIZ	MIDTERM	FINAL
2	Michelle	Yuen	76	72	79
3	Paul	Concha	93	83	84
4	Lynda	Hanks	87	95	98
5	Joshua	Bingaman	62	74	71

At the very bottom of the Excel window is the **Status bar**, which displays error and status messages or indicators. To the right of the Status bar are three Page View buttons—*Normal*; *Page Layout*, and *Page Break Preview*. Page Layout shows how the spreadsheet would look on the printed page and Page Break Preview shows where on the spreadsheet page breaks will be made. To the right of the Page View buttons is the **Zoom slider** which you use to magnify or reduce the view of the current spreadsheet.

Just above the Status bar, along the bottom is the **Sheet tabs line**, where you can see tabs for the different worksheets within the file. By default, an Excel workbook opens with three worksheets. You can add additional sheets by clicking the *New Tab* icon to the right of the sheet tabs; the number of worksheets permitted is limited only by your computer's available memory. Multiple worksheets allow you to organize the data in the worksheet in meaningful ways. For instance, you could create a Company Payroll Workbook with separate sheets for each department. Data can easily be entered into multiple sheets simultaneously, and it is easy to reference a cell or range on one sheet in another worksheet.

Moving Around the Spreadsheet

Spreadsheets are usually too large to be viewed on the screen in their entirety. To view other parts of the spreadsheet, you must *scroll* the cell pointer up and down the worksheet or across it using the mouse, the arrow keys, or other cursor movement keys. When the cell pointer reaches the edge of the current screen, the screen will shift to follow the cell pointer in the direction in which it is moving.

Clicking the mouse pointer on any cell makes that the current active cell. At the right and at the bottom of the Excel worksheet window are the vertical scroll bar and the horizontal scroll bar. Clicking the arrow buttons on these scroll bars moves your window one row up/down or one column right/left. You can also click on any point inside these scroll bars or drag the scroll box itself, to scroll faster.

You can also use the keyboard to navigate around the spreadsheet. When Excel is in READY mode (the current mode is displayed on the Status bar), various keys will behave as follows:

Excel Keyboard Pointer-Movement Keys

Key	Function
LEFT ARROW	Moves left 1 cell
RIGHT ARROW	Moves right 1 cell
UP ARROW	Moves up 1 cell
DOWN ARROW	Moves down 1 cell
[SHIFT]+[TAB]	Moves left 1 cell
[TAB]	Moves right 1 cell
[PAGE UP]	Moves up 1 screen
[PAGE DOWN]	Moves down 1 screen
[CTRL]+[HOME]	Moves to upper left corner
[CTRL]+[END]	Moves to lower right corner of the active area

Using the Mouse

Like the keyboard, you can use the mouse to choose commands, highlight ranges, resize windows, and perform many other tasks. There are some actions that you perform only with a mouse, such as dragging the border of a cell to increase column width. Whenever a selection is to be made with the mouse, use the left mouse button. Clicking the right mouse button brings up a shortcut menu with an abbreviated set of commands that are relevant to the current selection or active element.

Spreadsheet Commands

Commands are tools provided by spreadsheet software to manipulate the spreadsheet in various ways. For example, there are commands for copying data, formatting your worksheet, or printing your worksheet. Some commands affect the entire worksheet, but others only affect certain cells or ranges.

Some commands are performed by clicking a button, others by selecting an item in a drop-down menu or panel, or by selecting a check box or radio button.

Each tab on the Ribbon contains commands related to a different aspect of working with spreadsheets, and within each tab, commands are further organized into related groups.

The **Home tab** contains the most commonly accessed commands: for formatting fonts, text, numbers, and cells; for applying styles to cells, and for editing, inserting, and deleting rows, columns, and cells. The **Insert tab** contains commands for adding tables, illustrations, charts, links, and special text elements and objects to a spreadsheet. The **Page Layout tab** contains commands for managing the overall appearance and layout of your spreadsheet. The **Formulas tab** has commands for working with formulas and functions, and the **Data tab** contains commands for managing your raw data as well as any data sources linked to your spreadsheet. Commands for proofing, commenting, and handling changes are located on the **Review tab**, while the **View tab** allows you to modify the workbook view, zoom levels, and the Excel window.

Some tabs are context sensitive, and hidden unless you are working with a specific type of spreadsheet element. For example, tabs with commands for manipulating charts will not appear unless a chart is inserted into your spreadsheet and selected. If you are working with special Excel add-in modules, such as Adobe Acrobat, you may also have tabs with commands for working with these modules. You can also create and name custom tabs, with the commands of your choice, by right-clicking the Ribbon and selecting *Customize the Ribbon*.

Some of the buttons on the Ribbon have arrows, indicating that a menu of commands or gallery of options will appear when you click on that arrow. For example, if you click the arrow beside the *Underline (U)* button on the Home tab (in the Font group), a short menu will appear allowing you to apply a standard underline to the currently selected text or a double underline.

Some commands on the Ribbon include text boxes that you can type values directly into, and these may also include an arrow, indicating there are values you can select from a drop-down menu. To the bottom right of some groups of commands you will also see a small, diagonal arrow. This is a dialog box launcher, and clicking it will open a dialog box with a full set of options and commands related to that group of commands. For example, clicking the dialog box launcher in the Font group on the Home tab opens the Font section of the Format Cells dialog box, which allows you to select multiple options for formatting the font within a cell.

You can choose a command from a menu by using the mouse to click on the command or by using the arrow keys on the keyboard to select the command and pressing [Enter]. Some commands can be executed by pressing a series of keys, called a keyboard shortcut, such as [CTRL]+[C]. The keyboard shortcut for a command is listed beside the command in a menu or displayed in the command's ScreenTip when you mouse over the button. Using a keyboard shortcut will activate the command without your needing to select it from the menu. For example, the *Paste* command button on the Home tab displays "Ctrl + V" in its ScreenTip. Pressing the keyboard sequence [CTRL]+[V] (the [Ctrl] key followed by the [V] key) will execute the Paste command.

When you choose a command on a menu it is performed immediately, unless an ellipsis ("…") or arrow is displayed beside it. If the command includes an ellipsis, clicking on that command will open up a dialog box or window that includes additional settings or commands to choose from. If the command includes an arrowhead, pointing to that command will reveal a submenu that includes related commands or options.

In addition to using the mouse to press buttons and select menu items and options, or using keyboard shortcuts, you can also execute commands by using Office 2010's Key Tips. Key Tips allow you to locate and execute any command on the Ribbon by pressing a sequence of keys on the keyboard.

To use Key Tips, you first press [ALT] on the keyboard to display the Key Tips for each tab on the Ribbon. These Key Tips are displayed in small boxes on the Ribbon. You press the key for the tab you wish to open. This opens the selected tab, which displays Key Tips for each command or group of commands on the tab. You then press one or more keys to locate and execute a command.

For example, to execute the *Double Underline* command, you first press [ALT] on the keyboard to activate and display Key Tips in the Excel window. You then press [H] to select the Home tab, then [3] to select the Underline menu, and then [D] to select the Double Underline command. Pressing [ESC] at any time will return you to the previous command, and you can press [ESC] multiple times to bring you out of Key Tips mode altogether.

Setting up a Worksheet

Consult with your technical support specialist about how to install and configure Excel for your particular computer system and whether you are allowed to make a backup copy of the program.

To illustrate how spreadsheet software works, we will be developing a simple spreadsheet with which you are already familiar. Let's start by creating a course roster containing the student names and grades for a quiz, a midterm, and a final exam. The final product will look like Figure 2-1.

Assuming Excel has been properly installed, and you are using Windows 7 as the operating system, you start by clicking the *Start* button, pointing to *All Programs*, pointing to *Microsoft Office*, and then finally clicking *Microsoft Office Excel 2010*. In some cases, Excel will already be placed on the Quick Start Menu, which is a list of programs that you commonly use. In this case, click *Start* and you will see a list of programs above. Click on *Excel* if it is present. Excel will open up with a blank worksheet. You can now start working with your worksheet.

How to Enter Data into a Worksheet

The student roster illustrated in Figure 2-1 is a very simple list. You need only enter data regarding the student's names and grades. No calculations are required. You can start at cell A1 and enter your column headings. Enter FIRST NAME in cell A1, LAST NAME in B1, QUIZ in C1, MIDTERM in D1, and FINAL in E1.

You enter data into a cell by moving the cell pointer to the cell, typing in the entry. The insertion point indicates where the next character you type will appear. Each character you enter also appears in the Formula bar. When you are finished typing in the entry, press [ENTER] to move to the next cell down or [TAB] to move to the next cell across.

In addition to pressing [ENTER] or [TAB], you can complete a cell entry by clicking on another cell or by pressing one of the arrow keys on the keyboard. This will complete the entry and move the cell pointer to another cell as directed by the mouse or the arrow key. You can also click the *Enter* button on the Formula bar (this only appears after data has been entered into the current cell.) If you do this, the cell entry will be confirmed, but the cell pointer will remain in the current cell.

You can complete your roster by entering the student names in cells A2 through B5, the quiz grades in cells C2 through C5, the midterm grades in cells D2 through D5, and the final grades in cells E2 through E5.

How to Change Column Widths

You will notice that the first two column headings, FIRST NAME and LAST NAME, are truncated. This occurs because the column widths are at the default width of 8.43 characters[1]. Both of these headings have more characters than this and Excel cuts off both entries at the right edges of the cells. (However, were the cell to the right of Column A or B empty, the heading would carry over to display in the next blank cell.)

Sometimes pound signs (#####) will appear in a cell containing a numeric value. This happens when the column width is too narrow to accommodate the number of places in the numeric value plus additional punctuation for decimal points, commas, dollar signs, etc.

You can make column widths smaller or larger by using the **Column Width** command. Let's reset the column for student names in our example to 20 characters.

First, select the range for which you would like to adjust the column width. You can select a range by first clicking at the center of the cell and then holding the mouse button down while dragging the mouse pointer to the opposite corner of the range. To select more than one range at a time, keep the [CTRL] key pressed while selecting the next range. In our example, we need to select an entire column, which can be done in an easier manner. Every column in the worksheet has column headings (A, B, C, etc.) just above the first row of the worksheet. Clicking on a column heading selects the entire column. Click on Column A and you will find the whole column highlighted.

On the Home tab of the Ribbon, click *Format* in the Cells group and the Format drop-down menu will appear. Click *Column Width*. This opens the Column Width dialog box. Enter the desired width, *20* (for 20 characters), in the *Column width* text box and then click the *OK* button.

You can also change column widths by using the mouse. Position your mouse on the border between two column headers (such as B and C) to show the horizontal resize pointer ↔ and drag to the right or left. If you position the mouse directly on the line between the two letters and rapidly double-click, the column will be

---

[1] Measured according to the font specified as the workbook's default font.

auto fitted to the exact size needed to display the contents of all the cells in the row or column.

Values and Labels

Excel has two types of cell entries: *values* and *labels*. Values are numbers, functions, or formulae. Labels are used for text entries within your spreadsheet. Labels cannot be used in calculations.

As long as there is a letter in the cell, Excel will recognize the entry as a label, even if the entry begins with a numerical character. The entry will always be treated as a value if the beginning character is one of the following:

> = + - $

Position the cell pointer on the student first name *Michelle*. Then position it on the column heading FIRST NAME. You will notice that the formula bar displays Michelle, then FIRST NAME. Any cell containing a letter is considered a label. The entries can be aligned left, right, or center, but labels are left-aligned by default.

Aligning Labels

You can right-align the labels above the grades by selecting them and clicking the *Align Text Right* button or center them by clicking the *Center* button, both located in the Alignment group on the Home tab. Alternatively, you can click the Alignment group's dialog box launcher to open the Alignment tab of the Format Cells dialog box. Practice aligning labels by selecting QUIZ, MIDTERM, and FINAL and right aligning them within their cells.

Numbers in Excel

In Excel, a number cannot contain spaces and is limited to only one decimal point. The method for changing cell formats for displaying a number will be discussed later. A number can be entered in scientific notation, or it can end with a percent sign (%) to indicate percentage. When a number ends with a percent sign, Excel will divide the number that precedes the sign by 100.

Let's review the student roster you've entered. At this point, the labels will all be right-aligned except for FIRST NAME and LAST NAME, and the numbers will be right-aligned as well. The width of columns A and B will be 20 characters, and the width of the rest of the columns will remain at the default value of 8.43 characters. The worksheet will look like Figure 2-1.

How to Edit Data

There are three ways you can edit a cell entry:

1. You can enter data into a cell that already contains information using the same procedure for entering data into an empty cell. This will cause the new data to replace the earlier entry.

2. You can also use the [F2] key (also called the Edit key) to edit data in a cell. Position the cell pointer on the cell you wish to edit and press the [F2] key. This will switch Excel into EDIT mode. The easier way to switch into the EDIT mode is to click inside the Formula bar on the edit line (where the contents of an active cell appear). You can also double-click a cell to edit its contents.

3. Position the cell pointer on the cell you wish to edit and then position your cursor in the Formula bar at the point where you want to make the change. Press the [ENTER] key when you have finished making the correction.

Erasing Worksheet Data

To delete data in a cell, click inside the cell and then click the *Clear* button in the Home tab's Editing group. In the menu that displays, click *Clear Contents*. You can also simply press the [DELETE] key or right-click a cell and then select *Clear Contents* from the shortcut menu.

If you want to delete an entire range of cells, you first have to select the range that you want to delete. If the range you want to delete is A1:B2 (4 cells), click cell A1, hold the mouse button down, and drag the mouse pointer to B2. This procedure highlights the range selected. Once the range is selected, you can press the [DELETE] key or use the *Clear Contents* command.

If you wish to delete both the contents and the formatting of the cell, it is necessary to click the *Clear* button on the Ribbon and then select either *Clear Formats* or *Clear All*. If you do not clear the formatting when you delete the contents, you may occasionally create errors—such as numbers being displayed as dates. This can happen because certain formatting occurs automatically, i.e., keying a date into a cell will cause that cell to be formatted for a date even after the date itself is deleted.

Moving Data

It is a good idea to document each worksheet you create. Figure 2-2 illustrates how the worksheet we just created could be documented. Cell A1 explains the purpose of the worksheet. Cell A2 provides the name and location of the worksheet file. Cell A3 identifies the author of the worksheet and the date it was created.

We need to make room for this documentation at the top of the worksheet by moving the worksheet down five rows. To do this, first highlight the range A1:E5 using the mouse. On the Home tab of the Ribbon, in the Clipboard group, click *Cut*. This will send the data in the selected range to the Clipboard so it can be pasted elsewhere using the Paste command. Then click in cell A6 (which is where you want the upper-left corner of your selected range to be) and click the *Paste* button on the Ribbon (also in the Clipboard group).

You could also move the grades data down by inserting rows above. To insert one row at a time above a selected cell, click *Insert* on the Home tab of the Ribbon, in the Cell group, and then click *Insert Sheet Rows*. To insert multiple rows at a time, you can first highlight the number of rows you would like to insert. For instance, if you want to insert three rows at the beginning of your worksheet, you would select the first three rows using the mouse and click *Insert* and then *Insert Sheet Rows*, and this will add three rows above the selected rows. You can use the same procedures to insert single or multiple columns using the *Insert Sheet Columns* command.

Once you have moved the worksheet down, you can enter the documentation in cells A1 through A3 so that your worksheet looks like Figure 2-2. Note that the contents of these cells seem to extend into the blank cells in Columns B through F because the cells to the right of A1 to A3 are empty.

How to Save Files

You will learn more about formatting and organizing the worksheet in the case problems later in this book. Let's save the practice worksheet for future use. To save a file, you use either the Save or the Save As command. These Save commands will make an exact copy of your worksheet on disk, including any special formats and settings you have specified.

First, click the File tab. This replaces the view of the worksheet with a full-page display of file-related commands, called the Backstage View. The Backstage view is where you manage the file itself, rather than the spreadsheet data in the file. File commands are listed in the left pane, and further information and options for these commands appear in the panes to the right.

At the top of the left pane, click *Save*. If this is the first time that you are working on this file and saving it, this will open the Save As dialog box. Excel will provide a default filename (book1.xlsx) in the *File name* box. You can click inside this box,

Introduction to Spreadsheet Software 19

Figure 2-2

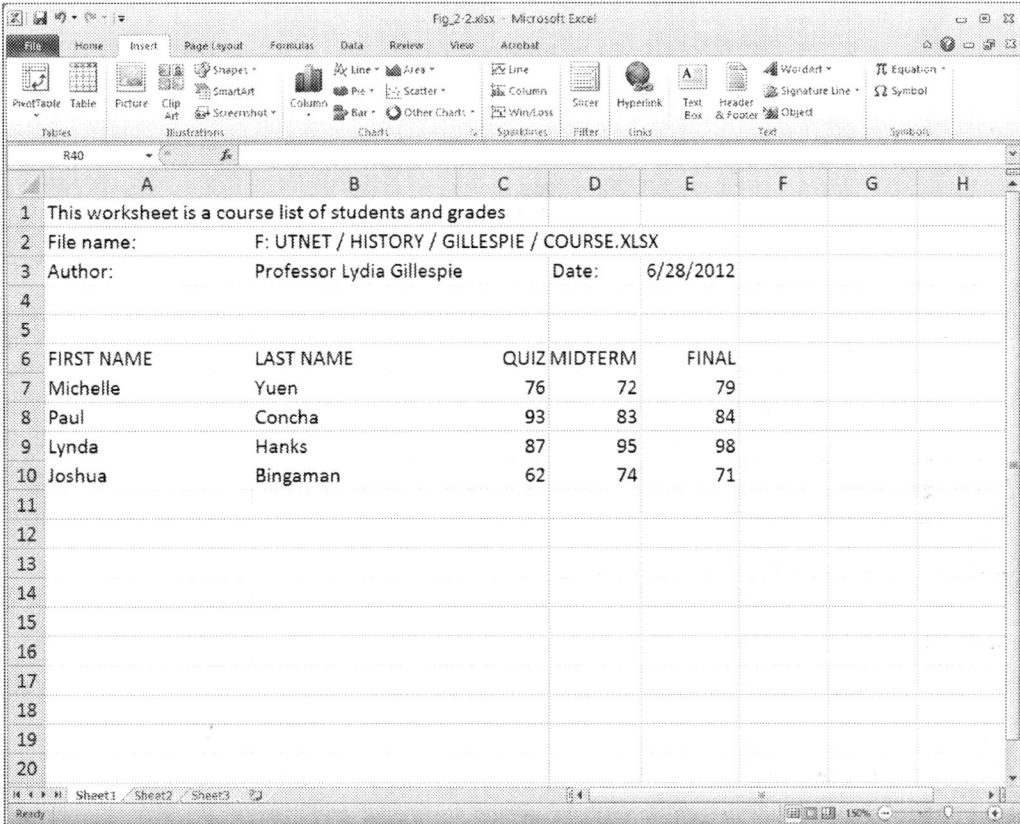

delete the default name, and type in a name (such as *Course*) that you choose for the worksheet. The *Save in* box indicates the drive and folder in which Excel will store the file. (The drive and folder are established during configuration, but they can be changed.) You can change the folder in which you want to save the file by clicking the *Save in* list arrow.

Enter the name you have assigned to your worksheet file in the *File name* box and click *Save*. Let's call the worksheet COURSE. The file name can contain uppercase or lowercase letters, numbers, and most symbols. When you save a file, Excel will automatically assign a three or four character extension, depending on the type of file you are saving. The extension *.xlsx* is used for an Excel 2010 or 2007 workbook. You could choose to save the file in a new location or using other formats (including Web page or XML format) using the *Save As* command. If you want your file to be compatible with earlier versions of Excel, click the arrow at the right of the *Save as* type box and select *Excel 97-2003 workbook (*.xls)* as the file type.

> Be sure to save COURSE.xlsx after you use it for a tutorial. You can save it under the same name after each tutorial session. Most of the changes you make to your worksheet during a tutorial will be required by subsequent sessions. Follow tutorial instructions to determine what changes to your worksheet must be saved or erased.

Ending Your Excel Session

To exit Excel, click the *Close* button at the far right of the Title bar. It is a good practice to save all your files and close them before quitting. If you have not saved a file, Excel brings up a dialog box that asks if you want to save the file before the program closes. Click the *Yes* button to save the file or the *No* button to discard the changes and exit. Clicking on *Cancel* takes you back into Excel in READY mode.

Spreadsheet Design Principles

Like any helpful tool, Excel worksheets can be abused and misused, especially if worksheets are carelessly built, poorly documented, and based on false assumptions. These problems can be minimized by following a few basic principles of spreadsheet design that have emerged over the last decade.

Your spreadsheets can be more easily understood by using a five-section design. In the first section, at the top, enter the company name and a title for the spreadsheet that accurately reflects the subject matter of the spreadsheet. After the title, the spreadsheet is organized into four sections: Documentation, Assumptions, Input and calculations, and Ranges. These sections are illustrated in Figure 2-3.

The purpose of the documentation section is to describe where the spreadsheet is stored, who created it, when, what ranges are used, and what macros are used. Try to keep your descriptions simple and to the point. You can divide the Documentation section into five separate lines. In companies, spreadsheets and other documents are often stored on network drives, or special project drives,

The third section in a spreadsheet is used for assumptions. Assumptions are used throughout spreadsheets to drive the calculations in formulas. It is important that all the basic assumptions used to create the output are clearly identified. In Figure 2-3, we are assuming an annual sales growth figure of 10%. This could, of course, change, and assumptions are frequently changed in spreadsheets to test various "what-if" scenarios. For instance, the results of this worksheet will be different if we change the assumption for annual sales growth to 5% or to 15%. By isolating

Introduction to Spreadsheet Software 21

Figure 2-3

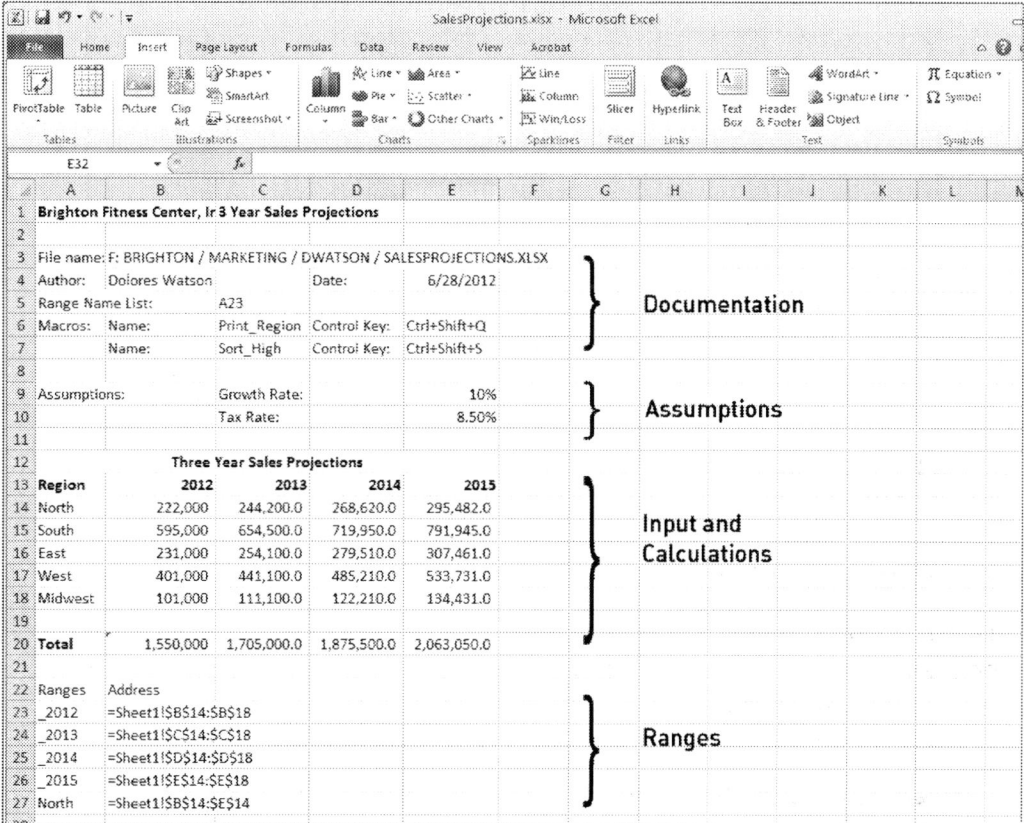

the assumptions in a specific section, it is very easy to change the spreadsheet as conditions change.

The fourth section is the input and calculations section. The input data are the raw data that are supplied by the author of the spreadsheet. In the spreadsheet illustrated here, the data consist of the names of the sales regions and the actual sales figures for 2012. Calculated results are also displayed in this section. For instance, in this spreadsheet, the sales for 2012 are raw data that reflect actual sales in 2012. Sales numbers to the right for years 2013 to 2015 are calculated based on the assumed 10% sales growth rate. Also, the totals for all columns are calculated results produced by Excel.

The fifth section in a spreadsheet, Ranges, provides a list of the ranges used in the spreadsheet and their address locations.

22 *Solve it!*

The worksheet files on your data disk are designed to encourage you to use these spreadsheet design principles, with the first lines of each worksheet file reserved for documentation. The *Solve it!* worksheet files provide much of the data for the input section of the worksheet. You will then complete the input and calculation sections of the worksheet to develop the solution for the spreadsheet case. If required by the problem, you can add an assumptions section by inserting rows above the input section or by moving the input section down several rows.

3

Spreadsheet Management Software Cases

Spreadsheet Case 1
IceBlast Cleaning

Problem:	Develop a client prospect tracking system
Management skills:	Organization Controlling
Excel skills:	Entering Labels, Dates and Hyperlink Fields Worksheet formatting Printing
File:	ICEBLASTCLEANING_Q.xlsx

Tye White is a sales representative with IceBlast Cleaning, a small industrial cleaning firm located in Henderson, Kentucky. His boss has instructed him to increase sales by 12% by attracting new clients. White locates the names of small businesses by using telephone directories, mailing lists, and the Internet. He makes a list of these sales prospects, noting the company name, telephone number, and the owner's name and email address if available. Then he starts telephoning or emailing them to describe IceBlast Cleaning's services.

If White's prospects are interested but not ready to sign up, he contacts them again one week later. Sometimes White forgets whether he has called or emailed a prospect and either contacts them again or forgets to follow up at all. Therefore,

23

24   Solve it!

White needs a way to keep track of prospects and contacts that he can easily consult and update.

Load the worksheet file ICEBLASTCLEANING_Q.xlsx. This worksheet contains a list of some of White's prospects and information. Use your spreadsheet software to create a prospect tracking system that White can read on screen and print out.

The worksheet should list each prospect's name, telephone number, email address, and the date and manner of the last contact. It should also include a column for *Follow Up* in which White can enter a *Yes* or *No* to indicate whether additional contact is required. To locate names more easily, organize the prospect list in alphabetical order by last name.

A spreadsheet's appearance and structure are both extremely important if you want to effectively use the information it contains. Professional spreadsheets are formatted in ways that allow you to quickly locate and digest their information. The format should also allow you to easily make changes and update data. This case shows you how to develop professional level, maintainable spreadsheets that can be easily understood by others.

Tasks:

There are five tasks to this problem:

1. Create new columns and appropriate column headings to capture the required information. There should be column headings for *Company, Last Name, First Name, Telephone, Email Address, Date Called,* and *Follow Up*. The column headings for *Company, Last Name,* and *Date Called* already appear on the worksheet. Center the title of the sheet across all of the columns.

2. Create appropriate widths for each column, and then decide whether to left justify, right justify, or center the column labels. Some of the worksheet columns have already been widened for you.

3. Be sure to format the cells containing the dates to display the name of the month. The email address should be formatted as a hyperlink field so that White can launch his email program by simply clicking on the field. White needs to make follow-up calls to Sonny Heyman and Jane Weisgarber.

4. White has just found two more prospects, Tim Sheley and Candy Sedlock, both of whom need follow-up calls. Sheley heads Castle Property Rentals and was first contacted on 7/29/12. His phone number is 270-555-1923. Sedlock works for Central Freight Management Services and was first

contacted on 7/13/12. Her phone number is 270-555-4974. Add information about these prospects to the prospect list by inserting new rows in the appropriate places in the worksheet to ensure that the company names remain in alphabetical order. Create fictitious data for other contacts to fill in the spreadsheet.

5. Improve the appearance of the log by bolding and underlining column labels. Print a report of the log with a footer that shows the date of printing and your name. You should be able to print this worksheet on one 8-1/2 x 11-inch page.

Time Estimates
Expert: 30 minutes
Intermediate: 45 minutes
Novice: 1.5 hours

Excel Tutorial for Spreadsheet Case 1

This case draws upon the data entry skills you have already acquired while developing COURSE.xlsx in Chapter 2 and upon new skills for formatting and printing spreadsheets. You will need to use COURSE.xlsx again for this tutorial.

How to Retrieve a Data File

Begin by starting the Excel application. When the spreadsheet screen appears, your next step will be to load the data file COURSE.xlsx. Do this by clicking the File tab at the left of the Ribbon and clicking *Open* in the Backstage view that displays. The Open dialog box will appear.

You may need to specify various settings within the Open dialog box in order to locate and load the file. The four items that must be set are the *file name,* the *file type,* the *folder,* and the *disk drive.* A list of files of the type specified for the disk drive and folder appears in the File List window. To change the settings to retrieve COURSE.xlsx, first ensure that *All Excel Files, Excel Files,* or *All Files* appears in the *Files of type* list box. If it does not immediately appear, it can be changed by clicking the list arrow next to the *Files of type* list box, revealing a list of file types Excel can open. To move up and down the list, click the arrows on the scroll bars next to the list. Select the required file type with the mouse pointer.

Use the *Look in* list arrow to select the Folder and Disk Drive where COURSE.xlsx is stored and display it in the *File name* box. The files are listed alphabetically, so if the desired file is not visible, you can move down the list using the scroll bar.

Double-click the COURSE.xlsx file to open it. Alternatively, you can simply select the file or type *COURSE.xlsx* directly in the File Name box. When the settings are correct, click the *Open* button or press the [Enter] key.

How to Insert or Delete Columns and Rows

Suppose you wanted to add lines under the column headings in your student roster. You can insert columns and rows in an Excel worksheet in either of two ways: (a) through the Ribbon command *Insert Sheet Rows* (accessed through the *Insert* button in the Cells group of the Home tab), or (b) clicking the right mouse button to open the shortcut menu and then selecting *Insert*. This opens the Insert dialog box with four options:

- Shift Cells Right
- Shift Cells Down
- Entire Row
- Entire Column

By selecting *Entire Row* from the options presented and clicking *OK*, you can insert a blank row.

You can also select an entire row and then select *Insert* from the shortcut menu or open the Insert menu on the Home tab of the Ribbon and click *Insert Cells*. To select an entire row, move the mouse pointer over the row number at the left of the worksheet and press the left mouse button. To select multiple rows, keep the left button depressed and drag up or down.

You will now insert the blank line into your student roster. To do so, select any cell in the row immediately below the column headings—that is, move to row 7; it doesn't matter which column the active cell is in. In the Cells group on the Home tab of the Ribbon, click the arrow on the *Insert* button. On the menu, select *Insert Sheet Rows*. You will notice that a blank row is inserted in row 7 and the data that was previously located in rows 7 through 10 has been moved to rows 8 through 11.

You can delete one or multiple rows and columns using the same principles used in inserting rows and columns. There are two ways of accessing the *Delete* command in Excel: (a) through the Delete menu on the Home tab of the Ribbon (also in the Cells group) or (b) through the shortcut menu activated by the right mouse button. If entire rows or columns are highlighted when these commands are selected, the effects will be immediate: the row(s) or column(s) will disappear.

Spreadsheet Management Software Cases 27

Figure 3-1

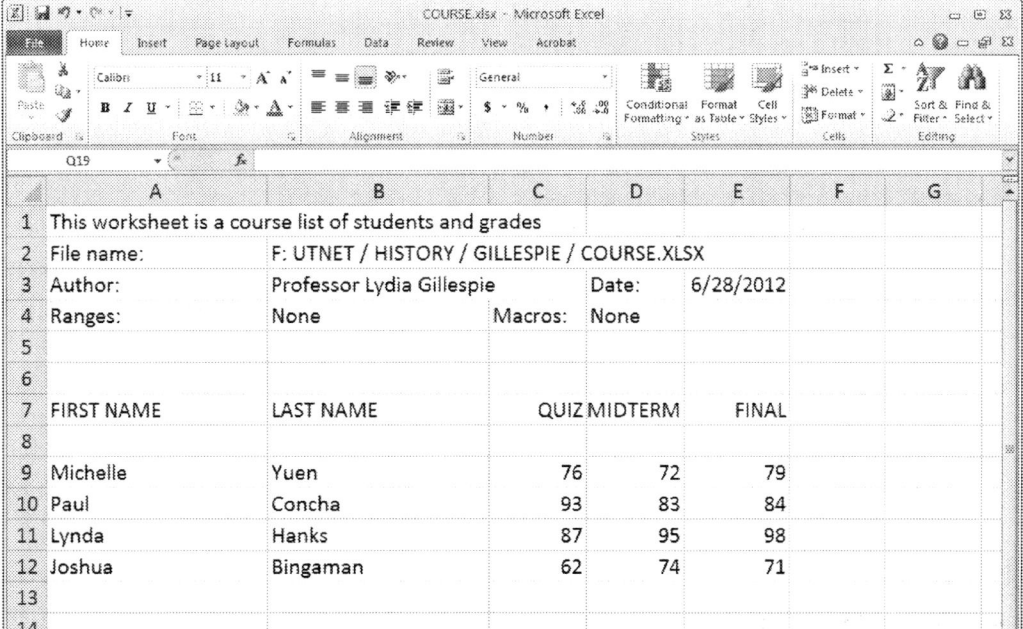

To make the worksheet documentation section conform to the spreadsheet design principles introduced in Chapter 2, let's add a fourth line to the documentation section. Use the first four cells in Row 4, starting in cell A4, to enter *Ranges: none Macros: none*. (We will add macros and range names in later tutorials.) Then insert a row so that there are two rows between the documentation section and the course list itself. Your worksheet screen now looks like Figure 3-1.

Moving and Copying the Contents of Cells

After using the *Insert Rows* command again, Row 8 will be blank. You can now add separator lines in this row to further set off the column headings from the data on the list.

This is a convenient time to explain some commonly used and helpful operations:

A *move* is referred to as a *cut and paste* in Excel. This involves simply relocating the contents of one or more cells. A *copy* reproduces the contents of the cells. The cut and copy commands are designed to be accompanied by a paste operation. The cut or copy designates *from where* the cells are cut or copied, while the paste designates *to where* they are being placed.

28 Solve it!

As with most operations in Excel, there are several ways to cut and copy:

1. Using the *Cut*, *Copy*, and *Paste* buttons on the Ribbon, located in the Clipboard group on the Home tab
2. Using the *Cut*, *Copy*, and *Paste* commands on the shortcut menu
3. Using the keystrokes for Cut [CTRL-X] Copy [CTRL-C], and Paste [CTRL-V]
4. Using the mouse pointer to drag and copy

Each of these is worth exploring at least once, and you can decide which method you find to be the most convenient. Generally speaking, most users use two of the methods listed. For example, some users will cut and copy using the mouse to drag and copy within a small area in a spreadsheet, and then use one of the other techniques to cut and copy between larger areas. Once you become familiar with each method, you will see that they are very similar. They all require you to specify a source range of cells, an operation (cut or copy), a destination or target range, and the Paste function.

It is worth explaining the mouse method of cutting and copying since it is extremely useful. This method applies to a single cell or a multiple selection. When you move your mouse pointer to the border of a selection on the worksheet, it transforms from a white cross to the Move pointer, a four-headed arrow. This is the signal that you can now perform the drag or copy.

To drag (or cut) the contents of the selection, press the left mouse button, continue to hold it down, and move the pointer. As you move the pointer across the worksheet, a shadow of the selection will also be moved until the mouse button is released to designate the destination of the drag. This operation may require some practice, but it will become second nature very quickly and you will find it to be an important editing function.

To perform the mouse copy, the actions are nearly identical to the drag (cut). The mouse pointer is moved to the border of the selection and the cross turns into an arrow. At this time, press and hold down the [CTRL] key. A small tell-tale plus sign will appear next to the arrow, indicating that we are performing a copy rather than a move. Drag the selection as we did for the move; when the mouse button is released, you will see that the copy operation has been completed.

With practice, you will realize that each of the different cut and copy methods results in identical results.

Returning to COURSE.xlsx, we now want to insert some decorative separators into the cells in Row 8 to distinguish the headings from the body of the table. To do this, we will enter the equals sign [=] and select the *Alignment Fill* command to fill the cell width with this symbol.

First, type = and click the *Enter* button ✔ on the Formula bar to enter = in cell A8. Now click *Format* in the Cells group on the Home tab of the Ribbon and then click *Format Cells* to open the Format Cells dialog box. This box has six formatting tabs: *Number, Alignment, Font, Border, Fill,* and *Protection.* Select *Alignment* by clicking on the tab label at the top of the dialog box. In the Text Alignment section, select *Fill* from the *Horizontal* drop-down menu and then click the *OK* button or press [ENTER]. The cell will be filled with the = sign.

Once you have set up the first cell, you can replicate it in all the cells in Row 8 below the column heads. Do this by using the *Copy* command. First, click the *Copy* button on the Home tab of the Ribbon. Notice the moving "marching ants" border around cell A8, indicating a copy or cut source. Next, select cells B8, C8, D8, and E8 (referred to as range B8:E8). Do this by moving the mouse pointer to cell B8, depressing the left mouse button, and dragging to the right until the desired range is selected. Now click the *Paste* button on the Ribbon. This will copy the formatting and contents of cell A8 to the range selected. When you are finished, press [ENTER] to finalize the copy and paste action. Your worksheet should look similar to Figure 3-2. In Excel 2010, the *Paste Options* button permits you to set formatting

Figure 3-2

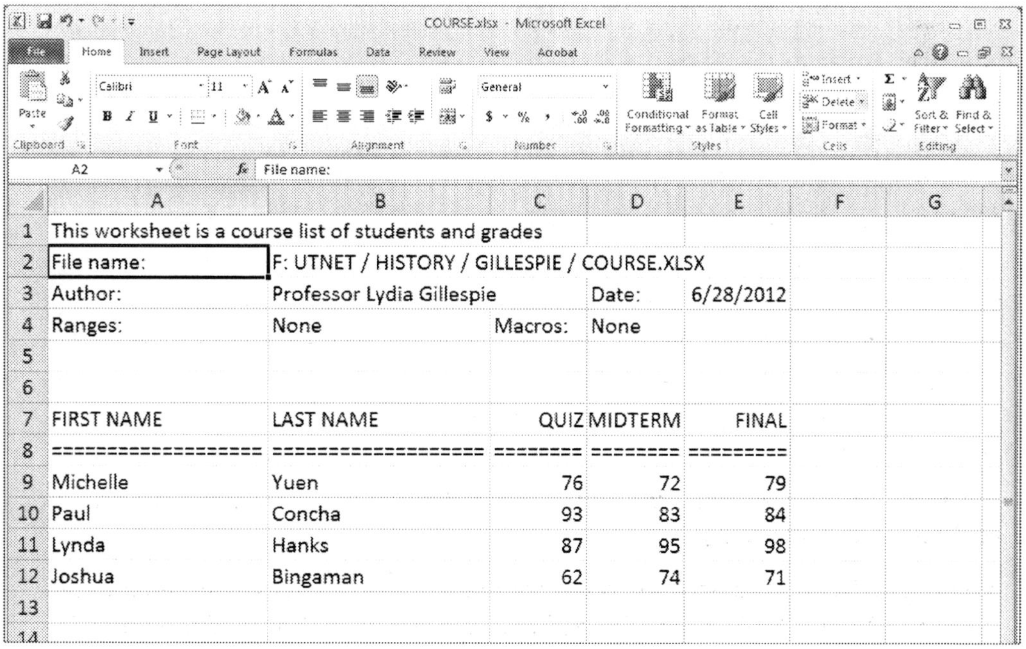

options for the data you have just pasted. Since you do not need to consider additional formatting, you may disregard the button.

Printing Your Worksheet

To print a simple worksheet such as your student roster, which is one page or less, you need only know the basic printing commands. Select the *Print* command on the left pane of the File tab to display printing options as well as a preview of the printed page at the far right. The various settings here can be explored later, however, for our purposes, simply accept the default settings and click the large *Print* button at the top of the right pane.

In this case, Excel will just print the page containing the student roster. Features can be adjusted, including paper size, page orientation, scaling, margin sizes, alignment, header and footer contents and options, print titles, page print sequence, and print area. You will find many of these settings in the Page Setup group of commands on the Page Layout tab of the Ribbon. To access the full set of Page Setup commands, click the dialog box launcher for the Page Setup group to open the Page Setup dialog box. Before printing, the appearance of your page can be observed in Print Preview so paper need not be wasted. To return to Print Preview in the Backstage view, you can click *Print Preview* on the Page tab of the Page Setup dialog box.

As Excel is printing your page, a small message box appears stating which page is currently being printed. This box contains a *Cancel* button, which you can choose if you want to stop the printing.

Changing Excel's Printer Options

The printing options in Excel can be changed in the Page Setup dialog box. The Page Setup dialog box has four tabs: *Page*, *Margins*, *Header/Footer*, and *Sheet*.

On the Page tab, you can choose specific features pertaining to individual pages being printed. The first option is Orientation—that is, whether the page is printed in landscape (horizontal wide, vertical narrow) or portrait (horizontal narrow, vertical wide) mode. The second option, Scaling, permits you to scale the size of the print up or down a specific percentage, or scale to fit a certain number of pages where the computer determines the percentage scaling. The Paper size option permits you to change the paper size between various standard sizes (e.g., Letter, Legal, Executive, A4, etc.). The next option allows you to change the print quality. The final option, First page number, permits you to specify the starting page. To print from the start, enter 1 or *Auto*; otherwise enter the page number from which you wish to begin.

On the Margins tab, you can change the margins that border the pages. The size of the margins on each page's edge can be specified in particular units (inches, centimeters). At the top right and top bottom are the Header and Footer settings, which specify the distance between the edge of the page and the header or footer. The last options are whether to center the print subject horizontally or vertically on the page.

On the Header/Footer tab, you can change the appearance of the headers and footers of the printed pages. The operation and options of headers (appearing at the top of every page) and footers (appearing at the bottom of every page) are the same. Each includes a number of default sample headers, a list to which you can add. Selecting *Custom Header* or *Custom Footer* permits you to change the header or footer. Each is split into thirds: left, center, and right. In each or any of these sections, you can enter text or click a button to insert any of the following: current page number, total number of pages, date, time, file path, file name, sheet name, or picture. You can change the fonts of any text using the *Format Text* button and format an inserted picture by using the *Format Picture* button.

On the Sheet tab, you can change the print features pertaining to the worksheet. First, you can specify precisely the range on the worksheet you want to print. This is done by clicking the *Collapse Dialog* button to the right of the Print Area list box, and then highlighting the range on the worksheet. The next option lets you specify Print Titles, which are either rows or columns that are to appear on every printed page. These are useful for lists or tables that extend beyond the confines of a single page. The next group of options allows you to select whether or how to print the following sheet elements: *Gridlines, Black and white, Draft quality, Row and column headings, Comments,* and *Cell errors*. The final option is the *Page Order*—that is, whether to print down and across or across and down.

Save COURSE.xlsx with the changes you made during this tutorial session. You will need it for the next spreadsheet case.

32 Solve it!

Spreadsheet Case 2
Pout Cosmetics

Problem:	Evaluate the effectiveness of an e-commerce company's Web site and advertising sites
Management skills:	Analyzing Organizing
Excel skills:	Formulas Absolute and Relative Addressing Formatting Printing
File:	POUTCOSMETICS_Q.xlsx

Pout Cosmetics, headquartered in Providence, RI, manufactures and sells trendy, inexpensive cosmetics. They have been in business since 2008 and have 13 store locations in the northeastern United States. Annual revenue from all the stores has been increasing each year, with 2012 revenues totaling $6,750,000. Pedro Archuleta, Director of Sales for Pout Cosmetics, recognized the potential market in online sales and had an outside Web development firm create an e-commerce site for the company. The site has had moderate success, but Archuleta would like to increase its effectiveness by turning more visitors into shoppers and decreasing the number of attempted buyers.

The company has been attempting to increase the number of online customers by placing advertising for their Web site on other Web sites. When users click on these ads, they are automatically transported to Pout's Web site. Data on Pout's Web advertising campaign is summarized in the weekly Marketing Trends Reports (MTR) produced by their Web site analysis software, which appears in the POUTCOSMETICS_Q.xlsx file.

- *Visitors* are the number of people who visited Pout Cosmetic's Web site by clicking on an ad for their site that was placed on an affiliated Web site.

- *Shoppers* are the number of visitors referred by ads who reached a page in their Web site designated as a shopping page.

- *Attempted buyers* are the number of potential buyers referred by ads who reached a Web site designated as a page for summarizing and paying for purchases.

- *Buyers* are the number of buyers referred by ads who actually placed an order from their Web site.
- *Source* indicates the specific Web site from which visitors came to Pout's Web site.

In trying to increase the number of on-line customers, Archuleta must determine the Web site's success in converting visitors to actual buyers. He must also look at the abandonment rate—the percentage of attempted buyers who abandon the Web site just as they were about to make a purchase. Low conversion rates and high abandonment rates are indicators that a Web site is not very effective and needs work.

Archuleta also wants to increase the effectiveness of his advertising dollars by increasing the size of the Pout Cosmetic ads on the sites where it advertises.

Tasks

There are five tasks in this problem:

1. Create new columns for the percentage of visitors who became shoppers, the percentage of shoppers who became attempted buyers, and the percentage of attempted buyers who became buyers. Also, create a column that shows the percentage of visitors from each advertising source. Create meaningful headings and display them wrapped above the columns and in bold.

2. Create formulas to total each column so you can determine the total number of Visitors, Shoppers, Attempted Buyers, and Buyers, as well as the Percentage of Visitors from each Source.

3. Create formulas to calculate the percentage of visitors who became shoppers, shoppers who became attempted buyers, and attempted buyers who became buyers. Calculate the percentages on the totals of these categories as well. Calculate the percentage of total visitors who came from each source, utilizing absolute addressing so that the results of the formulas can easily be copied down each column.

4. Format the spreadsheet so the percentages are displayed with the percent sign.

5. Print the spreadsheet with the data *centered* both horizontally and vertically on a single page, and include a centered header with Archuleta's name. Include your name and today's date in the footer.

Excel Tutorial for Spreadsheet Case 2

This case draws upon all of the skills acquired in Spreadsheet Case 1, plus new skills for using formulas, formatting, and absolute and relative addressing. You will once again use COURSE.xlsx for this tutorial.

Suppose you want to expand your worksheet by including each student's final grade. You must add an extra column and label for FINAL GRADE, and you must calculate the final grade for each student. The final exam counts for 50% of the final grade, the midterm for 35%, and the quiz for 15%.

Formulas

To compute the final grade, you must use a formula. A *formula* tells Excel what manipulations to perform on specific cell contents. The cells are specified using their cell references (e.g. A11, C3). Mathematical operators specify arithmetic operations. They are:

^	Exponentiation
*, /	Multiplication, Division
+,-	Addition, Subtraction
%	Percent (i.e. 75% represents 0.75)

Operations are always performed left to right within a formula in their order of precedence. The order of precedence in Excel corresponds to the order of the above list. Exponentiation will always be performed first, followed by multiplication and division, and then addition and subtraction. Percent amounts are evaluated when they are encountered.

Parentheses can be used to override the order of precedence. Operations inside parentheses will be performed before those outside the parentheses. The order of operations remains the same within the parentheses. When multiple sets of parentheses are employed, the operations within the innermost set of parentheses will be performed before those within the next set. Thus, the formula for Michelle Yuen's final grade would be:

=C9*.15+D14*.35+E9*.5

Note that the first character in the formula is preceded by an = sign. To be treated as a formula rather than a label, a formula must begin with an equals [=] sign. (The reason for the $ symbol and use of these cells is explained below.) Thus, a formula to add the contents of cells A6 and B6 must be expressed as =A6+B6. If you try to type this formula as A6+B6, it will be treated as a label.

Formula Errors

If you try to enter a formula with a logical or mathematical error, Excel will display a message box stating what error has occurred. To proceed, you must click the *OK* button. If you want further information on the error, you can select the *Help* button, which will provide a broader explanation of the error. Once the problem is corrected, you can continue.

Another common problem is the circular reference, which is a formula that directly or indirectly refers back to the same cell in which it resides. For example, if you try to enter the formula =A12+B12 into cell B12, an error box will appear stating a circular reference has occurred. This is because cell B12 is an operand in the operation, as well as the cell that holds the result of the calculation.

Absolute and Relative Addressing

Suppose we want to make our worksheet more flexible for future changes. The professor may decide that the quiz should only contribute 10% toward the final grade and the midterm will not count for 50%. In that case, the formula for the final grade must be adjusted to change the percentage weight applied to the midterm and the quiz.

You could, of course, re-enter the new formulas, but an easier way to keep track of the percentage weight assigned to each grade would be to list the percentages assigned to each grade in an unused portion of the spreadsheet. Formulas would reference the cell addresses where these percentages reside rather than the percentages themselves.

Set up an Assumptions section in the upper left-hand corner of your worksheet. First, move the course list down so that the column labels are in Row 14. Then, enter the label "ASSUMPTIONS" in cell A7, and format cell A8 in the same manner as cells A15:E14. Below the underlining, in cells A9 through A11, enter the labels "Quiz," "Midterm," and "Final Exam."

In cells B9 through B11, enter the percentage weights for each of these grades: .15, .35, and .5.

Develop a formula for a student's final grade to reference the cells where these percentages reside. It is never good practice to use the percentages themselves in a formula; always use a cell reference. Enter the formula for Michelle Yuen's grades into cell F16.

=C16*$B$9+D16*$B$10+E16*$B$11

The $ designates an absolute address. An *absolute address* is one that will not change when that address is copied. Excel's default is to treat an address as a *relative address*, meaning that when you copy or move a formula, the addresses of the cells in the formula will be automatically adjusted to fit the new location. A relative address has no $ symbols. Any formula with multiple cell references can have absolute, relative, and mixed addresses (see the next section) all in the one formula.

Relative addressing means that you can copy the formula in cell F14 for Michelle's grade to cell F15 for Paul, and the formula will automatically adjust to add the proper cell addresses (the addresses without the $ sign) for Paul's grade. The formula bar will show the formula in F15 to be

=C17*$B$9+D17*$B$10+E17*$B$11.

Mixed Addressing

There will be certain situations where you will want to combine relative and absolute addressing; that is, you will want to create a cell reference that is part relative and part absolute. Either the column letter or the row number remains constant.

For example, an address of $B21 means that absolute addressing will be used on the column portion of the address, but relative addressing will be used on the row portion. Conversely, an address of B$21 means that absolute addressing will be used on the row portion of the address, and relative addressing on the column portion. You will need to use relative, absolute, and mixed addressing throughout your *Solve it!* Spreadsheet Cases.

Formatting

Suppose you want to express the percentages in your Assumptions section as 50% rather than .5. You can change the format in which numeric information appears by using Excel's Format Cells commands.

First, select the cells you want to change by selecting the range *B9:B11*.

On the Home tab of the Ribbon, click *Format* and then click *Format Cells* to open the Format Cells dialog box. This box has six formatting tabs: *Number, Alignment,*

Font, *Border*, *Fill*, and *Protection*. To change the format of numbers, select the Number tab. The *Category* list box displays the different types of numerical formats. Select *Percentage* in the Category list box. Type *0* into the *Decimal places* spin box, and click the *OK* button.

You should see the effects of this formatting on the three figures in the Assumptions area of the worksheet. They will be displayed as percentage figures: 15%, 35%, and 50%. Excel often provides shortcuts to frequently used commands and operations by allocating buttons on the Ribbon. In this case, Excel has a *Percent Style* button % in the Number group on the Home tab. To format selected cell(s) with a percent style, you can simply press the *Percent Style* button.

The different Number categories listed on the Numbers tab of the Format Cells dialog box are:

- *General:* This is the default format for all new worksheets. With the General format, the values are displayed in their natural state. No suppression or compression of formatting is permitted. Scientific notation will be used to display numbers that are too large or too small to be displayed normally. The General format displays up to 11 digits.

- *Number:* The Number format displays a fixed number of decimal places, negative values in red, negative values in brackets, and combinations of these characteristics.

- *Currency:* This format places a dollar sign before each number and uses commas to separate hundreds from thousands, etc. There are options for zero or two decimal places, and for red or black negative values.

- *Accounting:.* The Accounting format displays four accounting formats, keeping the dollar sign to the left of the cell, showing negative values in brackets, and displaying zero values as hyphens.

- *Date:* This format displays dates in a variety of different ways and can be used by Excel in mathematical calculations. Default date formats include:

d/mm/yy	(Example 2/02/80)
d-mmm-yy	(Example 2-Feb-80)
d-mmm	(Example 2-Feb)
mmm-yy	(Example Feb-80)

To use date and time formats, you must use one of the Excel date and time functions (such as =DATE, =DATEVALUE, =TIME, =TIMEVALUE, or =NOW) to enter dates and times into your worksheet. Excel date functions will be treated in more detail in Spreadsheet Case 8. A date can also be entered as a label if it is not involved in any calculations.

- *Time:* This format can represent times in a number of formats where they can be used by Excel time functions in mathematical calculations.
- *Percentage:* The Percentage format displays numbers as percentages. The default decimal places are zero and two.
- *Fraction:* This format displays numbers as fractions, separating whole numbers and the fractional parts.
- *Scientific:* The Scientific format displays data in exponential scientific notation.
- *Text:* This format displays the values as labels rather than values.
- *Special:* The Special format is used to format zip codes, zip codes + 4, phone numbers, and social security numbers.
- *Custom:* The Custom format can be used to create custom formats for numbers such as product codes.

Copy the final grade formula to the rest of the student entries. Add a column heading "FINAL GRADE" to cell F14, and match the formatting of cell F15 to the other cells in the row. Your worksheet should look like Figure 3-3.

Totaling the Values in a Range

This case requires totalling values in each column so that Pout Cosmetics can determine the total number of Visitors, Shoppers, Attempted Buyers, and Buyers on the Web site. The =SUM function of your spreadsheet software can help you do this. The =SUM function calculates the sum of all of the values in a specified range. The form of the =SUM function is:

=SUM(range)

For example, if you want to total the percentages in the Assumptions section of your sample worksheet to make sure they add up to 100 percent, you could use the =SUM function instead of the formula =B9+B10+B11. The values in range B9:B11 can be totalled much more easily by entering in cell B12:

=SUM(B9:B11)

Spreadsheet Management Software Cases 39

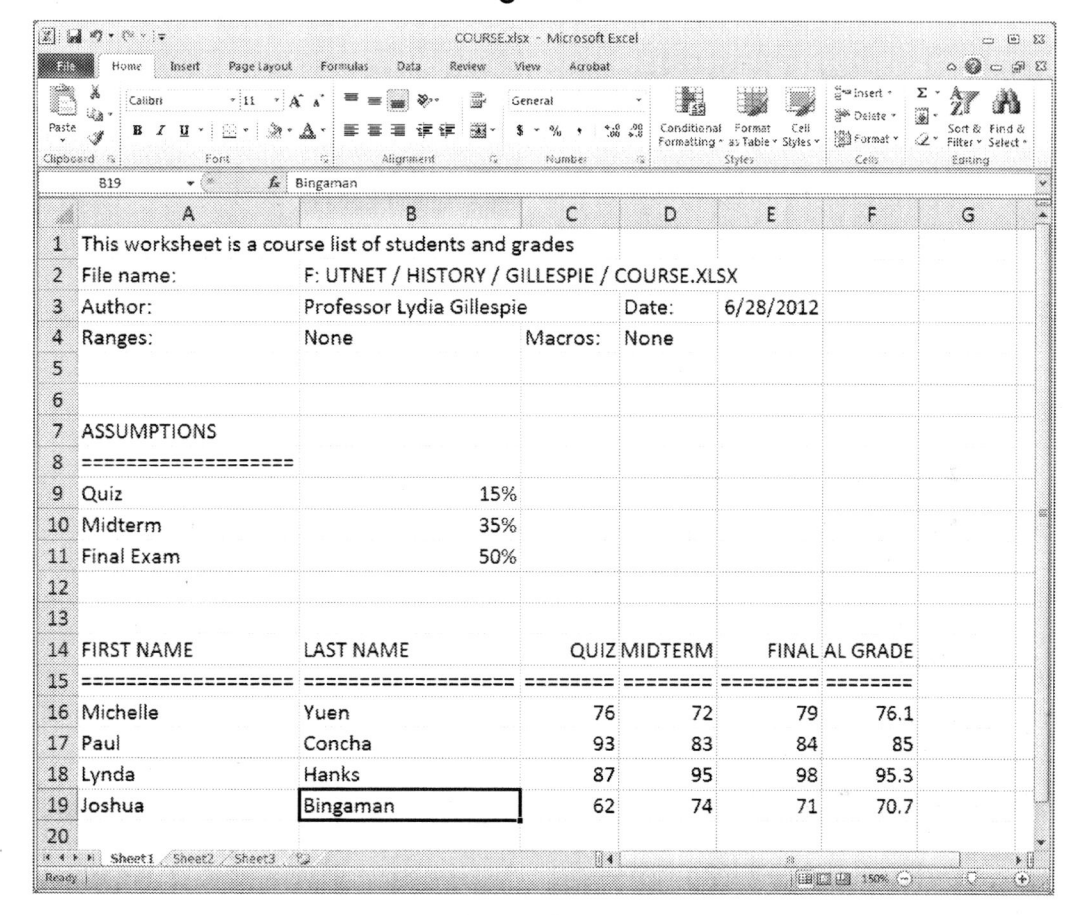

Figure 3-3

	A	B	C	D	E	F	G
1	This worksheet is a course list of students and grades						
2	File name:	F: UTNET / HISTORY / GILLESPIE / COURSE.XLSX					
3	Author:	Professor Lydia Gillespie		Date:	6/28/2012		
4	Ranges:	None		Macros:	None		
5							
6							
7	ASSUMPTIONS						
8	==================						
9	Quiz		15%				
10	Midterm		35%				
11	Final Exam		50%				
12							
13							
14	FIRST NAME	LAST NAME	QUIZ	MIDTERM	FINAL	AL GRADE	
15	==================	==================	========	========	========	========	
16	Michelle	Yuen	76	72	79	76.1	
17	Paul	Concha	93	83	84	85	
18	Lynda	Hanks	87	95	98	95.3	
19	Joshua	Bingaman	62	74	71	70.7	
20							

Excel provides a shortcut for this formula: the *Sum Function* button Σ.

This button appears in the Editing group on the Home tab, and if clicked, the =SUM function will be placed in the current cell and a sample range will be assumed, typically above or to the left of the current cell. All you have to do is press [Enter] to complete the operation. Try the button as well as entering the function yourself. When entering the function, select the range to sum using the cursor keys or the mouse rather than typing the range. This tends to be easier and more accurate; typing is more prone to error.

Save COURSE.xlsx with the changes you made during this tutorial session. You will need it for subsequent Spreadsheet Cases.

40 Solve it!

Spreadsheet Case 3
New Generation Roofing Payroll

Problem:	Develop a payroll register
Management skills:	Organization
Excel skills:	Formulas Absolute and relative addressing Creating an Assumption Area for variables
File:	NEWGENERATION_Q.xlsx

New Generation Roofing is a family-owned company in Albany, NY, that produces roofing materials. It has 3,700 employees and an operating budget of $14,500,000. All employees except the eight members of the company's founding family are on the firm's automated payroll system. The family members are paid through a separate confidential payroll, which is processed manually because it contains highly sensitive information, such as salaries and bonuses. Like other salaried employees, they are paid monthly.

Myriam Legg, executive assistant to the founder, Mike Ramsey, is in charge of preparing this confidential payroll. She must make all of the calculations for salary changes, deductions, and net pay using a calculator. She then enters the results onto a Payroll Register sheet. A Payroll Register is a report prepared for each payroll period that lists the names, gross pay, deductions, and net pay of all employees, and the total gross pay, deductions, and net pay for that payroll period as well as the net amounts deducted and paid to date. Legg writes out the checks by hand.

This is a very time-consuming process that prevents Legg from fulfilling other responsibilities. Mike Ramsey would like to use his time more productively for coordinating meetings and managing correspondence. Also, there is a danger of miscalculations, which would incite the wrath of the family members. Ramsey and Legg would like to automate the process as much as possible while maintaining strict confidentiality.

Legg feels there are so few checks to write that this part of the process could remain manual. However, many hours could be saved if all of the payroll calculations and the preparation of the Payroll Register report could be automated.

Open NEWGENERATION_Q.xlsx, which displays the names of the executive family members, their social security numbers, and annual salaries. You should develop a worksheet that creates a Payroll Register report for these employees. The worksheet should automatically calculate monthly gross pay, net pay, and all deductions. It should also provide totals for each of these categories for the current pay period and add this period's amounts to the year-to-date totals.

Monthly gross pay can be computed by dividing annual salary by 12. Federal withholding tax should be set to 26% of gross pay. State withholding tax should be set to 9% of gross pay. For the tax year 2012, FICA (the employee Social Security deduction) is 7.65% of the first $94,200 earned during the year. The Medicare deduction is 1.45% of gross pay for all wages earned during the tax year. Since this is the first pay period of 2012, FICA and Medicare deductions must be taken for all employees for this payroll. Group health insurance is $250 per month. All of these family members have elected to participate in a profit sharing plan to which they contribute 7.5% of their gross pay each month.

Tasks

There are five tasks to this problem:

1. Complete the column labels to include gross pay, all deductions, and net pay. Also, include a column for gross pay to date that will be used in future months.

2. Make all appropriate format changes for numbers and percentages. Columns containing numbers should be formatted to show two decimal places to the right of the decimal point.

3. Create an assumptions section for all deductions and other variables in the upper left of the worksheet and label it Assumptions. This way, you can easily make changes in deductions and formulas using the addressing function of the spreadsheet software. By keeping all assumptions in a clearly defined assumptions section, you can make changes rapidly in the worksheet to respond to changing tax laws or other regulations. Listing variables also allows all assumptions to be clearly visible and reported.

4. Use formulas to calculate monthly gross pay, all deductions, and net pay. Be sure these formulas reference the appropriate cells in the assumptions section of your worksheet (e.g., $A$56) rather than actual values (e.g., 20%). Provide totals for gross pay, net pay, and each deduction category so that

Legg can track the company's expenses for the pay period. Widen columns if necessary.

5. Print the spreadsheet on a single sheet. Include your name and today's date in the footer.

Additional Problems

1. The family members have decided to contribute 1% of their gross pay each month to the local Goodwill. Modify the Payroll Worksheet to implement this plan.

2. The company feels it should be withholding 35% of gross pay for federal tax. Modify your worksheet to change the federal withholding tax deduction and print the new version.

Time Estimates
Expert: 30 minutes
Intermediate: 1 hour
Novice: 1.5 hours

There is no tutorial for this case because it uses skills introduced in earlier chapters.

Spreadsheet Case 4
Benchmark Consultants

Problem:	Analyze financial ratios
Management skills:	Decision Making
Excel skills:	Formulas Spreadsheet control Reporting
File:	BENCHMARK_Q.xlsx

Benchmark Consultants is a small investment advising firm that has just opened in Yuma, Arizona. It is trying to take market share from large brokerage houses by offering custom advice to clients on long-term investing, rather than recommending the stock-of-the-week strategy touted by its competitors. Benchmark focuses on wealthy families and retirees who have financial assets to invest.

Clients may call or visit to seek expert advice about specific stocks in which they are interested. Ahmoud Khatan, a young pediatrician, has expressed interest in two firms in the drug retail sector, and he wants to know which one, if either, would be a good investment. These firms are CVS and Walgreens, both of which are listed on the New York Stock Exchange.

CVS Caremark Corporation operates in the retail drugstore industry in the United States with over 7,300 retail and specialty pharmacy stores in 44 states, the District of Columbia, and Puerto Rico. The company also does business online under the CVS.com name. It is a Fortune 500 company, and for 2011, annual sales were over $100 billion.

The Walgreen Company is the nation's leading drugstore chain. Walgreens has 7,847 stores in 50 states and Puerto Rico and also does business online. In 2012, annual sales were $72 billion.

To make sound recommendations, Benchmark analysts must carefully examine a company's financial statements. The purpose of financial statements is to identify the major sources, uses, and flows of funds within an organization. The three principal financial statements used in business are income statements, balance sheets, and cash flow statements.

44 Solve it!

Income statements (also called operating statements) summarize the income, expenses, and profits of businesses for a specified period. The purpose of income statements is to show the profitability or unprofitability of firms during a specified period, usually a year, quarter, or month.

Balance sheets identify the assets, liabilities, and owners' (or shareholders') equity of a firm at a particular point in time. The difference between assets and liabilities is net worth or equity (literally what the organization is worth net of all other factors). Cash flow statements provide detailed information on total receipts and disbursements of cash. Cash flow statements are like checking account registers for individuals.

Certain financial ratios based on figures from financial statements have been traditionally used to assess a company's financial health and performance. There are five kinds of financial ratios that you can apply to assess the financial position of a firm.

1. Liquidity Ratios

Various liquidity ratios measure a firm's liquidity, its ability to draw on cash and other current assets to pay its financial obligations. Two commonly used liquidity ratios are the *current ratio* and the *quick ratio*, or *acid test*.

(a) $$\text{Current Ratio} = \frac{\text{Current Assets}}{\text{Current Liabilities}}$$

(b) $$\text{Quick Ratio w(Acid Test)} = \frac{\text{Current Assets} - \text{Inventory}}{\text{Current Liabilities}}$$

The current ratio is the most commonplace measure of short-term solvency. If current liabilities are rising faster than current assets, this may be a harbinger of financial difficulty. The quick ratio measures the firm's ability to pay off short-term obligations without relying on the sale of inventory, which is the least liquid of the firm's current assets.

2. Asset Management Ratios

Another group of ratios measures how effectively a firm is managing its assets. One of these is the *total assets utilization ratio*, which measures the utilization or turnover of all of the firm's assets.

$$\text{(c)} \quad \text{Total assets utilization} = \frac{\text{Sales}}{\text{Total Assets}}$$

3. Debt Management Ratios

These ratios determine the extent to which a firm uses debt financing. If equity, or owner-supplied funds, accounts for only a small portion of a firm's total financing, the risks of the firm are borne mainly by creditors. On the other hand, by raising funds through debt, owners can control the firm with a smaller investment of their own. If the firm returns more on the borrowed funds than it pays in interest, the return on the owner's capital is magnified, or leveraged. An important ratio is the *debt ratio*, which measures the percentage of a firm's total funds provided by creditors.

$$\text{(d)} \quad \text{Debt ratio} = \frac{\text{Total Liabilities}}{\text{Total Assets}}$$

Creditors prefer low debt ratios, whereas it may be advantageous for owners to seek higher debt to leverage their money and earnings. However, a debt ratio that is too high signals trouble repaying loans and too much reliance on borrowed money to pay for the firm's operations.

4. Profitability ratios

Profitability ratios illustrate the combined effects of liquidity, asset management, and debt management on profits. Important profitability ratios measure the *return on total assets (ROA)*, the *return on common equity (ROE)*, or return on stockholders' investments, and the *profit margin on sales*.

(e) Return on Total Assets (ROA) = $\dfrac{\text{Net profit after taxes}}{\text{Total Assets}}$

(f) Return on Equity (ROE) = $\dfrac{\text{Net profit after taxes}}{\text{Net worth (equity)}}$

(g) Profit Margin = $\dfrac{\text{Net profit after taxes}}{\text{Sales}}$

5. Market Value ratios

These ratios help indicate what investors think of the company's past performance and future prospects. The market value ratios (and stock price) will be high if a firm has strong liquidity, asset management, debt management, and profitability ratios. The most widely used market value ratio is the *price/earnings ratio*.

(h) Price/Earnings Ratio = $\dfrac{\text{Price per share}}{\text{Earnings per share}}$

To evaluate a firm's financial ratios properly, you must compare its ratios to ratios for comparable businesses. You can find financial ratio data on comparable businesses in publications like Dun and Bradstreet's *Industry Norms & Key Business Ratios* and Robert Morris's *Annual Statement Studies*. Both publications group businesses and provide financial ratio data classified by standardized industry classification codes.

Tasks

There are five tasks in this case:

1. Examine the 2011 income statements and balance sheets of CVS and Walgreens, which can be found by loading the file BENCHMARK_Q.xlsx. All data are based on the publicly available 2011 annual Form 10K reports of these firms. You can find the 10K reports either at the EDGAR database maintained by the Securities and Exchange Commission (http://www.sec.

gov/edgar.shtml) or from the firms' Web sites (usually in a section called Investor Relations).

2. Print out the financial statements so you have a hard copy to work with. Review them very closely.

3. Assign range names to the balance sheet and income data that will be used to calculate the financial data. Create a table of range names below the worksheet. Format the ranges with the income statement and balance sheet data to display a comma with one decimal place. Format the ranges with the financial ratios, earnings per share, and stock price to display two decimal places.

4. Calculate the eight financial ratios outlined above for each company at the end of the financial statements. Print out the ratios for both companies.

5. In a single paragraph, write an analysis of both companies. Based on the information provided in this case, is each firm financially sound? Which would make the better investment? Review the financial statements of both companies for any items that might help explain their financial position.

Additional Problems

1. Obtain the current stock price for each of these companies and recalculate the Price/Earnings ratio.

2. Use a search engine on the Web to get additional information on these companies from their home sites and also from two financial sites that cover these stocks. Some good sources are Hoover's (www.hoovers.com), Google Finance (finance.google.com), and Yahoo Finance (finance.yahoo.com). How do professional analysts feel about investing in these companies? Do you agree?

Time Estimates

Expert: 45 minutes
Intermediate: 1 hour
Novice: 1.5 hours

48 Solve it!

Excel Tutorial for Spreadsheet Case 4

You do not need to use range names for the solution to this case, but you may choose to use them when you use different formats for different ranges in your worksheet.

In COURSE.xlsx, name the range with the student grade data as GRADES. Also name each of the cells holding the percentages.

Naming Ranges

You can name a range with the *Define Name* command. To name the range of student grades as GRADES, highlight the cells from C16:F19, open the Formulas tab on the Ribbon, and click *Define Name* in the Defined Names group. This opens the New Name dialog box with the percentage range reference already inserted into the *Refers to* text box. Type the name GRADES in the *Name* text box and click the *OK* Button.

You can alternatively click the *Define Name* button, select the range once within the dialog box, and type the name. Use either procedure to name cell B9 *Quiz*, cell B10 *Midterm*, and cell B11 *Final_Exam*.

Creating a Table of Range Names

You can document your range names in a table in your worksheet using the *Use in Formula>Paste Names* command. Place the table in an unused portion of the worksheet where it will not overlay any data. The spreadsheet design principles introduced in Chapter 2 suggest placing the range name table below the left-most portion of the worksheet. For the table's column heads, type RANGES into cell A22 and ADDRESSES into cell B22. Copy cell A15 into cells A23 and B23. Now, to create the range name table, click inside cell A24. On the Formulas tab on the Ribbon, in the Defined Names group, click *Use in Formula* and then click the *Paste Names* command. The Paste Name dialog box opens listing the named ranges.

The purpose of this dialog box is to paste a selected name in the formula bar. However, we are using the alternative purpose of the dialog box—pasting a list of range names and their references onto the worksheet. To do this, click the *Paste List* button. Your worksheet should resemble Figure 3-4. The pasted list of range names is static, so if you add or delete range names, you will have to paste the list again. Also, be careful that the pasted list does not overlay existing data.

Figure 3-4

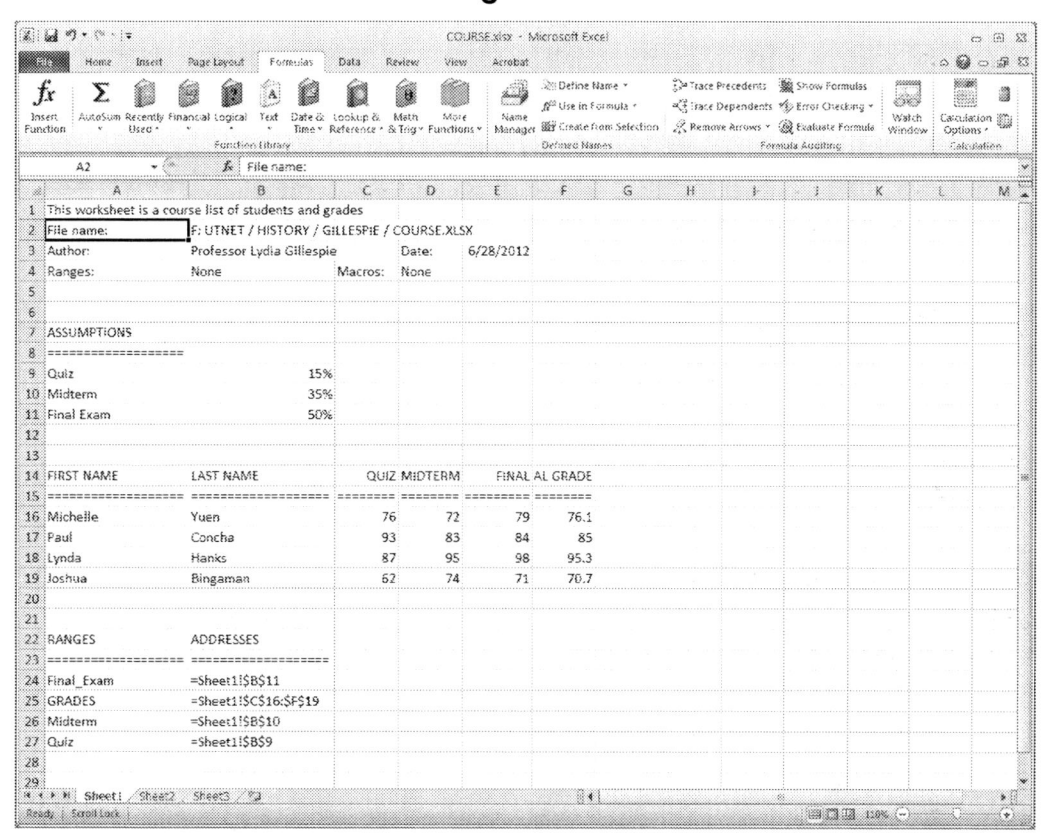

	A	B	C	D	E	F	G
1	This worksheet is a course list of students and grades						
2	File name:	F: UTNET / HISTORY / GILLESPIE / COURSE.XLSX					
3	Author:	Professor Lydia Gillespie		Date:	6/28/2012		
4	Ranges:	None	Macros:	None			
5							
6							
7	ASSUMPTIONS						
8	===================						
9	Quiz		15%				
10	Midterm		35%				
11	Final Exam		50%				
12							
13							
14	FIRST NAME	LAST NAME		QUIZ	MIDTERM	FINAL	AL GRADE
15	===================	===================	========	========	========	========	
16	Michelle	Yuen		76	72	79	76.1
17	Paul	Concha		93	83	84	85
18	Lynda	Hanks		87	95	98	95.3
19	Joshua	Bingaman		62	74	71	70.7
20							
21							
22	RANGES	ADDRESSES					
23	===================	===================					
24	Final_Exam	=Sheet1!$B$11					
25	GRADES	=Sheet1!$C$16:$F$19					
26	Midterm	=Sheet1!$B$10					
27	Quiz	=Sheet1!$B$9					

Spreadsheet Case 5
The Town of Medford

Problem:	Prepare a budget for a small municipality
Management skills:	Planning Decision Making
Excel skills:	Formulas Spreadsheet control Reporting
File:	MEDFORD_Q.xlsx

The town of Medford has a population of 9,782 and is located in Blaine County, Oklahoma. Each November, Carrie Kozak, the town manager, works with the Mayor and the Board of Trustees to develop the town's budget for the forthcoming year. The town's main source of revenue is the local property tax, but it also receives some aid from the state government and some revenue from miscellaneous licenses and fees.

The town leaders want to hold to their campaign promises of raising taxes by only 4%. Their community has become very environmentally conscious, and they do not want to encourage new businesses that would add to the traffic congestion or pollute the air. They fear revenues may be declining because the state of Oklahoma is facing severe financial problems and wants to cut the state aid it provides to local governments.

Carrie Kozak wants to develop a budget that can be supported by anticipated revenues. Anticipating continued cutbacks in state aid, Kozak would like to develop preliminary budgets for the next two years. That way she can plan ahead if major changes are required. If planned expenditures exceed revenues, Kozak, the Mayor, and the Trustees must develop an alternative budget that is balanced. Can they develop a balanced budget without raising local property taxes?

Open the file MEDFORD_Q.xlsx, showing the actual receipts and disbursements for the Town of Medford in 2012. Kozak wants to use this budget as the basis for projecting the town budget for the next two years.

One way to analyze a budget is to estimate the amount of each category of cash receipts and disbursements. The projected outflow of funds is subtracted from the projected inflow. If the amount of outflow is greater than the amount of inflow, the town must secure additional funds to pay for its expenditures or it must reduce its spending. For instance, the town could raise taxes or borrow money to meet its costs, or it could reduce some of its expenses.

In projecting the next two years' budgets, Kozak wants to use the following assumptions: She expects the state will reduce its aid to the town by 6% each year. Historically, expenditures for employee salaries and benefits have been rising 13% annually. She expects all other expenditures to rise at a rate of 6% annually and miscellaneous receipts to rise 5% annually. The town's expenditure for debt service to pay off previous loans will remain constant. Can the town balance its budget if it keeps its promise not to raise taxes beyond 4% or go further into debt?

Tasks:

There are five tasks in this case:

1. Print out and review MEDFORD_Q.xlsx.

2. Create an Assumptions section of the worksheet to identify factors in your calculations of receipts and disbursements. Make sure formulas reference cells in the Assumptions section wherever possible.

3. Calculate the receipts and disbursements for each of the categories on the worksheet for 2013 and 2014. Calculate total receipts and total disbursements. The case has been simplified so that all revenue is collected in the year it is due.

4. Complete the worksheet by subtracting total receipts from total disbursements in 2013 and 2014. Print the results.

5. Write a brief analysis of the projected 2013 and 2014 budgets for the town of Medford. If these budgets don't balance, what steps would you recommend be taken by the town? Revise your worksheet to incorporate your recommendations, save it under another name, and print it out again. Keep revising the worksheet until you have developed a balanced budget. Is there some way for the town to come up with a balanced budget without raising taxes?

Additional Problem

1. What if state aid is not reduced but instead increases by 5% for the next two years? What impact would this have on the budget? Revise your worksheet and save it under a different name. Print out and analyze the results.

Time Estimates

Expert: 30 minutes
Intermediate: 1 hour
Novice: 1.5 hours

There is no tutorial for this case because it uses skills introduced in earlier chapters.

Spreadsheet Case 6
Pickled Sisters

Problem:	Develop a breakeven analysis model for a start-up venture
Management skills:	Planning Decision Making
Excel skills:	Formulas Graphics Worksheet organization
File:	PICKLEDSISTERS_Q.xlsx

Pickled Sisters, Inc. is a newly formed, two-person company located in Yuba City, California, that produces organic pickles and preserves from local ingredients. The pickles and preserves are packaged in traditional jelly jars with hand-drawn labels. Its founders, sisters Celia Renwick and Viola Kidwell, have arranged to sell this new collection of spreads in a network of organic food stores and supermarkets, as well as local tourist shops. Viola Kidwell, who handles the finances, believes that a huge demand for natural homemade style products makes this a promising business opportunity.

Before Pickled Sisters invests heavily in advertising, cooking equipment, warehouse rental, and office space, they must know if there is a future for this type of business and at what point they can expect it to produce a profit. Viola Kidwell has not done any formal market research, but she would like to sell each twelve-pack of jars to retailers for a wholesale price of $39.95.

This is a classic problem for all businesses—determining what objectives they must meet to produce a profit or to minimize losses. What Kidwell must do is utilize the managerial accounting concept of breakeven analysis. *Breakeven analysis* establishes the *breakeven point*, which is the number of units that Pickled Sisters must sell to yield no profit and incur no loss. Any units sold beyond the breakeven point will represent profit, and a sales volume below the breakeven point will put the firm at a loss.

To perform breakeven analysis, a company must examine its operating costs. Some of these costs are fixed and do not change over the range of the operations activity regardless of how many units of an item the company produces or sells. Variable costs, on the other hand, increase as production increases and decrease as production decreases.

In the case of Pickled Sisters, Inc., fixed costs are the rent for a large office-storage-preparation area ($12,000 per year), the cost of a commercial stove ($7,200), the cost of large cooking equipment, such as bowls, pots, and sterilizers ($950), and the cost of an initial advertising campaign ($5,550). Pickled Sisters' variable costs are the cost of supplies like fruit, vegetables, sugar, jars, packaging, and shipping. Kidwell has calculated that the cost of preparing and packaging each twelve-pack of jars is $15.60 and the cost of shipping each package is $1.95. Both sisters have decided not to take a salary right away. Until the business starts producing a profit, they will live off their savings, which amount to $164,000.

Once a product's costs have been determined, the contribution margin per unit must be calculated. The contribution margin per unit is the difference between the selling price per unit and the variable costs per unit. (The contribution margin per unit = average selling price per unit - variable costs per unit.) Once the contribution margin per unit has been determined, one can then calculate the breakeven point. In a company such as Pickled Sisters, Inc., which produces only a few products, the formula for the breakeven point would be calculated by dividing the total fixed costs by the contribution margin per unit.

Often the best way to display the results of breakeven analysis is in graphic form. It is also useful to use breakeven analysis to generate pro forma income statements that convert unit data to dollars and display projected sales revenue.

Tasks:

There are four tasks in this case:

1. Load the data file PICKLEDSISTERS_Q.xlsx. Create a worksheet that displays the total fixed cost and the total variable cost per unit for one case of preserves from Pickled Sisters, Inc. Calculate the contribution margin per unit and the breakeven point. Include an Assumptions section that identifies variable factors used in calculations. Assign range names to the variables to be used in the calculations.

2. Use your results to generate pro forma income statements using the framework supplied on the data file. A pro forma income statement is a projection of future incomes, not actual incomes earned. Include two projections of sales and income below the breakeven point and two above it. Include a projection of sales and income right at the breakeven point. The income data

below the breakeven point should reflect zero sales and sales at half of the breakeven units. The income data at the breakeven point should reflect sales at 1.0 times the breakeven units. The income data above the breakeven point should reflect sales at 1.5 and 2.0 times the breakeven units.

3. Create a line chart (graph) to display the most important data from the pro forma income statements and the breakeven point. The X-axis of the chart should display the range, indicating units sold in your pro forma income statements. The first data series should display fixed cost (which will be constant). The second data series should display total cost figures. The third data series should display revenue figures. Give your chart (graph) a title, and supply titles for the X and Y axes. Supply legends for all of the data series. The point on the chart where the data lines for total cost and revenue intersect is the breakeven point.

4. Be sure to name and save your chart as well as your worksheet. Print both the chart and the worksheet including your name in the footer. Examine your output. Write a one-paragraph statement analyzing the results of the breakeven analysis. Is Pickled Sisters, Inc. a worthwhile business venture for the sisters?

Additional Problem

1. Kidwell has been told that the cost of the glass jars will rise 7% in a few weeks. Jars account for approximately 15% of the production and packaging cost for each case shipped. What impact will this have on her breakeven analysis?

Time Estimates

Expert: 45 minutes
Intermediate: 1 hour
Novice: 2 hours

Excel Tutorial for Spreadsheet Case 6

This case draws upon all of the skills acquired in previous Spreadsheet Cases, plus new skills for creating and printing graphs, or charts as they are known in Excel. You will need to use COURSE.xlsx again for this tutorial.

Creating Charts with Excel

Excel provides excellent functions for generating charts to graphically display data on your worksheets. An Excel chart can be stored on a separate sheet or it can be embedded in the same worksheet as the data. With the chart embedded in the worksheet, you can instantly observe the effects of changing the data in the worksheet. The steps to achieve each of these graphs are identical.

We want to graph the grades of each test for every student. It is easier to select the range containing the data before selecting the *Insert Chart* command. Select the range *A16:F19*. This range contains the values representing the students' final grades as well as the students' names and their test grades. Open the Insert tab on the Ribbon. In the Charts group are seven button commands for adding different types of charts: *Column charts, Line charts, Pie charts, Bar charts, Area charts, Scatter charts,* and *Other (Stock, Surface, Doughnut, Bubble, and Radar)*.

Different types of charts emphasize different qualities or aspects of data, so it is important to choose the right chart type for the data and for your purposes. Displaying comparisons among different elements or changes over time are two of the most common uses of charts.

Major Excel Chart Types

The most important chart types are:

- *Area chart.* Each data series is shown as a shaded area, each added onto the previous area.
- *Bar chart.* Values are depicted as solid horizontal bars of differing lengths. This type is ideally suited to categorized data.
- *Column chart.* This chart is similar to the Bar chart except that bars are vertically aligned. Again, this type is ideally suited to categorized data.
- *Line chart.* Each data series is shown as points connected by a line. This type is used to show trends and values, typically over a time horizon at even intervals.
- *Pie chart.* A Pie chart is best used when showing values as a proportion of a whole or total. The values are represented as a slice of a circular pie. This is only used when there is a single data series.
- *Scatter chart.* A scatter chart shows the degree of a relationship between the numeric values on both the X and Y axes for several data series. This chart type is useful since it represents data with uneven intervals on the axes.

Click the *Line* button on the Ribbon to open a menu of options. The options include various types of line charts, some with 3-D visual effects. Hover the mouse over the types of line charts to view their Screen Tips, which explain more about each type of chart and how it is best used. Click *Line with Markers* to create this type of chart using the selected worksheet data.

Excel automatically recognizes the first and last names of the students as labels and creates a chart with a legend distinguishing each student. The chart is inserted over the selected data. At the same time, three Chart Tools tabs, specific to working with charts, display on the Ribbon: Design, Layout, and Format. The Design tab contains commands for working with the chart as a whole: changing the type of chart, selecting the data it is based on, the basic chart layout and style used. The Layout tab includes commands for modifying the layout of the chart: whether or not to hide elements, such as labels, axes, background, etc.; and the Format tab contains commands for applying styles: colors, fills, and more to chart elements and text.

To move the chart to its own sheet, click *Move Chart* in the Location group on the Chart Tools: Design tab. This opens the Move Chart dialog box. Select the *New sheet* option, leave the default sheet name of *Chart 1*, and click the *OK* button. This creates a new sheet entitled *Chart 1* in your workbook that displays just the chart.

Notice the Chart1 tab at the bottom of the screen. This is where the newly created chart is stored. To move between the chartsheet and the worksheet, simply click the respective tab at the bottom of the screen.

Graph Formatting

Excel provides extensive features for formatting objects within charts. Although the *Insert Chart* command has produced an attractive chart, further enhancements can be made to improve some of its aspects. You can select virtually any object in an Excel chart and adjust its features. You can select objects in a chart using the arrow keys to step through each of the objects that can be changed or simply select the object with the mouse.

Objects that can be selected are: Axis (X and Y), Axis Title, Chart Title, Chart Area, Plot Area, Data Series, Data Point, Legend, Legend Key, Legend Entry, and <Chart Type> Group.

Once the object is selected, you can open the Format tab and click the Shape Styles dialog box launcher to open the Format <Object> dialog box. Alternatively, you can right-click an object and select the *Format <Object>* command on the shortcut menu to open this dialog box.

The Format <Object> dialog box contains different tabs for adjusting different aspects of the object.

For example, select the Y axis by clicking on it (click to the left of the chart, so that just the Y axis and labels are selected). A gray outline, with circles at each corner and small squares along each side indicates that the object is selected. Open the Format tab on the Ribbon. In the Shape Styles group, click the Shape Styles dialog box launcher on the Ribbon. This opens the Format Axis dialog box, which contains tabbed sections. The tabs displayed depend on the object selected: The tabs for the Format Axis dialog box are Axis Options, Number, Fill, Line Color, Line Style, Shadow, Glow and Soft Edges, 3-D Format, and Alignment.

Select the Axis Options tab. The settings here permit you to change the minimum value, the maximum value, the major interval value, and the minor interval value (unit) of the axis. Other settings also let you specify where the X axis crosses, whether the scale is logarithmic, whether the values appear in reverse order, and whether the X axis crosses at the maximum value.

Currently the graph has all the data points congregating at the top of the chart. It would be preferable for the data to be spread more evenly up the chart. To do this, we would adjust the minimum value of the Y axis to 60. To do so, first select the *Fixed* radio button beside Minimum. This permits manual entry of fixed values. Now enter *60* in the Minimum value text box and click the *Close* button. Your chart should now resemble that in Figure 3-5.

Other tabs used in Format <Object> dialog boxes include:

- *Number.* Lets you change the presentation of values
- *Fill.* Lets you apply a fill (interior color or pattern) to an object
- *Alignment.* Lets you change the arrangement and orientation of objects
- *Border (or Line) color.* Lets you apply and modify object borders or lines
- *Border (or Line) styles.* Lets you modify the style (width, dashes, arrow settings, etc.) of borders or lines
- *Shadow.* Lets you apply and modify a shadow effect
- *3-D Format.* Lets you apply and modify a 3-D effect
- *Marker Options/Fill/Line Color/Style.* Lets you format and modify the type of marker or icon used for data points

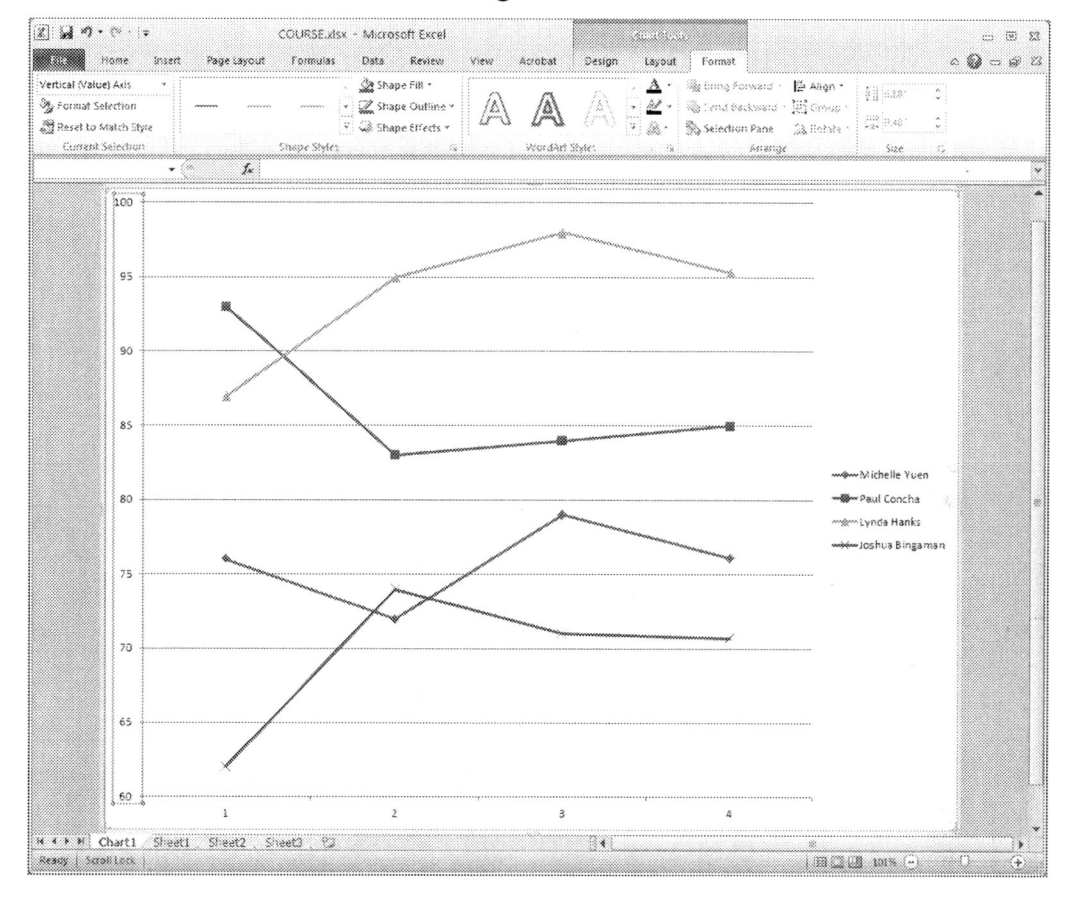

Figure 3-5

Embedding a Chart in a Worksheet

All the features discussed for a chart in a separate chartsheet apply equally to a chart embedded in a worksheet. Charts are embedded by default in the worksheet when they are created.

You can move a separate chart back to its worksheet by clicking *Move Chart* on the Chart Tools: Design tab and selecting *Object in* in the Move Chart dialog box. Do so now to move the chart back to Sheet 1. When you do so, the workbook opens Sheet 1 with the chart selected. You can tell that the chart is selected, or active, because of the pale border around the chart. At the corners and along the sides of this border are three dots, indicating places at which you can drag the border to increase or decrease the size of the chart. A selected chart can be seen in Figure 3-6.

When a chart is deselected, the border disappears and is replaced by a thin border. To select an embedded chart, simply place the mouse pointer over the chart and

Figure 3-6

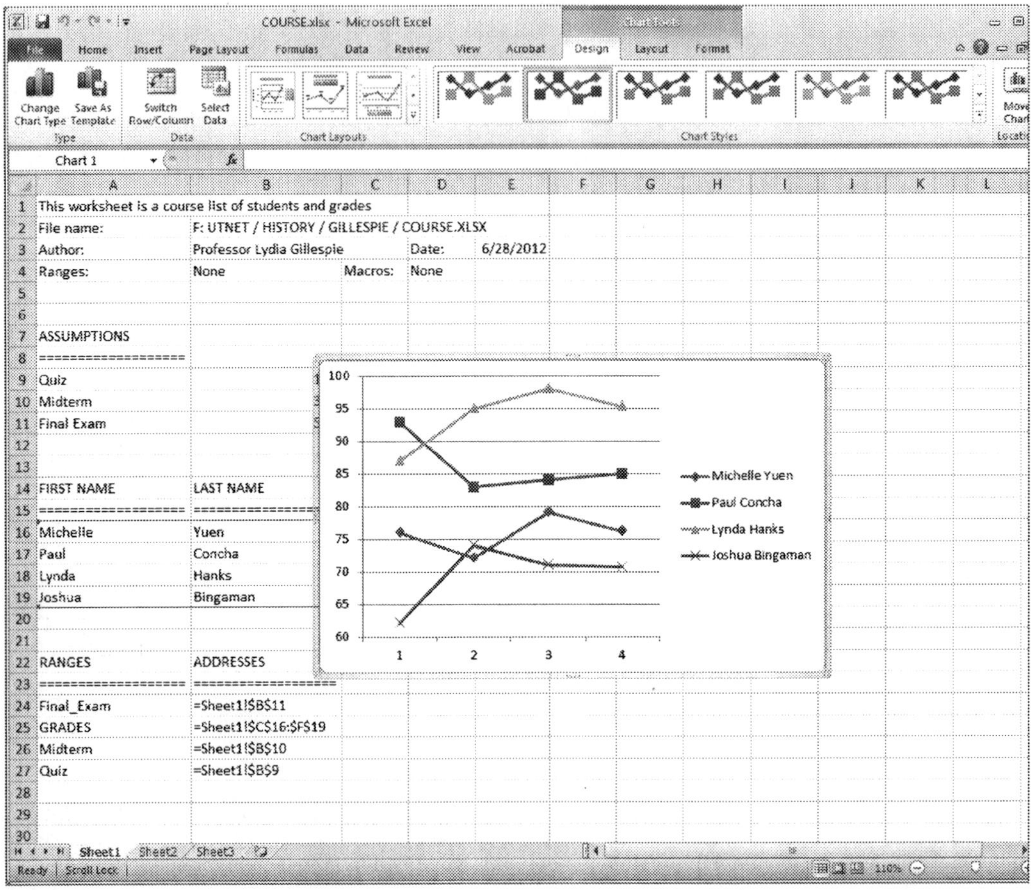

click the left mouse button. To resize the chart, grab the border at one of the sizing locations (with the three dots) and drag it in the desired direction. To move the chart, grab the selected chart anywhere inside the border and drag to the new location. To delete the selected chart, simply press the [DEL] or [Delete] key.

Printing and Saving a Chart

Excel chartsheets can be printed in exactly the same way as Excel worksheets, as described in the Tutorial for Spreadsheet Case 1. The *Print Preview* and *Page Setup* operations apply in the same way as for a worksheet also.

A chart is saved when the workbook in which it resides is saved, as described in the Tutorial for Spreadsheet Case 1.

Spreadsheet Case 7
Fortress Fasteners

Problem:	Develop an inventory control system
Management skills:	Organizing Controlling
Excel skills:	Spreadsheet control Logical functions
File:	FORTRESS_Q.xlsx

Fortress Fasteners, Inc. in Twin Falls, Idaho, wholesales small hardware items like bolts, nuts, and washers to local builders and contractors. The hardware business is highly competitive, but Fortress has acquired a long list of clients by always stocking high quality items within the budgetary limits specified by clients.

Because the company is relatively new, Robin Weiss, the general manager, has been tracking the supplies kept in inventory by using a traditional, manual ledger sheet. This process is time-consuming, and errors have sometimes resulted in missed production deadlines due to inadequate inventory. In response, Weiss has increased the level of safety stock to avoid running out in the future. This increase, however, raises operating costs, and Fortress needs to keep these down to remain competitive. Weiss has decided to implement her own inventory control system using a PC and spreadsheet software.

To ensure efficient use of funds, a good inventory control system will maintain an inventory level that is neither overstocked nor understocked. It will match existing inventory levels against desired levels so that understocked items can be reordered.

There are two basic models for accomplishing this. The first is to use a *reorder level system*, which merely ensures that required items are ordered with sufficient lead time to arrive when needed in the production process. The second is to use a system that determines the least expensive quantity to order, or most economic quantity. This approach, based on the *economic order quantity model*, strikes a balance between carrying costs (e.g., taxes and insurance) and procurement costs (e.g., ordering, shipping, and receiving costs).

Ordering in large quantities reduces procurement costs, but it also raises carrying costs. The *economic order quantity* represents the number of units where procurement costs equal carrying costs. The exact size of the economic order quantity depends upon the estimated amount of the product needed each year, its unit cost, the fixed cost of placing and receiving an order for the item, and the carrying cost for the item in inventory, expressed as a percentage of inventory value. The formula for calculating an item's economic order quantity is:

$$EOQ = \sqrt{(2FU/CP)}$$

where:

> EOQ = the item's economic order quantity
> F = the fixed cost of ordering the item
> U = the amount of the product needed each year
> C = the item's carrying cost, expressed as a percentage of inventory value
> P = the item's unit cost

The calculation of the economic order quantity often results in a fractional amount that must be rounded to the next whole number to determine the economic order quantity.

Load the data file FORTRESS_Q.xlsx. This file contains a list of items that Fortress keeps in its warehouses, the balance on hand, the balance on order, unit cost per item, estimated annual usage per item, and the order point. The order point is the number of units of an item in inventory that triggers the decision to order more items. There is usually a lead time period (for example, two weeks) between the time an order is placed and the time it is actually fulfilled. Reordering while some inventory is still in stock reduces the possibility of an out-of-stock situation.

Assume that the order cost is a fixed cost of $115.00 for all items in this problem. Also, assume that the inventory carrying cost is 25% of the inventory value for all items in this problem.

Tasks

There are four tasks in this case:

1. Above the table of data, insert rows to hold Assumptions for carrying costs and order costs.

2. Add the following columns to the worksheet to track:

    a. *Balance Available* that can be calculated by adding balance on hand + balance on order

b. *Order Quantity* for those items in need of reordering; if the balance available is less than the order point, calculate the economic order quantity. If the balance available is greater than the order point, put a zero in the column for order quantity. Use the =IF and the =SQRT functions, and be sure to use absolute cell references when referring to the fixed and carrying costs.

3. Develop a method for identifying any stock items that need reordering on the worksheet. (**Hint:** One way is to add a column containing a formula to print an asterisk next to needed stock items.)

4. Write a short paragraph suggesting some enhancements to this application to make it a better management tool.

Time Estimates

Expert: 1 hour
Intermediate: 1.5 hours
Novice: 2 hours

Excel Tutorial for Spreadsheet Case 7

This case draws upon all of the skills acquired in previous Spreadsheet Cases, as well as new skills for using the logical functions of your spreadsheet software and the =SQRT function. You will once again need to use COURSE.xlsx for this tutorial.

Excel includes a set of logical functions that enable the software to perform conditional tests and evaluate a condition in your worksheet. Depending on whether the condition is true or false, different values will be returned to cells.

The most important conditional function in Excel is =IF. The =IF function enables you to test one or more conditions in your worksheet and perform different tasks depending on the outcome of the test. The form for the =IF function is:

=IF(condition, action if true, action if false)

This formula tests the *condition* to determine if specific results or cell contents are true or false. The *action if true* portion contains specific instructions to execute if the result of the test is true. The *action if false* portion contains another set of instructions to execute if the result is false. The instructions to be executed can return cell contents that are labels as well as values.

64 Solve it!

To perform conditional tests, the =IF function and other conditional functions require logical operators. These operators help establish the relationship between two numbers, strings, or cell references.

Logical Operator	Meaning
=	Equal
<	Less than
>	Greater than
<=	Less than or equal to
>=	Greater than or equal to
<>	Not equal

To establish relationships between two or more conditional tests, Excel provides Logical Functions.

Logical Functions	Description
AND (*logical1, logical2, ...*)	Returns TRUE if each *logical* condition is true; returns FALSE otherwise
OR (*logical1, logical2, ...*)	Returns TRUE if any *logical* condition is true; returns FALSE otherwise
NOT (*logical*)	Returns TRUE if *logical* is FALSE; returns FALSE otherwise
TRUE()	Returns TRUE always
FALSE()	Returns FALSE always

The logical functions NOT, AND, and OR contain conditional tests to result in a single TRUE or FALSE. The following are examples of logical statements using =IF, using the logical operators, and using the logical functions:

=IF(A5>20,B5,0) means that if the value in cell A5 is greater than 20, you will use the value in cell B5. Otherwise, assign the number zero.

=IF(AND(B11<>0,G11=1),10,0) means that if the value in cell B11 is not equal to zero and the value in cell G11 equals 1, you will assign the number 10. Otherwise, assign the number 0.

=IF(OR(E13="Profit",F15>=G15),"Surplus","Deficit") means that if either cell E13 contains the label "Profit" or the contents of cell F15 are greater or equal to the contents of cell G15, you will assign the label "Surplus". Otherwise, assign the label "Deficit".

Spreadsheet Management Software Cases   65

The second and third examples just above show that logical functions can have more than a single condition as the =IF conditional test.

For your student roster, you can develop a conditional test to print an asterisk (*) after the name of any student whose final grade is less than 80. In cell G16, add a formula that will examine the student's final grade. If the grade is less than 80, an asterisk will appear in the cell next to the final grade. If the grade is greater than or equal to 80, a character string consisting of a blank space will be placed in the cell. The formula for this would be as follows:

=IF(F16<80,"*"," ")

Copy this formula into range G17:G19. Observe on your screen and in Figure 3-7 that the final grades for Michelle Yuen and Joshua Bingaman will be followed by an asterisk. The final grades for the other students will be left blank.

Figure 3-7

	A	B	C	D	E	F	G
1	This worksheet is a course list of students and grades						
2	File name:	F: UTNET / HISTORY / GILLESPIE / COURSE.XLSX					
3	Author:	Professor Lydia Gillespie		Date:	6/28/2012		
4	Ranges:	None		Macros:	None		
5							
6							
7	ASSUMPTIONS						
8	================						
9	Quiz		15%				
10	Midterm		35%				
11	Final Exam		50%				
12							
13							
14	FIRST NAME	LAST NAME		QUIZ	MIDTERM	FINAL	AL GRADE
15	================	================	========	========	========	========	
16	Michelle	Yuen		76	72	79	76.1 *
17	Paul	Concha		93	83	84	85
18	Lynda	Hanks		87	95	98	95.3
19	Joshua	Bingaman		62	74	71	70.7 *
20							
21							
22	RANGES	ADDRESSES					
23	================	================					
24	Final_Exam	=Sheet1!$B$11					
25	GRADES	=Sheet1!$C$16:$F$19					
26	Midterm	=Sheet1!$B$10					
27	Quiz	=Sheet1!$B$9					
28							

The =SQRT Function

The =SQRT function is one of a series of functions that perform mathematical, statistical, and trigonometric operations. The =SQRT function calculates the square root of a positive number. The form of this function is:

=SQRT(number or cell reference)

For example the square root of the average of Heather Smith's quiz and midterm grades would be =SQRT((C14+D14)/2)

You do not need to save COURSE.xlsx with the modifications you made during this tutorial session.

Inserting Functions

Excel provides a facility that makes it easier to retrieve or enter functions. You can activate it by pressing the *Insert Function* button *fx* on the Formulas tab of the Ribbon, located in the Function Library group of commands.

Press the *Insert Function* button now. This will display the Insert Function dialog box. Select the function that you want to use. In the *Search for a function* text box, you can enter a question describing what you want to do. Otherwise, you can use the *Or select a category* list box to select a major category of formulas (e.g., Financial, Statistical, Logical, etc.). For example, if you want the IF function, select *Logical* from the *Or select a category* list box, and then scroll down the list in the *Select a function* list box until IF appears.

Select *IF*, and then press the *OK* button to open the Function Arguments dialog box. In this second and final dialog box, you type your logical test in the top box, your desired output for a true result in the middle box, and your desired output for a false result in the bottom box. When you have completed the Function Arguments dialog box, click the *OK* button to close the dialog box and enter the desired formula in the selected cell.

Nested functions use a function as one of the arguments within another function. (Arguments are the values that functions use to perform operations or calculations.) To create a nested function, follow the same general procedure as described above for creating a formula with the IF function. First, click in the cell where you want to place a formula. Second, open the Insert Function dialog box and select your desired function. Third, enter the arguments required for the nested function and then click *OK* to close the dialog box.

When entering arguments for nested functions, you can type the desired cell references into the relevant text boxes in the Function Arguments dialog box. However, to avoid typographic errors, click the *Collapse Dialog* button at the right end of an argument's text box to collapse the large dialog box to a small rectangular one and then do the following:

- Select the worksheet cell(s) needed to create the first part of your formula.

- Click the *Expand Dialog* button at the right end of the small dialog box to return to the Function Arguments dialog box.

- Tab to the second argument box, collapse the dialog box, select the desired cells for that part of the formula, and re-expand the dialog box.

- When you have filled in all the required argument boxes in the Function Arguments dialog box, click *OK* to close it.

Spreadsheet Case 8
Laser Plastics, Inc.

Problem:	Develop an employee benefits billing reconciliation program
Management skills:	Organizing Controlling
Excel skills:	Nested functions Spreadsheet control
File:	LASERPLASTICS_Q.xlsx

Laser Plastics, Inc., located in Decatur, AL, manufactures precision engineering plastic, rubber, and metal components for a variety of industries, including transporation, medical, construction, and food and beverage. Laser Plastics sells these specialized components to other manufacturers for incorporation into their products. Laser Plastics is a subsidiary of Apex Global, a multinational corporation that has its headquarters in Ho Chi Minh City, Vietnam, its manufacturing plants in Cambodia, Mexico, and Taiwan, and sales offices in Vietnam, Japan, and the United States. The corporation employs more than 8,000 people worldwide. Laser Plastics, Inc., employs 340 people and has annual revenues of $71,350,000.

Each Apex subsidiary location is in charge of the selection and administration of health insurance benefits for its employees. Health insurance premiums are tiered by the number of dependents insured under each employee. Laser Plastics pays for the cost of health insurance premiums for each employee, and employees must contribute to the cost of dependent care.

Toni Acuna is responsible for reconciling the monthly insurance invoice issued by Laser Plastic's health insurance provider, Lydel Healthcare. Each month, she must add new employees and delete terminated ones. She must also ensure that the total amount billed from Lydel matches her records. Acuna has been processing the invoice manually and has encountered an increasing number of discrepancies over the past few billing cycles. She spends a considerable amount of time going through the invoice employee-by-employee, trying to rectify the difference between the invoice issued by Lydel and her own records.

Her boss, James Yi, has suggested that Acuna automate the billing reconciliation process by creating a spreadsheet that automatically calculates the monthly premium based on the number of dependents each employee insures. The rates for insurance year 2012 are: $270 for 0 dependents (employee only), $412 for 1 dependent (employee plus 1 spouse or child), and $540 for 2 or more dependents (employee plus 2 or more dependents).

Laser Plastics pays for the employee portion ($270) of the health insurance premium, while the employee is responsible for the dependent portion through a payroll deduction. Acuna must inform Payroll if an employee is responsible for a portion of his or her health insurance premium so it can be deducted monthly from the employee's paycheck. Her spreadsheet must also include this amount.

Load the file LASERPLASTICS_Q.xlsx. It has employee names and the number of dependents they insure. Acuna will use this data, as well as additional data listing new hires and terminations for the month, to calculate the monthly insurance cost. She will also calculate the amount of payroll deductions for the month.

Tasks

There are four tasks in this case:

1. Add the heading *Premium* to the headings row and create a formula that will calculate the amount of premium based on the number of dependents. (**Hint:** This formula is comprised of nested IF functions.) Since premiums usually rise annually, remember to use absolute addressing in the formula.

2. Add two more employees: Jacob Hoopes and Ronny Barino. Jacob has a wife and two children he wants to cover under Laser Plastic's insurance, and Barino wants to insure his wife.

3. Add the heading *Emp Contribution* (Employee Contribution) to the headings row and create a formula that will calculate the amount of premium for which each employee is responsible.

4. Sort the data in order by Number of Dependents and then by Employee Last Name.

Time Estimates

Expert: 1 hour
Intermediate: 1.5 hours
Novice: 2 hours

Excel Tutorial for Spreadsheet Case 8

As discussed in Tutorial for Spreadsheet Case 7, nested functions use a function as one of the arguments within another function. You do not have to use distinct functions when you nest. You can also nest the same function. In this tutorial, we will discuss how you can nest the IF function to create powerful functions that display a range of variables.

Let's review the structure of the IF function. The form for the =IF function is:

=IF(condition, action if true, action if false)

This formula tests the *condition* to determine if specific results or cell contents are true or false. The *action if true* portion contains specific instructions to execute if the result of the test is true. The *action if false* portion contains another set of instructions to execute if the result is false. The instructions to be executed can return cell contents that are labels as well as values.

Up to seven IF functions can be nested as *value_if_true* and *value_if_false* arguments to construct more elaborate tests. For this tutorial, we will be nesting four functions to calculate the letter grade of each student.

Notice that the simple IF statement uses parentheses in its argument:

=IF(condition, action if true, action if false)

When you create a nested IF statement, you must use everything in this argument except the closing parenthesis and the equal sign. A sample nested IF argument would look like this:

=IF(condition, action if true, action if false, IF(condition, action if true, action if false, IF(condition, action if true, action if false, IF(condition, action if true, action if false)))

Notice that the end of the argument contains all of the closing parentheses for each of the nested arguments.

In this tutorial, we will use the COURSE.xlsx file. We have previously calculated the numerical value of the final grade as the FINAL GRADE column. Now we will calculate the final grade as a letter grade. The breakdown of the letter grades is as follows:

A	90 - 100 points
B	80 - 89 points
C	70 - 79 points
D	60 - 69 points
F	< 60 points

In cell G14, create a heading called *LETTER GRADE*, and below it insert separator marks as in cells A15 through F15. Clear the contents of cells G16 through G19. In cell G16, type in the following formula:

=IF(F16>90,"A",IF(F16>80,"B",IF(F16>70,"C",IF(F16>60,"D","F"))))

Use the Fill Handle to copy the formula into cells G17 through G19. Your spreadsheet should look like Figure 3-8. Save COURSE.xlsx with the changes you made during this tutorial session. You will need it for the next Spreadsheet Case.

Figure 3-8

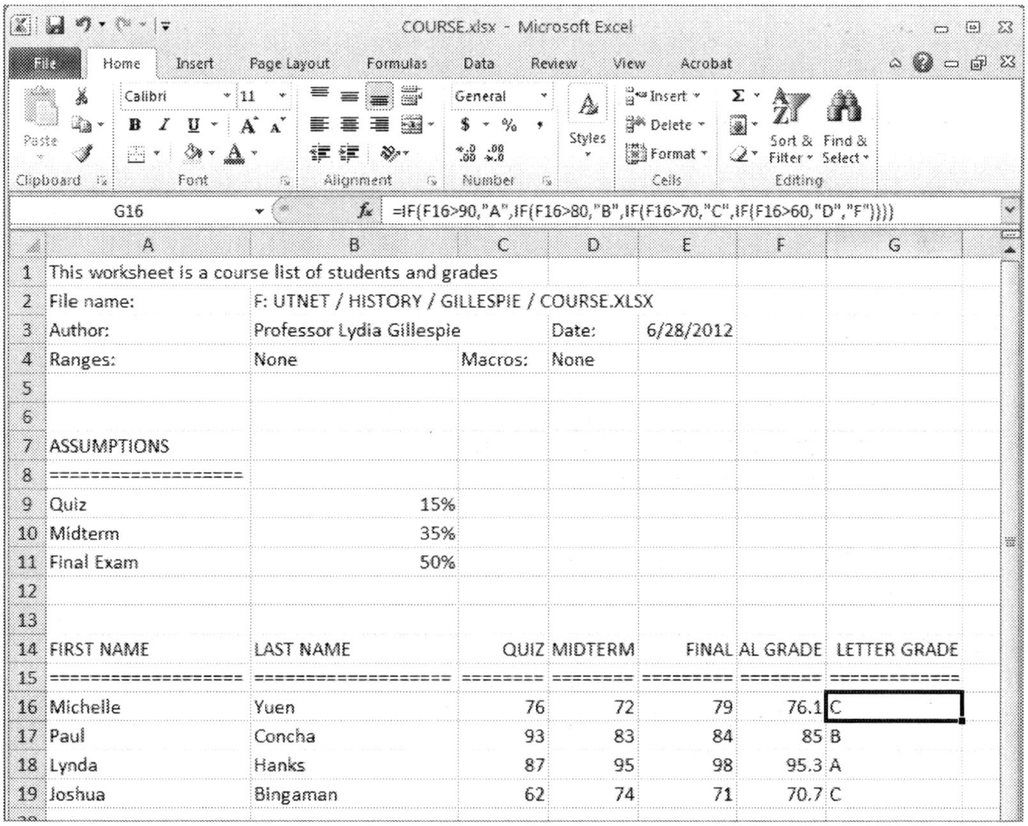

	A	B	C	D	E	F	G
1	This worksheet is a course list of students and grades						
2	File name:	F: UTNET / HISTORY / GILLESPIE / COURSE.XLSX					
3	Author:	Professor Lydia Gillespie		Date:	6/28/2012		
4	Ranges:	None		Macros:	None		
5							
6							
7	ASSUMPTIONS						
8	================						
9	Quiz		15%				
10	Midterm		35%				
11	Final Exam		50%				
12							
13							
14	FIRST NAME	LAST NAME	QUIZ	MIDTERM	FINAL	AL GRADE	LETTER GRADE
15	================	================	========	========	========	========	============
16	Michelle	Yuen	76	72	79	76.1	C
17	Paul	Concha	93	83	84	85	B
18	Lynda	Hanks	87	95	98	95.3	A
19	Joshua	Bingaman	62	74	71	70.7	C

72 Solve it!

Spreadsheet Case 9
KBC Media

Problem:	Determine a relationship between defects and production volume
Management skills:	Controlling Planning
Excel skills:	Regression analysis Graphics
File:	KBCMEDIA_Q.xlsx

KBC Media in Tallahassee, Florida, is a medium-sized DVD replicating company. KBC has been able to take advantage of a growing market, and its business has expanded dramatically. Since opening twenty years ago, the company has doubled its workforce and more than quadrupled its production.

KBC Media's customers are radio program syndicators and small recording companies. Many defective DVDs go undetected until people try to use them. KBC's customers feel that any incidence of defect threatens their reputation and credibility, and has set high quality standards to ensure their viability in the marketplace.

A zero defect rate is an impossibility, but KBC management has mandated a rate below one defective DVD per ten thousand. Unfortunately, KBC's defect rate has been steadily rising. Ester Nicodemus, KBC's Quality Control Supervisor, wonders if the rise in defects comes from the company's growth and increased production volume.

To meet production demand, KBC has had to double its labor force. Its recent recruits tend to be fresh out of high school or job retraining programs. KBC's own internal training has been minimal because many of its positions, such as pressers and packagers, do not involve special technical skills. Nicodemus feels many workers do not pay close attention to quality control procedures, nor do they operate equipment as carefully as they should.

Senior management has ordered Nicodemus to curb the rise in DVD defects. KBC's sales targets are to obtain orders for 15,000,000 DVDs by 2013 and 20,000,000 by

2014. Nicodemus wants to institute a stronger training program and higher quality controls, but she needs some data to convince senior management that, if unchecked, the frequency of defective DVDs will worsen. In addition to predicting future defect levels, Nicodemus also wants to use this data as a baseline to gauge the success of her quality control problems.

Open the data file KBCMEDIA_Q.XLS. It shows KBC's production volume and defects per 10,000 DVDs from 2003 to 2012. Nicodemus will use this data to determine the historical relationship between frequency of defects and production volume so she can predict the level of defects in the future.

You can predict the level by performing a regression analysis, a statistical method for measuring the relationship between two or more variables. If the relationship is between only two variables, the method is called *simple regression*. If the relationship is between more than two variables, the method is called *multiple regression*. We have simplified this case for instructional purposes so that only two variables—incidence of defects and production volume—will be analyzed.

A regression analysis results in an equation that describes the behavior of one dependent variable in terms of other variables, called *independent variables*. In this case, there is only one independent variable, production volume, and one dependent variable, incidence of defects. The regression analysis also produces statistics that measure the strength of the relationship between the independent and dependent variables. You can visualize regression analysis as a way of drawing the "best line" through a series of data points.

You can then use the regression equation to forecast future incidence of defects given projected production volumes. Some popular business applications for regression analysis are determining the relationship between a product's price and cost of production, or determining the level of sales to be generated by an advertising campaign.

Tasks

There are four tasks in this case:

1. Carefully examine the data file, KBCMEDIA _Q.xlsx, which you have just opened. Use the regression analysis commands of your spreadsheet software to perform a simple regression analysis. In Excel, the Regression dialog box allows you to perform regression analysis. To open the Regression dialog box, select the Data tab on the Ribbon, and in the Analysis group, click *Data*

Analysis. In the Data Analysis dialog box that opens, select *Regression* in the Analysis Tools list box and click *OK*.

(Note: If the Analysis group is not present, you will need to load the Analysis ToolPak first. To do so, follow the instructions provided in the Case 9 Tutorial that follows.)

2. In the Regression dialog box, for the dependent variable (Input Y Range), select the level of defects range. For the independent variable (Input X Range), select the production volume range. For your Output Range text box, select a cell to the right of your data so that the regression analysis does not overwrite any existing cell contents.

3. To the right of your data, create a column for the *Regression Line*. Calculate the Regression Line as follows:

   a. Multiply the value of the X Variable 1 Coefficient by each value of the independent variable (Pieces Produced).

   b. Add the value of the constant (i.e., Intercept of Coefficients).

   c. Be sure to apply absolute cell referencing to the X Variable 1 Coefficient and Intercept of Coefficients.

   d. Copy the formula into the remaining rows (i.e., down to the final year of known data). Print out the worksheet and the Regression Output. Put your name in the footer of all printouts.

4. Construct an XY (Scatter) type chart showing the independent variable (Pieces Produced) on the X-axis, the dependent variable (Percent Defective) on the Y-axis, and the Regression Line. Entitle the graph as *Production Volume vs. Defects, 2003-2012*. If needed, add an explanatory legend. Print out this graph.

5. Extend the independent variable range with values of 15,000,000 for 2013 and 20,000,000 for 2014. Then extend the regression line to predict future levels of defects. Revise your graph to incorporate this data and print again. Entitle this graph *Production Volume vs. Defects, 2003-2014*.

Time Estimates

Expert: 45 minutes
Intermediate: 1.5 hours
Novice: 2.5 hours

Excel Tutorial for Spreadsheet Case 9

This case expands on graphics and other spreadsheet skills that you have previously used and introduces the use of an Excel command for regression analysis. You can use your sample student roster (COURSE.xlsx) if you expand it to include a column for the students' ages.

The professor and school administration want to see if there is any correlation between student age and academic performance. In cell H14, enter the column heading *AGE*. Copy cell G15 to cell H15. Place ages in corresponding cells in range H16:H19. Assign the age of 27 to Michelle Yuen, 25 to Paul Concha, 23 to Lynda Hanks, and 18 to Joshua Bingaman.

The number of students on this worksheet is too small a sample to be statistically valid in actual life. Nevertheless, the worksheet will illustrate the concept of regression analysis and the Excel Regression Analysis tool. Excel provides a variety of Analysis Tools that can be accessed through the Data Analysis dialog box. To open the dialog box, open the Data tab on the Ribbon and click *Data Analysis* in the Analysis group.

> **Note:** If the *Data Analysis* group does not appear in the Data tab, the Analysis ToolPak add-in has not been loaded. (An *add-in* is a file that provides additional functions, commands, and menus.) To add the Analysis ToolPak, click the File tab and then click *Options* in the left pane to open the Excel Options dialog box. Click *Add-Ins* in the left pane of the dialog box. At the bottom of the right pane, make sure *Excel Add-ins* is selected in the Manage list box and click *Go*. In the Add-Ins dialog box that opens, place a check mark beside *Analysis ToolPak* and click *OK*. If an alert window opens, asking if you should install the add-in now, click *Yes*. It may take a few minutes for Microsoft Office to complete the installation. (To install the Data Analysis add-in file on a stand-alone computer, you may need the Office 2010 or Excel 2010 application disks. In a networked environment, the file may already exist on the network. Consult your instructor if you have difficulty installing the file.)

1. In the Data Analysis dialog box, scroll down the list as needed, click *Regression* and press the *OK* button. To determine the relationship between students' ages and final grades, you will want to make age the independent variable (x) and final grade the dependent variable (y).

    The Regression dialog box (see Figure 3-9) requires that you specify the ranges that hold the dependent values and the independent values.

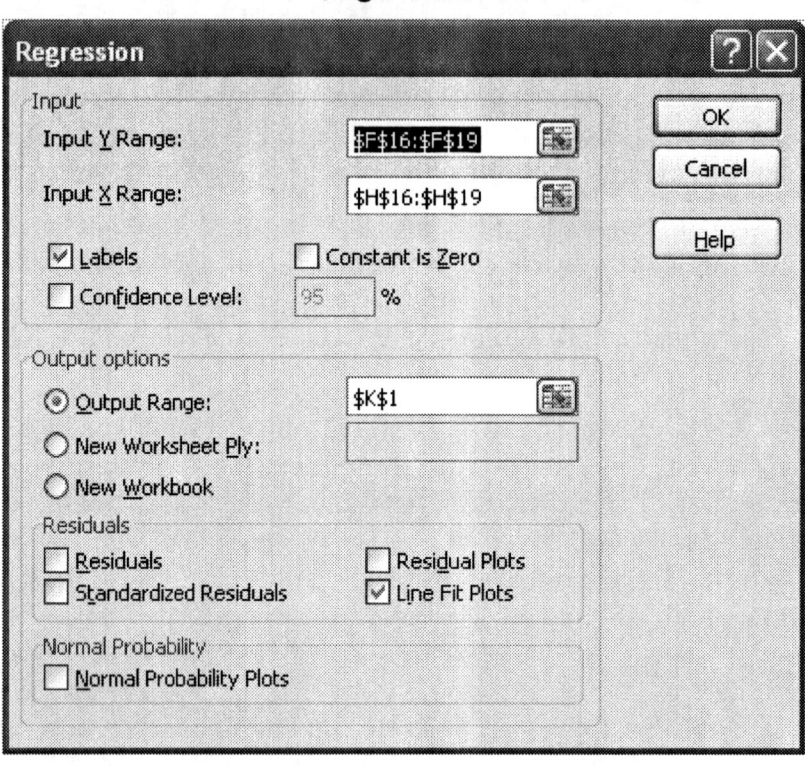

Figure 3-9

2. At the *Input Y Range* setting, specify your dependent variable. In the window provided, enter the range *$F$16:$F$19* (the range for final grades). Alternatively, since this dialog box also permits you to select ranges on the worksheet, select the Final Grades range using your mouse.

3. At the *Input X Range* setting, specify one or more independent variables. In the window provided, enter the range *$H$16:$H$19* (the range for students' ages). As with the Y range, ranges on the worksheet can be selected with the mouse.

4. Select the *Labels* check box to indicate that the selected ranges include the Labels in the first row. (Another input setting available is the *Constant is zero* check box, which lets the user force the Y intercept to zero. We will not use this setting for this problem.) If you wanted to apply confidence intervals to the regression in addition to the default 95% levels, you would click the *Confidence Level* check box. Leave this box unselected.

5. The Output options section of the dialog box contains several option buttons and check boxes. Three output options are available: (1) *Output Range* deposits the output on the same sheet and asks for the upper-left cell reference of the output range. (2) *New Worksheet Ply* creates a new worksheet in the same

workbook and (optionally) asks you to name the new worksheet. (3) *New Workbook* creates an entirely new workbook and places the output in cell A1 of its first worksheet. Select the *Output Range* option button and enter the cell reference *$K$1* in the available window. (Generally, you should allocate a blank worksheet area so that the resulting analysis does not overlay existing data.)

6. Excel provides four check boxes for residual values: *Residuals, Standardized Residuals, Residual Plots,* and *Line Fit Plots. Residuals* are the differences between the actual values and predicted values using the regression coefficients for the same dependent values. The plots will be embedded charts in the worksheet where the output tables will appear. Choose the *Line Fit Plots* setting to compare the actual values and the predicted values.

The final check box is for *Normal Probability Plots.* You would add a check mark here to create a chart to plot normal probability. Leave this check box unselected. Click the *OK* button to start the regression calculations. Your output should look like Figure 3-10.

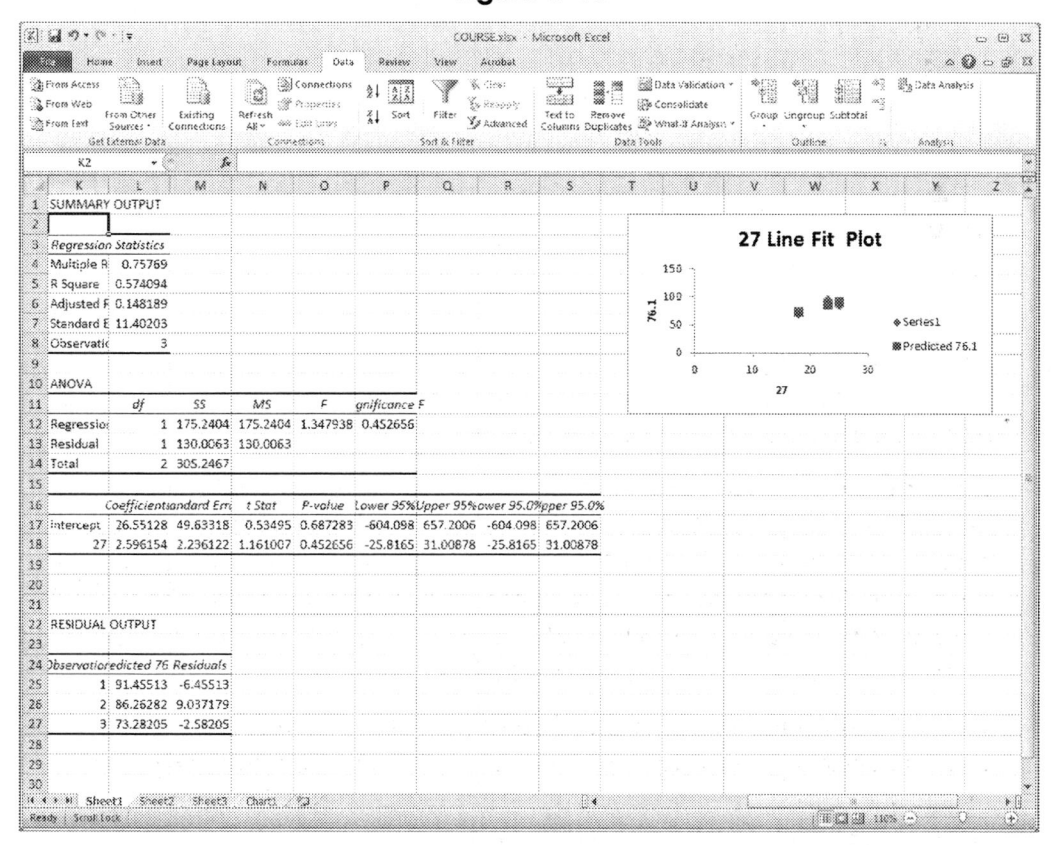

Figure 3-10

Spreadsheet Case 10
Cylon Computers

Problem:	Develop an accounts receivable system
Management skills:	Organize
	Control
Excel skills:	Date Math
	Database querying and extraction
	Lookup Functions
	Data Functions
File:	CYLON_Q.XLS

Cylon Computers, based in Corvallis, Oregon, provides assistance to computer and cable users who have hardware, software, or connectivity problems with their electronic equipment. Cylon was founded in 2005 by four Computer Engineering majors who were frequently asked to help their family and friends with installing, upgrading, and connecting their game machines, TVs, and computers. At first they served only local people, but news of their skill spread, and today Cylon employs 87 people, including a full-time administrative assistant and a part-time accountant. Gross revenues now total almost one million dollars annually!

Cylon has remained essentially a small, friendly business. Three of the original founders have gone on to careers with large corporations, but one, Estelle Gilkey, has taken over and she is now trying to build the business even more. Cylon's customers now include several small businesses as well as individuals. Gilkey fears that the firm does not generate as much revenue as it could to pay the bills and maintain a healthy growth curve. She suspects that one of the reasons for this is that too many bills are outstanding. The business has been run on a largely goodwill basis. They have maintained some of their key accounting records manually, and they have had to remember the names of the people who had not paid up.

Now Gilkey would like her accounts receivable organized and automated so she can easily locate late payers. Load the data file CYLON_Q.xlsx to see the outline of the accounts receivable file. It contains a sample of Cylon's accounts receivable list as of June 30, 2012. Gilkey would like to type in today's date (for this case, June 30, 2012) whenever she accesses the file and then automatically calculate the days outstanding for each account. She also would like to produce an aging report that automatically classifies the records according to 4 aging categories of lateness: Current (30 days or less), 31-60 days, 61-90 days, and Over 90 days.

Gilkey would also like some reporting mechanism to identify the most seriously late payers (over 90 days) so she can contact them and, if necessary, provide their names to a collection agency. She wants to sort the accounts receivable file first by Overdue Category and then by Invoice Amount. She would also like to have a listing of customers who are more than 90 days late with outstanding balances.

Tasks

There are five tasks to this problem:

1. Calculate the number of days each invoice has been outstanding. This is the difference between the invoice date and today's date. Format the result as a number.

2. Classify the invoices using formulas into the four aging categories shown on the worksheet. (**Hint:** Use a lookup function to classify the invoices.) Display overall invoice totals.

3. Sort the database in descending order using the *Overdue Category* as the primary sort key and in descending order using the *Invoice Amount* as the secondary sort key. Print the sorted database (including the information you just provided on categories of lateness).

4. Using the sorted database from Task 3, use the *Advanced Filter* command of your spreadsheet software to extract (copy) a report that shows the relevant information on customers more than 90 days overdue. Print this report.

5. Use the math function SUMIF to total the invoice amounts by *Overdue Category*.

Time Estimates

Expert: 1 hour
Intermediate: 2 hours
Novice: 3 hours

80 Solve it!

Excel Tutorial for Spreadsheet Case 10

This case requires new skills utilizing Excel data management capabilities, along with math, lookup, and date functions. Save a new version of the COURSE.xlsx file for this tutorial that does not include the regression analysis data or the range name table.

Excel Date Functions

To determine how many days an account is overdue, you must be able to calculate the difference between today's date and the date of a customer's invoice. You can calculate the difference by subtracting the earlier date from the later one and by formatting the result of the date calculation in **numeric** format.

Excel can represent any 20th or 21st century date as a serial number equal to the number of days after December 31, 1899. For example, January 1, 1900 is serial number 1 because it is the first day after December 31, 1899. Likewise, January 1, 2000 is serial number 36526 because it is day 36,526 in the number sequence. (Excel supports two date systems: the *1900* for the PC and the *1904* for the Mac.)

You can enter today's date by using the function =Today(). The date provided by the Today() function is updated to the current date whenever the spreadsheet is modified. The function =Now() is similar, but it provides the time as well as the date. Note that although these functions have no arguments, you must include the parentheses after the function name.

For practice purposes, modify your COURSE spreadsheet to include data about due dates for students' library books. You will then calculate the number of days overdue by subtracting the date due for each student's books from the report date.

Create a new range for book due dates in H14:H19. The first cell (H14) should contain the column label DUE DATE, and H16:H19 will contain date information for each student as follows:

Michelle Yuen:	2/27/12
Paul Concha:	6/30/12
Lynda Hanks:	4/16/12
Joshua Bingaman:	5/25/12

Enter the due dates for the students. In cell E21, enter the label REPORT DATE. In cell G21, enter the date of this student roster report (6/25/12). Enter a label for DAYS OVERDUE in I14. Using the Report Date and the student book due dates,

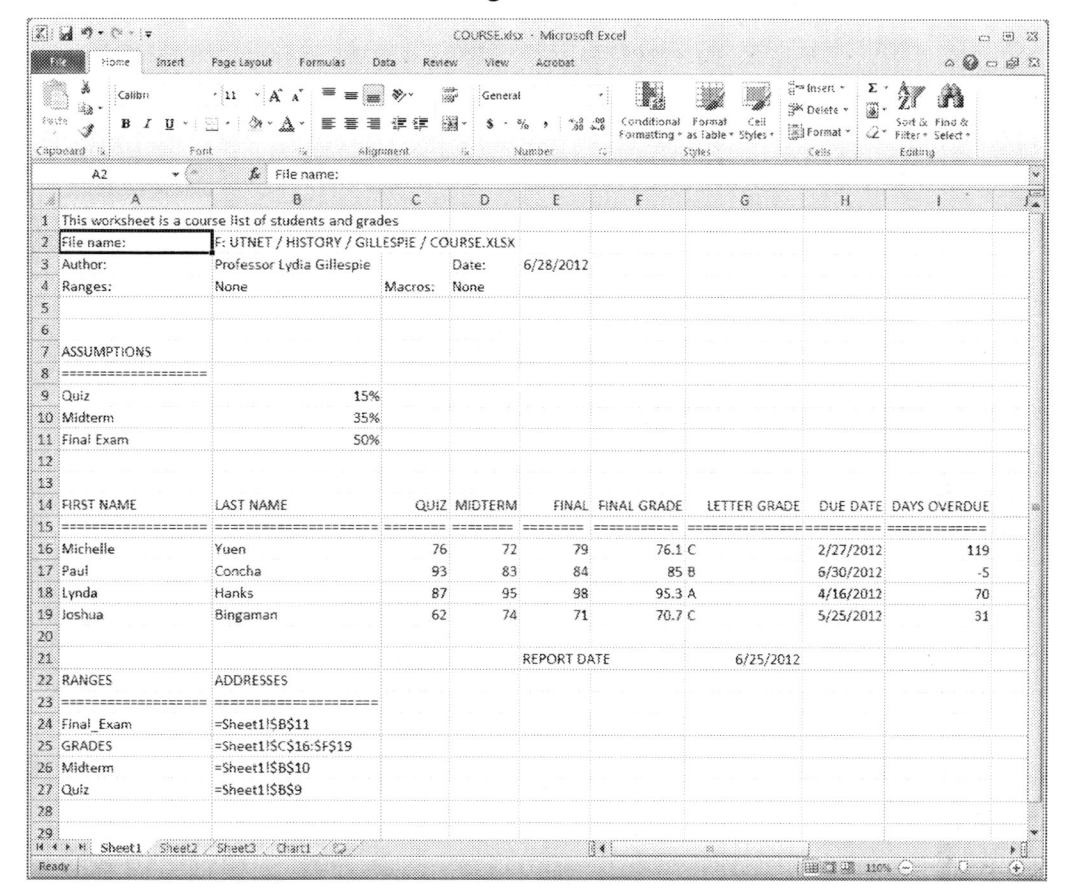

Figure 3-11

	A	B	C	D	E	F	G	H	I
1	This worksheet is a course list of students and grades								
2	File name:	F: UTNET / HISTORY / GILLESPIE / COURSE.XLSX							
3	Author:	Professor Lydia Gillespie		Date:	6/28/2012				
4	Ranges:	None	Macros:	None					
5									
6									
7	ASSUMPTIONS								
8	================								
9	Quiz	15%							
10	Midterm	35%							
11	Final Exam	50%							
12									
13									
14	FIRST NAME	LAST NAME	QUIZ	MIDTERM	FINAL	FINAL GRADE	LETTER GRADE	DUE DATE	DAYS OVERDUE
15	==========	==========	====	=======	=====	==========	===========	========	===========
16	Michelle	Yuen	76	72	79	76.1	C	2/27/2012	119
17	Paul	Concha	93	83	84	85	B	6/30/2012	-5
18	Lynda	Hanks	87	95	98	95.3	A	4/16/2012	70
19	Joshua	Bingaman	62	74	71	70.7	C	5/25/2012	31
20									
21					REPORT DATE		6/25/2012		
22	RANGES	ADDRESSES							
23	================	================							
24	Final_Exam	=Sheet1!$B$11							
25	GRADES	=Sheet1!$C$16:$F$19							
26	Midterm	=Sheet1!$B$10							
27	Quiz	=Sheet1!$B$9							

calculate the number of days each student's book is overdue. Perform the calculation by subtracting each student's due date from the report date. Be sure to format the cells in the DAYS OVERDUE column as *Numeric*. A negative number indicates that the book has that many days left before it becomes overdue. Your worksheet should look like Figure 3-11.

Mathematical Function =SUMIF

=SUMIF is a quick way to sum only those cells that meet a particular condition (e.g., all the unit sales on a specific day, such as Saturday). The format of the =SUMIF function is:

=SUMIF(range to be tested, criterion, range to be summed)

Note that the criterion may either be a cell, in which case the contents of the cell are matched, or an actual value in quotes. This would include text. For instance, in Figure 3-12 below, you can find out how many sales are made on Saturday by using the SUMIF function in cell B16.

If you are asking Excel to match a text criterion, put the text you want to match in quotes when using this function.

Lookup Functions

The =*VLOOKUP* function is often used to translate one set of values into another set of values based on a lookup table you create. For instance, let's say you want to translate students numerical test grades into letter grades. VLOOKUP can do that for you automatically.

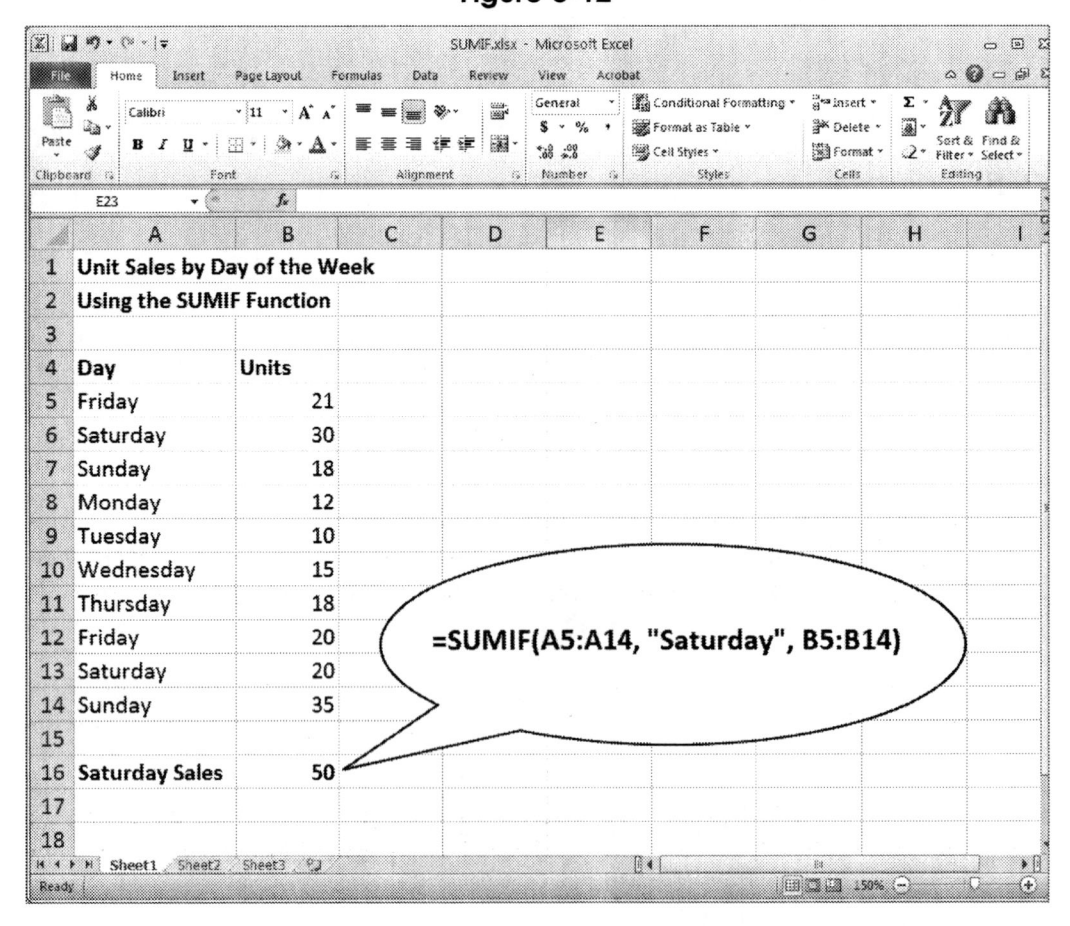

Figure 3-12

	A	B
1	Unit Sales by Day of the Week	
2	Using the SUMIF Function	
3		
4	Day	Units
5	Friday	21
6	Saturday	30
7	Sunday	18
8	Monday	12
9	Tuesday	10
10	Wednesday	15
11	Thursday	18
12	Friday	20
13	Saturday	20
14	Sunday	35
15		
16	Saturday Sales	50

=SUMIF(A5:A14, "Saturday", B5:B14)

The =VLOOKUP function obtains data from a list in much the same way one would manually look up information in a table. Often VLOOKUP is a simpler alternative to a complex =IF function. Note that the column containing the item being searched for must be sorted in ascending order and any lookup value outside the range of the table will return =N/A (not available). The format of the =VLOOKUP function is:

=VLOOKUP(Value to be looked-up, range in which to look, column with the result)

To see how the VLOOKUP function works, let's modify your COURSE.xlsx file to provide a comment for each student based on their final GPA (grade point average). Beginning in cell E24 create the VLOOKUP table of Teacher Comments shown below:

LOOKUP TABLE

0	F	FAIL
60	D	OK
70	C	GOOD
80	B	BETTER
90	A	BEST

Format the lookup table so that it is distinct from the rest of the worksheet.

Enter the label COMMENT in Cell J14. Now enter in Cell J16, the VLOOKUP argument: =VLOOKUP(F16,$E$25:$G$29,3) to display the comment based on the student's final grade reported in E16...E19. Copy this function down to J17:J19 so that comments will be provided for each student. Your spreadsheet should look similar to Figure 3-13.

On your own, you could also translate the students GPA into a letter grade using the same LOOKUP table. Note that with this lookup table, you could also replace the =IF functions used to display the letter grades.

When using =VLOOKUP, always be sure use an absolute address or named range for the look-up table. Test the results of any lookup function to be sure that all possible cases are covered, like a grade of zero or no grade at all.

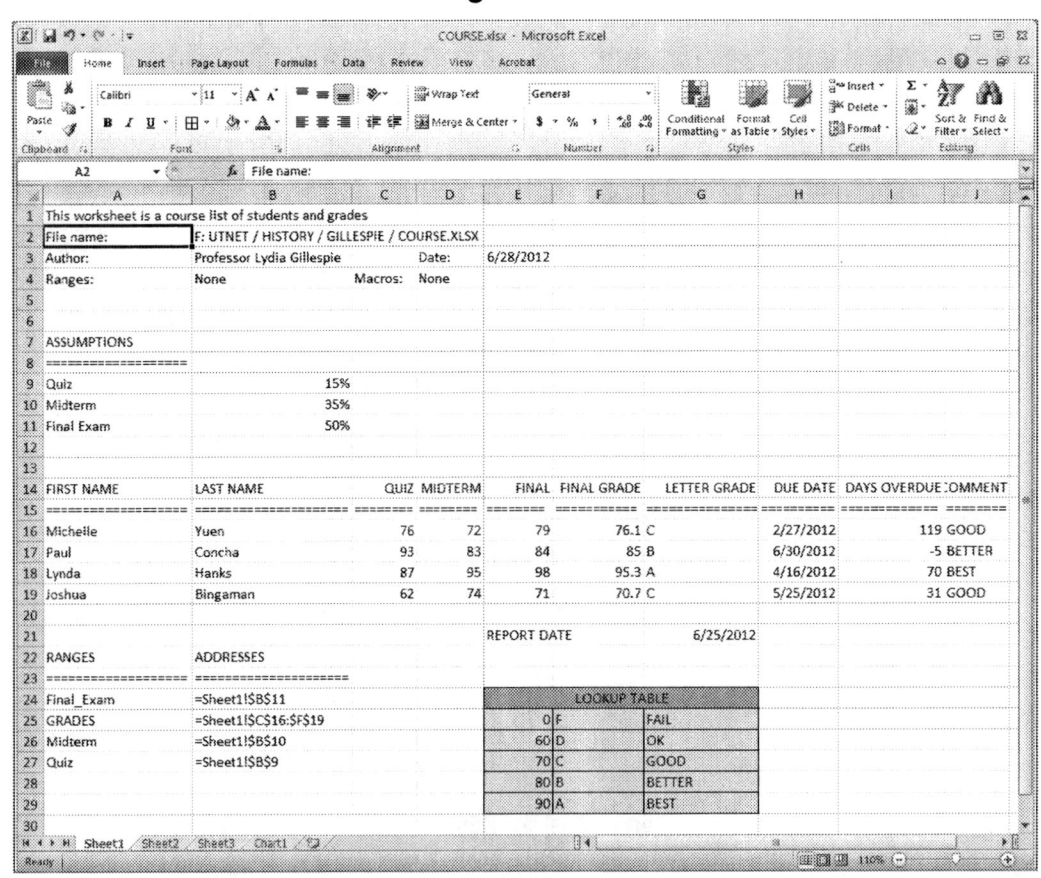

Figure 3-13

	A	B	C	D	E	F	G	H	I	J
1	This worksheet is a course list of students and grades									
2	File name:	F: UTNET / HISTORY / GILLESPIE / COURSE.XLSX								
3	Author:	Professor Lydia Gillespie		Date:	6/28/2012					
4	Ranges:	None		Macros:	None					
5										
6										
7	ASSUMPTIONS									
8	===========									
9	Quiz		15%							
10	Midterm		35%							
11	Final Exam		50%							
12										
13										
14	FIRST NAME	LAST NAME	QUIZ	MIDTERM	FINAL	FINAL GRADE	LETTER GRADE	DUE DATE	DAYS OVERDUE	COMMENT
15	===========	===========	====	=======	=====	===========	============	========	============	=======
16	Michelle	Yuen	76	72	79	76.1	C	2/27/2012	119	GOOD
17	Paul	Concha	93	83	84	85	B	6/30/2012	-5	BETTER
18	Lynda	Hanks	87	95	98	95.3	A	4/16/2012	70	BEST
19	Joshua	Bingaman	62	74	71	70.7	C	5/25/2012	31	GOOD
20										
21					REPORT DATE		6/25/2012			
22	RANGES	ADDRESSES								
23	==========	============								
24	Final_Exam	=Sheet1!$B$11				LOOKUP TABLE				
25	GRADES	=Sheet1!$C$16:$F$19			0	F	FAIL			
26	Midterm	=Sheet1!$B$10			60	D	OK			
27	Quiz	=Sheet1!$B$9			70	C	GOOD			
28					80	B	BETTER			
29					90	A	BEST			

Database Management with Excel

The student roster you have created in A14:JI9 in the COURSE.xlsx spreadsheet can be treated as a database where data can be extracted, sorted, and analyzed. Consider each row with data about a student as one *record* in the database. Within each row, each cell represents a *field* of that record. The headings at the top of each column, such as LAST NAME or QUIZ, represent *field names*.

With Excel, you can treat any collection of data organized into records and fields as a database. Fields in an Excel database may contain either labels (such as the student names in our roster) or numeric data (such as the student grades).

You can use various data commands with an Excel database to sort its records in numeric or alphabetical order, or to find and list records that match criteria that you specify. There are also several powerful database functions that help you analyze your data.

To streamline the data in the student roster database, delete the row that includes the separator marks, Row 15. Doing this will allow Excel to properly distinguish between the headers and the data in your database. Now, sort the student roster database and arrange it by the number of days overdue in ascending order. To sort, select any cell in the range A14:J19 that contains the data and the column headings. Open the Data tab on the Ribbon and click *Sort* in the Sort & Filter group. In the Sort dialog box that opens, you can add multiple levels of sorts. For example, you could sort by Letter Grade, and then alphabetically. To do so, you would first select LETTER GRADE in the *Sort by* list box under Column. To add a second level of sort, click the *Add Level* button. In the second row, select LAST NAME in the *Then by* list box. You can remove a level by clicking the *Delete Level* button.

For this exercise, perform a sort based on the Days Overdue column. In the *Sort by* list box, select *DAYS OVERDUE*, and then select *Largest to Smallest* for the order.

Notice a check box setting at the top of the Sort dialog box indicates whether the list includes or excludes headers (containing field names). The dialog box should already indicate that headers are present. If it does not, select the *My data has headers* check box. If you specify that the list does not contain a header row, the heading row will be sorted with the data.

To execute the sort, select the *OK* button. Your course roster will then sort so that Michelle Yuen, with 119 days overdue, will be first on the list, and Paul Concha, with 5 days left before his due date, will be last on the list (see Figure 3-14).

Filtering a Database

You can search an Excel database for specific records, and copy or extract records using the *Filter* or *Advanced Filter* commands. For example, you can filter your student database to produce a list of all students whose books are more than 45 days overdue.

The Filter and Advanced Filter do the same thing in different ways. An Excel filter enables the user to dictate criteria that will include some records and exclude others. The Filter command performs the filter operation on the list at the same location. The Advanced Filter command gives the user the option to filter on the same location as the list or to copy to a new location. The Advanced Filter also permits more complex criteria than the Filter, although the Filter satisfies most demands.

The Filter command is a simple but extremely effective tool to distill large amounts of data very quickly. To demonstrate its usefulness, highlight the range A14:J18. Now open the Data tab on the Ribbon and click *Filter* in the Sort & Filter group.

86 *Solve it!*

Figure 3-14

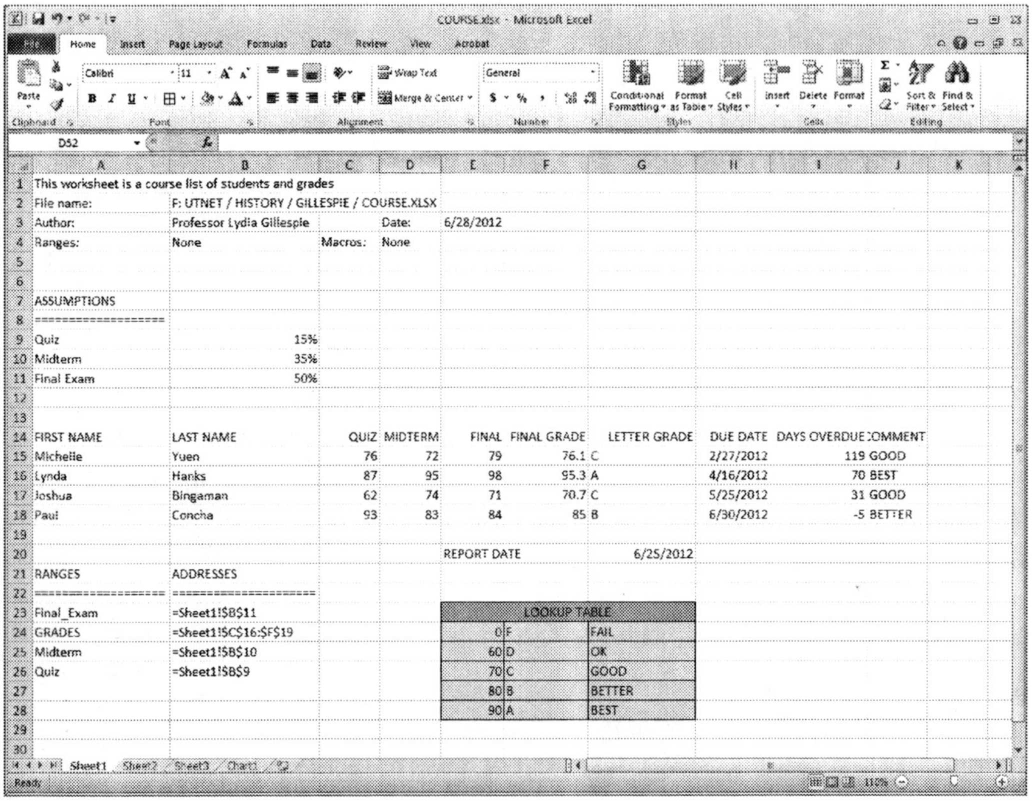

This action places drop-down list buttons next to each of the field names (column headers). It is with these buttons that a filter is performed. Press the list arrow on the *QUIZ* field. The top level of the *QUIZ* drop-down menu for each field contains options for sorting the values in the column, and selecting or excluding specific values. Selecting one of these specific values will display those records with that entry only. Click *Select All* to remove all checks beside specific values. Then click 76 on the *QUIZ* drop-down list and click *OK*. All entries other than those with 76 in the QUIZ field are hidden and the row numbers of the remaining entries are colored.

Open the *QUIZ* drop-down menu again and click *Select All* to return to a full list. Click *OK* to close the *QUIZ* drop-down menu. Select the *DAYS OVERDUE* drop-down menu and point to *Number filters* to open the submenu. The submenu contains options such as: Equals, Greater than, Between, and Custom filter. These options allow you to specify a condition or criterion for displaying a record. For example:

- The **Equals** option allows you to specify a value that a record must have for the Quiz field in order to display.

- The **Custom** option lets you enter a criterion for the current field.

- The **Between** option displays all rows that fall between the upper and lower limits you specify.

Select *Custom Filter*. The Custom AutoFilter dialog box permits one or two simple conditions connected with an OR or an AND. If the field being queried is text, the box for the first logical operator on the left should be an *equal to* or = sign. For our purposes, select *is greater than or equal to* (>=) as the logical operator. Then type *45* in the value window to the right of this logical operator box to represent DAYS OVERDUE >= 45 (greater than or equal to) 45 days. Press the *OK* button to execute the query. The list should have two records displayed now: Michelle Yuen and Lynda Hanks. If you wanted a separate permanent copy of the results of an AutoFilter query, you would have to copy them manually. To turn off the Filter, click *Filter* on the Ribbon.

The Advanced Filter command permits more advanced criteria than the Filter command. It requires criteria to be placed in a separate location on the worksheet. This is best done by copying the field names from the original list so no typing error can creep in. Copy the headings to A31:I31. Type >=45 under the DAYS OVERDUE heading in the criteria (cell I32).

Select any cell in the student grades list (A15:J18). Open the Data tab on the Ribbon, and in the Sort & Filter group, click *Advanced*. In the Advanced Filter dialog box, select *Copy to Another Location* to provide a separate list for the result of the query. For this Action setting, the *Copy to:* text box becomes active. Three references are now required for this dialog box: the *List Range*, the *Criteria Range*, and the *Copy to Range*. Select the ranges:

List Range	A14:J18
Criteria Range	A31:J32
Copy to Range	A33

It is not necessary to specify the end of the Copy to Range since you do not know the number of rows that will be copied. However, be careful because the copied rows will overlay any preexisting data in these cells.

The Criteria Range setting in the Advanced Filter dialog box tells Excel which records to search for in the database. Your search criteria may include one or several fields in the database. The criteria range will have at least two rows: one for the heading and one for the selection criteria.

The first criteria row **must** be the field names of all of the fields that will be referred to in your search criteria. The second row of the criteria range is where the various selection criteria are entered. You must enter each criterion directly below the field name to which it applies. Criteria may be numbers, labels, or formulas. A criteria range can be two or more rows long. For this example, there are two criteria rows: 31 and 32.

Select the *OK* button to execute the query. The resulting screen should look like Figure 3-15.

To search for exact matches of labels, enter the label used as a criterion exactly as it appears in the database. You can also search for similar, but not identical, label entries using special characters called *wildcards*. You can use wildcards in both Advanced Filter criteria and Filter criteria:

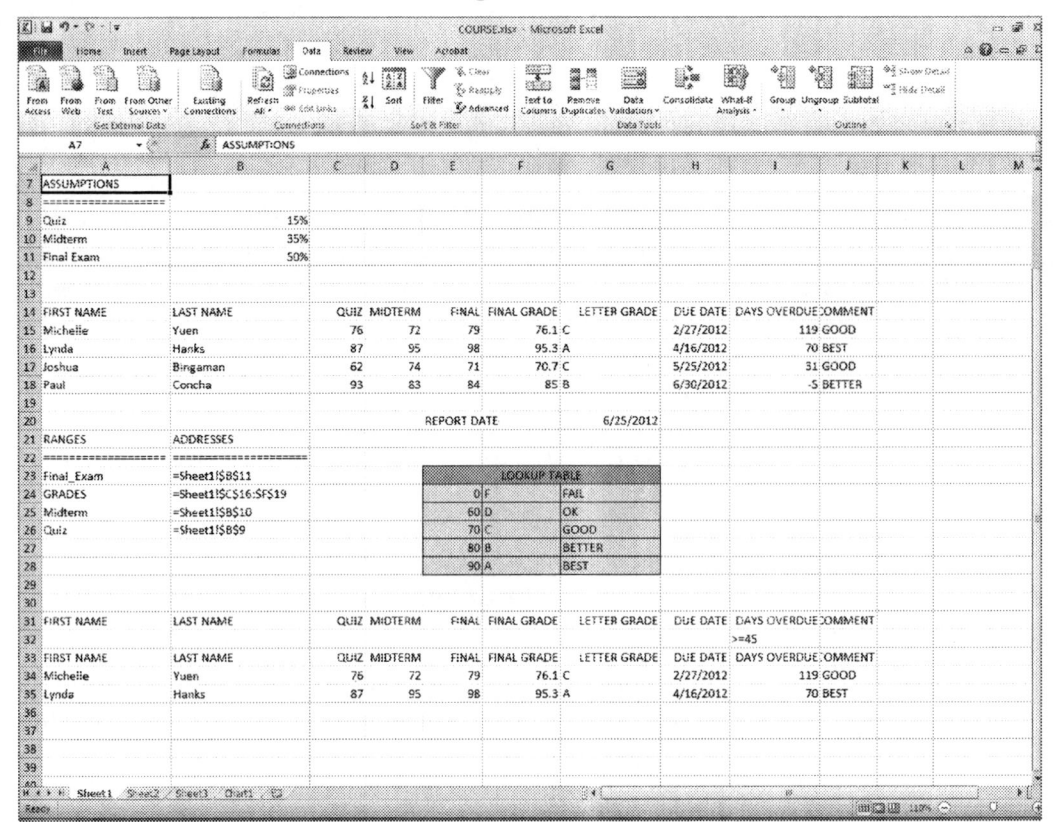

Figure 3-15

- "?" instructs Excel to accept any character in that specific position and can be used only for fields of the same length (for example, "b?t" matches "bit" or "bat," but not "beet").

- "*" instructs Excel to accept any and all characters that follow and can therefore be used for fields of unequal length (for example, "bat*" matches "batch" or "batter," but not "butter").

- The Copy to Range determines the destination of the extracted records and the field names are copied as well. This option is only active when the Copy to Another Location has been selected. The Copy to Range should be an unused area of the worksheet.

- The rows copied by the Advanced Filter will not reflect any subsequent changes to the original list.

90 Solve it!

Spreadsheet Case 11
Three Rivers Machinery

Problem:	Develop a sensitivity analysis for capital budgeting
Management skills:	Planning Deciding
Excel skills:	Two Input Data Table building Financial functions and Formulas
File:	THREERIVERS_Q.xlsx

Three Rivers Machinery, Inc., of Tyler, Texas, makes bearings and metal parts for the farm machinery industry. To increase productivity and profits, the company has started investing in new computer numerically controlled machine (CNC) tools, enabling it to design and make parts faster and with fewer defects. CNC machine tools have multiple tools and multi axes that operate under the control of a computer program entered by the machinist. Most machine shops today employ these sophisticated tools that can carve complex shapes out of solid metal. In keeping with the investment strategy, the company's production manager, Amie Sidwell, wants to spend $640,000 for a new CNC programmable machine. Sidwell estimates that the new tool will increase the firm's after-tax income by $130,000 each year over five years by reducing production costs. At the end of six years, Sidwell hopes to sell the tool for a total of $210,000. The sale price of the tool at the end of its useful life to the firm is the *salvage value*.

Purchasing new, expensive equipment or upgrading plant facilities often requires substantial investment to produce future benefits. Such investments are *capital expenditures*. The process of analyzing and selecting various proposals for capital expenditures is *capital budgeting*. A capital expenditure is not worthwhile unless it produces at least the same rate of return on the investment as if the expenditure were invested at a certain rate of interest that the firm specifies. Businesses use several methods for evaluating the desirability of capital expenditures. One widely used method is the *net present value method*.

You must compare the initial cost of the investment to the total cash flow from the investment. The total cash flow is the sum of the additional income produced by the investment plus the salvage value of the machine tool. You must discount the cash flow from the investment to account for the declining time value of money. A dollar earned ten years from now will not be worth one of today's dollars because you could invest today's dollar at a certain rate of interest. Ten years from now, you would have not only the dollar, but also the interest income from the period. For instance, $1000 invested at a 7% interest rate, compounded monthly, would be worth $2,010 at the end of 10 years.

To arrive at the return from the investment in today's dollars, first calculate the present value of the total cash flow from the new machine tool discounted at the target interest rate for borrowing money. This targeted discount rate is the minimum return on the investment desired by the company. Three Rivers Machinery wants a minimum return of 10% on its investment. Subtract the initial purchase price of the tool in today's dollars from the present value of the total cash flow from the investment to arrive at the net present value of the investment. If the net present value for the investment is positive, it is a worthwhile investment. If it is negative, you should reject the investment.

Since investments vary greatly with changes in interest rates, Sidwell wants to see whether or not the new machine tool makes a good investment under a wide range of situations. What if the interest rate and annual income from the new tool are lower (or higher) than originally assumed? Sidwell can perform a *sensitivity analysis* in a data table that shows how interest rate changes and annual income from the investment affect the net present value.

Tasks

There are five tasks in this case:

1. Review the data file THREERIVERS_Q.xlsx to see the assumptions for the problem and the basic outline of the template. Calculate the total additional income from the investment for the years 2012-2017.

2. Calculate the cumulative cash flow from the investment for 2012-2017. Use the =NPV function to calculate the present value of this amount. (**Hint:** In the Function Arguments dialog box, the Rate equals the interest rate required by the firm. Value 1 equals cumulative cash flow from the investment. You do not need data in the Value 2 text box.) Calculate the net present value of the investment by subtracting the cost of the investment from the present value.

92 Solve it!

3. Calculate the profitability index by dividing the present value of the cash flows by the cost of the investment, displaying 4 decimal positions for the profitability index. The profitability index is another capital budgeting method that helps firms compare the profitability of different potential investments. (For instance, if the present value of the total cash flow from an investment is 24,000 and the initial cost of the investment was 22,500, the profitability index would be 1.066.) Using this method, firms can compare various capital investment projects and select those with the highest profitability indices. You should reject any investment with a profitability index of less than one.

4. Develop a data table showing the impact of different interest rates and different annual additional incomes on the profitability index. In the top left corner of the data table range, key the formula in which the variables are to be tested. In this problem, it is the formula used to obtain the Profitablity Index. **Note:** Copying and pasting the value of a cell or manually typing in a value will cause the data table to yield incorrect data. The *Data Table* command uses the formula in the top left cell to create the values in the table. This cell must therefore contain a formula.

5. Enter the interest rates on the X axis beginning in the cell immediately to the right of the cell containing the Data Tables' formula. The interest rate should begin with a value of 7% and end with 13% in half percent increments. The interest rate is the X variable and should increment across the row. Enter the annual incomes from the investment on the Y variable down the column beginning immediately below the cell containing the formula. The annual income should begin with $100,000 and end with $160,000 in $10,000 increments. (**Hint:** Use the *Edit/Fill/Series* command of your spreadsheet software to set up these values on the data table.)

6. Finally, use the *Data/Table* command to open the Table dialog box, insert the appropriate values in the Data Table Dialog box, and then close the dialog box. To make comparisons more accurate, format the resulting Profitablility Indices with 4 decimal places.

7. Write an evaluation of the proposed purchase. Should Sidwell make the investment? Should it be rejected at all costs? Are there conditions

under which it would be worthwhile? If so, what are they? Utilize the information created by the Data Table command to support your conclusion.

Time Estimates
Expert: 1 hour
Intermediate: 1.5 hours
Novice: 2 hours

Excel Tutorial for Spreadsheet Case 11

This case requires knowledge of spreadsheet software's table-building features and Excel's =NPV function. You do not need the COURSE.xlsx file for this tutorial.

Sensitivity analysis is the process of exploring various *what-if?* situations to determine the impact of one or several variables on a model. Table-building automates the what-if? process so that sensitivity analysis need not be performed manually. Instead of performing repeated what-if? analyses, the Excel table-building function allows various values to be substituted for existing values in your worksheet. Excel will then generate a table to detail the results.

To demonstrate, create a new Excel worksheet that calculates sales commissions. Save the worksheet as CASE11_TUTORIAL.xlsx. See Figure 3-16 to view the spreadsheet format. You want to see the impact on commissions on sales of $5000 when they are based on different percentage rates. To fully display the data table on your worksheet screen, we will not enter documentation into the first four rows.

Set up your worksheet so that the labels PERCENT, SALES, and COMMISSION appear in cells A1, B1, and C1, respectively, and the values for percent (5%) and sales ($7500) that we want to use in our calculation are in cells A2 and B2, respectively. In cell C2, place the formula, =A2*B2, for calculating the commission. In cell A5, type *DATA TABLE 1*. In cell A7, type *Percent*, and in cell B7, type *Commission*.

You could enter different percentages in the A column and then copy the formula for commission calculation to appropriate cells in the C column. However, you can also use the Data Table command to perform this analysis automatically.

The Edit/Fill/Series Command

Before using these commands, you must enter the different percentage values in a column. Rather than enter each value individually, use the *Edit/Fill/Series* command. This command fills a range of cells with a series of numbers or dates that increase or decrease by a specified increment or decrement, or increase or decrease with a multiplicative growth factor.

First, in cell A9, type *.05*, and press *[Enter]*. Reselect cell A9, and on the Home tab, in the Editing group, click *Fill* and select *Series*. In the Series dialog box, select the *Columns* option button, and be sure that the Type is *Linear*. In the *Step value* text box, type *.01*. In the *Stop value* text box, type *.10*. Press *[Enter]* or click the *OK* button when finished. Format the cell range A9:A14 as percentages with no decimal points.

Alternately, if you did not have a required Stop value, but you did have a desired range for the series, you could select the range with the first cell containing the starting value and select *Fill>Series*. You would not specify a Stop value in the dialog box; instead, Excel would finish filling the series when it reached the end of the selection.

Data Table Command

After generating the column of interest rates in range A9:A14, you must enter either the formula for calculating commissions or the cell address from which to draw the formula. *This entry goes next to the column of percentages and one row above the first entry.* In cell B8, enter the formula =C2. (You could have also entered the formula for computing commission in cell B8.)

Select the range *A8:B14*, the range containing the percentage values, the formula, and the blank cell where the results will go. Next, open the Data tab on the Ribbon, In the Data Tools group, click *What-If Analysis* and click the *Data Table* command on the menu. The Data Table dialog box has two available settings: the Row input cell and the Column input cell. Since you are examining only the impact of changes in one variable—percentage—you will enter a cell reference in only one of these. The variable numbers you are examining are in a column, so you should enter the cell reference for the percentage variable. Enter the reference *A2* in the *Column input cell* and click the *OK* Button.

By entering only a single input cell reference in the dialog box, you are examining the impact of changes to one value in a formula. (If, instead, you had entered data in both the Row input cell and Column input cell, you would have shown the

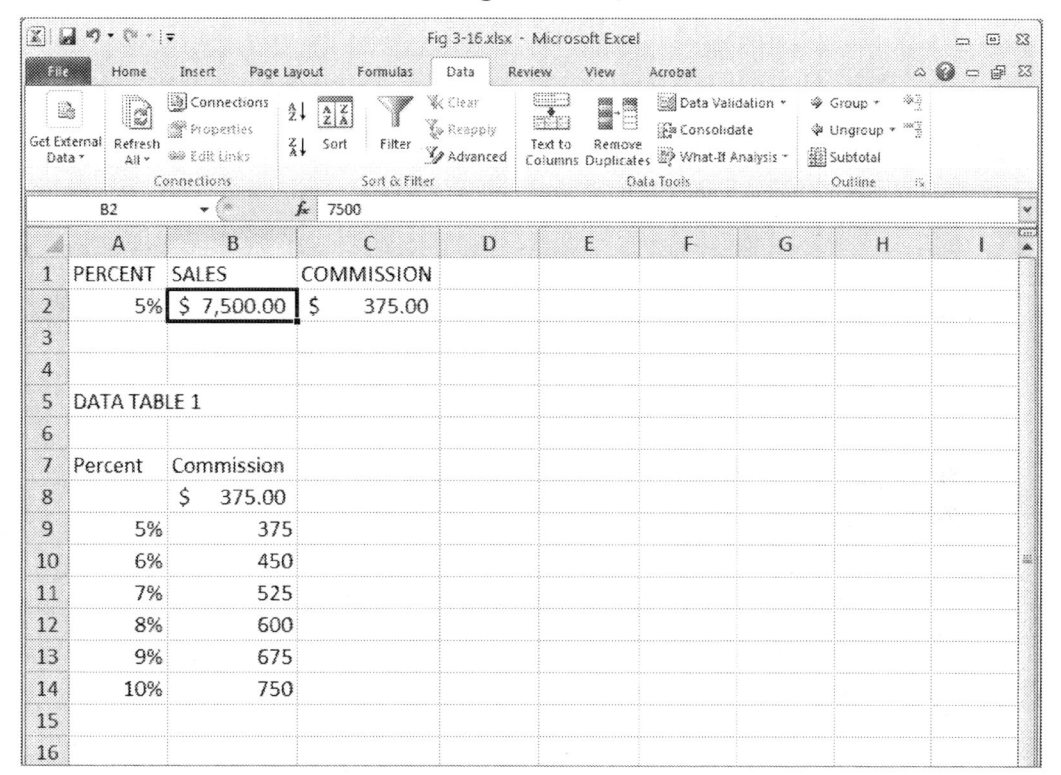

Figure 3-16

	A	B	C
1	PERCENT	SALES	COMMISSION
2	5%	$ 7,500.00	$ 375.00
3			
4			
5	DATA TABLE 1		
6			
7	Percent	Commission	
8		$ 375.00	
9	5%	375	
10	6%	450	
11	7%	525	
12	8%	600	
13	9%	675	
14	10%	750	

impact of changes to two values in a formula.) The results should look like Figure 3-16.

Now examine the impact on commissions if the sales amount, as well as the percentage, is variable. What happens when sales are $7500, $12,500, and $17,500? You would enter the values for our second variable (Sales) in the row just above the first entry of our first variable (Percentage). First, in cell D5, type *DATA TABLE 2*. In cell F7, type *Sales*. Then in cell range E8:G8, enter the Sales values: *7500*, *12500*, and *17500*. In cell range D9:D14, copy and paste the Percentage values that appear in cell range A9:A14. *You also must enter the address of the formula (=C2) in the cell directly above the first entry of the first variable.* (In your tutorial file, this would be in D8.)

Select the range of the table (D8:G14) and then, on the Data tab of the Ribbon, in the Data Tools group, click *What-If Analysis* and then *Data Table* . In the Table dialog

96   *Solve it!*

box, choose cell reference *B2* as the Row input cell and cell reference *A2* as the Column input cell. Click *OK*. The two-dimensional data table should resemble Figure 3-17.

Figure 3-17

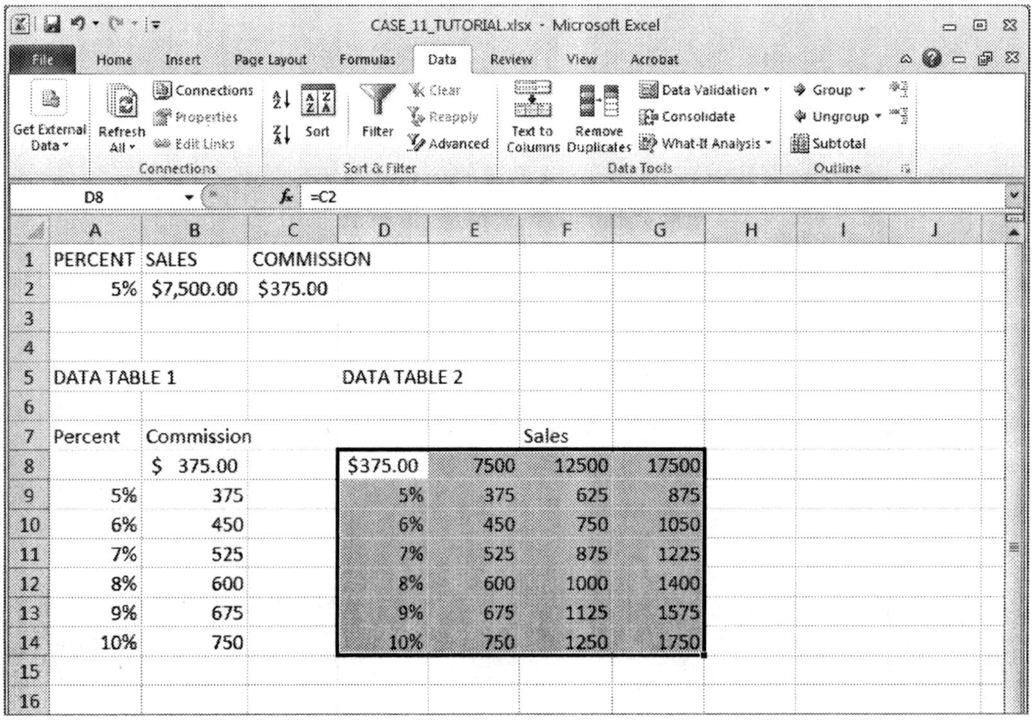

	A	B	C	D	E	F	G
1	PERCENT	SALES	COMMISSION				
2	5%	$7,500.00	$375.00				
3							
4							
5	DATA TABLE 1			DATA TABLE 2			
6							
7	Percent	Commission				Sales	
8		$ 375.00		$375.00	7500	12500	17500
9	5%	375		5%	375	625	875
10	6%	450		6%	450	750	1050
11	7%	525		7%	525	875	1225
12	8%	600		8%	600	1000	1400
13	9%	675		9%	675	1125	1575
14	10%	750		10%	750	1250	1750

Cell D8: =C2

Spreadsheet Case 12
FixRite Assembly

Problem:	Develop a parts inventory scheduling system
Management skills:	Controlling Deciding
Excel skills:	Sorting by Multiple Keys Macro Creation Creating Command Buttons
File:	FIXRITE _Q.xlsx

FixRite Assembly is a moderately-sized assembly company in St. Paul, Minnesota. The company specializes in assembling parts into various types of lawn mowers for larger companies. Jacob Hastings founded the company 13 years ago.

Business has grown steadily over the last few years, and scheduling both the supply and production sides of the business has become more complex than in the early years. Hastings' small amount of factory space limited the amount of inventory the company could keep on hand and restricted assembly operations to only one or two jobs at a time. The company has a difficult time getting all of its vendors to ship items on a timely basis. Production-job due dates also caused problems. For example, an order with a two-month deadline might take three months to complete. There simply was no system in place that linked outstanding orders to fulfill with the production of lawn mowers in the factory.

With uncertainty on both the supply and production sides, shipments of many of their component parts sometimes arrive late with little or no penalty to the supplier. However, Truman Assembly knows that maintaining superior customer loyalty in such a competitive industry requires that the company minimize the number of late shipments.

Thankfully, the company has solved its basic problems on the assembly side of the business. Better worker training, more space, and more efficient shipping services have enabled Truman to deliver products at the quality level that its customers desire and on time. However, Truman still has problems getting its vendors to deliver the small items it needs in a prompt and reliable manner. These delays make it hard to keep storage space needs and essential inventory as low as possible and have reduced profit margins.

Truman's purchasing director, Lee Chiang, recently started using spreadsheet software to track vendor inventory, inventory costs, and delivery performance. She laid out the worksheet, set up the fields and records that the company needs to track, and entered the main data about its vendors. However, Chiang now needs your help sorting the worksheet to make better use of the information.

Tasks

There are four tasks in this problem:

1. Create a macro that sorts the entire spreadsheet in ascending order by Vendor Name, then in ascending order by Item No., and then in descending order by Cost per Order. Name the macro *"VendorSort"*. Assign this macro control key sequence of [Ctrl] + [Shift] + [V].

2. Create two additional macros. The first should sort the spreadsheet column "DAYS OVERDUE" in ascending order to indicate which shipments arrived quickest. Name the macro *FastArrival*. The second should sort the same column in descending order to indicate the slowest shipments. Name the macro *SlowArrival*. Include a secondary sort to organize VENDOR NAMES alphabetically in ascending order in both macros. Assign these macros control key sequences of *[Ctrl] + [Shift] + [F]* for fast, and *[Ctrl] + [Shift] + [S]* for slow.

3. Create three Command buttons above the data area. Assign a macro to each button and label them appropriately as *Sort by Vendor, Sort by Slow Delivery,* and *Sort by Fast Delivery*.

4. Write a one-paragraph summary that identifies the fastest and slowest suppliers. Determine if your conclusion should change based on the additional factors of Item Cost and A/P (accounts payable) terms.

Time Estimates

Expert: 1 hour
Intermediate: 1.5 hour
Novice: 2 hours

Excel Tutorial for Spreadsheet Case 12

This case requires that you use Excel to build a *macro* to perform a sort on a list. A macro is, in essence, a recorded sequence of commands. The commands are contained in a module that can be stored in the current workbook or in a workbook of macros. You can execute a macro through the *Macro* menu on the View tab of the Ribbon or via an assigned control key sequence.

For this exercise, you will need COURSE.xlsx with some of the changes you made during the Spreadsheet Case 10 tutorial session.

Excel includes an extensive scripting language called Visual Basic. Several Microsoft applications can use this language. Excel allows macros to be recorded by transcribing a series of operations performed by users to the equivalent Visual Basic commands. The commands are stored in a module and can be edited using the Visual Basic Editor. Macros can be stored in the current workbook or in a Personal Macro workbook, making them accessible by any workbook.

You can record a macro by accessing the command *Macros>Record Macro* on the View tab of the Ribbon and naming the macro.

You can create a macro, for example, to automate the sorting of your student roster spreadsheet by number of days overdue in ascending order, the same task you performed during the tutorial for Spreadsheet Case 10.

To record an Excel macro, click the down-arrow of the *Macro* button on the View tab, in the Macros group. This opens a menu with more choices. From the menu, select *Record Macro* to open the Record Macro dialog box.

Recording a New Macro

Assign a meaningful name to the macro. The *Macro name* text-entry box is highlighted with the default name *Macro* followed by a number. Type *SortMacro* as the name of the macro to replace the selected default name. Macro names must begin with a letter and cannot contain spaces or punctuation marks. Otherwise, they can include letters, numbers, and underscores.

Assign a letter for the keyboard shortcut that a user can type to start the macro running. Type the capital letter *K* into the *Shortcut key* text box. Notice that Excel changes the shortcut to Ctrl+Shift+K to accommodate the capital letter.

From the *Store macro in* list, select *This Workbook*. If you are creating multiple macros to be used in more than one file, they can also be stored in a Personal Macro Workbook.

Describe the macro. In the *Description* text box, type *Sorts by the number of overdue days in ascending order.* (See Figure 3-18.)

To start recording, click the *OK* button. While you are recording, be careful to include only those commands, keystrokes, and typed items that are absolutely necessary to create the macro. Avoid mistakes, as Excel will include them in the macro if it is still recording. To turn off macro recording function, click *Macro* and then click *Stop Recording* on the View tab of the Ribbon. Excel will not record the Stop Recording command as part of the macro.

One of the most common problems when recording a macro is forgetting to stop recording! If this occurs, immediately select *Stop Recording*, delete the macro (on the Macro menu), and start over. To halt a macro that seems to be running forever (perhaps because you forgot to stop recording), hit the *[ESC]* key.

To automate the sorting of your student roster spreadsheet, record the following actions:

1. Select the range A14:J18.
2. Open the Data tab on the Ribbon and click *Sort*.
3. In the Sort dialog box, select *DAYS OVERDUE* in the *Sort by* list box.

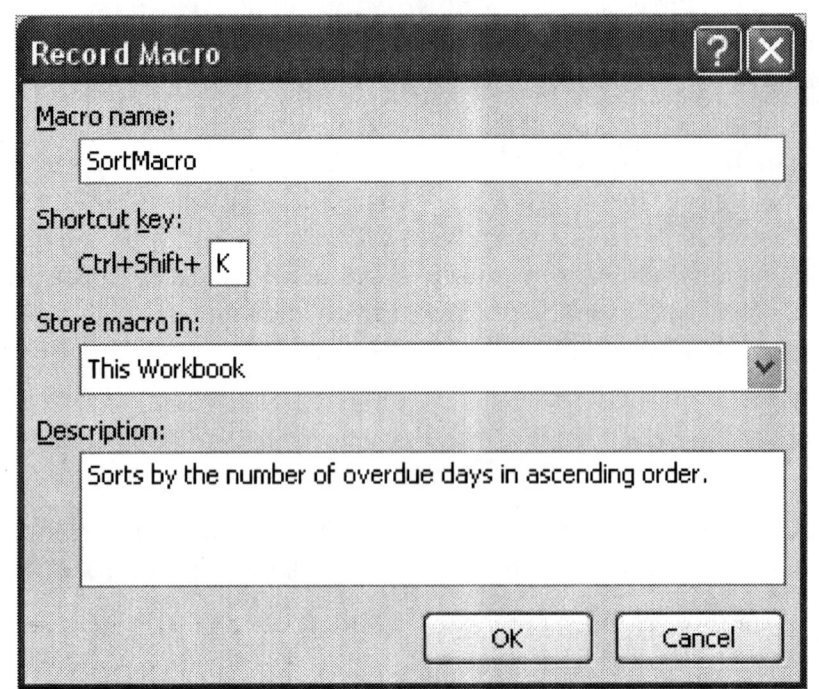

Figure 3-18

4. In the Order column, select *Smallest to Largest* for the sort.
5. Make sure that the *My data has headers* check box is selected.
6. Click the *OK* button to execute the sort.
7. To finish, open the View tab on the Ribbon, click *Macro* and then click *Stop Recording*. The macro stops recording.

To test the macro, first undo the changes you made while creating the macro so you can see if it works correctly. It is also a good idea to save a worksheet before running a macro for the first time. This way, if the macro has any problems that affect the data, you can revert to the saved version of your workbook.

To run the macro, open the *View* tab, click on the *Macro* command, and select *View Macros* from the menu. The Macro dialog box opens. Beneath the *Macro name* text box is a larger box listing all available macros. Click on your macro's name in this box. The name displays in the text box above, and the macro's description appears at the bottom of the dialog box. Click the *Run* button. You can also run the macro by hitting the control key sequence assigned to it. If the macro runs correctly, the spreadsheet will sort in ascending order.

Assigning a Macro to a Command Button

To make it even easier to run a macro, you can add it as a button on the Quick Access toolbar, and the button will appear every time you call Excel. (However, if you specify that a macro is saved for only the current workbook, the macro will not run in other workbooks.)

To create a Quick Access button, click the down-arrow to the right of the Quick Access toolbar, and click *More Commands*. This opens the Quick Access Toolbar section of the Excel Options dialog box, which allows you to modify the Quick Access toolbar. From the *Choose commands from* drop-down list, select *Macros*. In the list box on the left, scroll down to select *SortMacro*. Click the *Add* button to add *SortMacro* to the right pane, which lists the buttons in the Quick Access toolbar. (Notice that you can change the button that is used on the Quick Access toolbar by pressing the *Modify* button and selecting a new button icon to use in the Modify Button dialog box that opens.) Click *OK* to add the SortMacro macro to the QuickAccess toolbar and close the Excel Options window. Clicking on the *SortMacro* button will now cause the macro to run.

Viewing the Macro

Recording a macro and then viewing and editing it is a great way to learn Visual Basic. You can view your macro commands by opening the View tab, clicking *Macro* and then *View Macros*, and then selecting the *Edit* option from the Macro dialog box. The Visual Basic module for the macro will appear and can be edited. The module for the macro to sort the student roster spreadsheet would look like Figure 3-19.

As you can see, modules have a non-tabular format, and they lack the rows and columns typical of regular worksheets. Instead, data displays as lines of text against a white background.

Managing Your Macros

To easily write and edit macros, you should become familiar with the Visual Basic Editor. With the help of this editor, you do not have to learn Visual Basic itself to make simple edits to your macros. The editor enables you to edit macros, copy macros, rename macros, etc. Note also that recent versions of Excel have increased safeguards against computer viruses transmitted by macros. To set the level of security most appropriate for your spreadsheet activities, click the File tab and then click *Options*. Select *Trust Center* in the left pane of the Excel Options window. In the right pane, under Microsoft Office Excel Trust Center, click the *Trust Center*

Figure 3-19

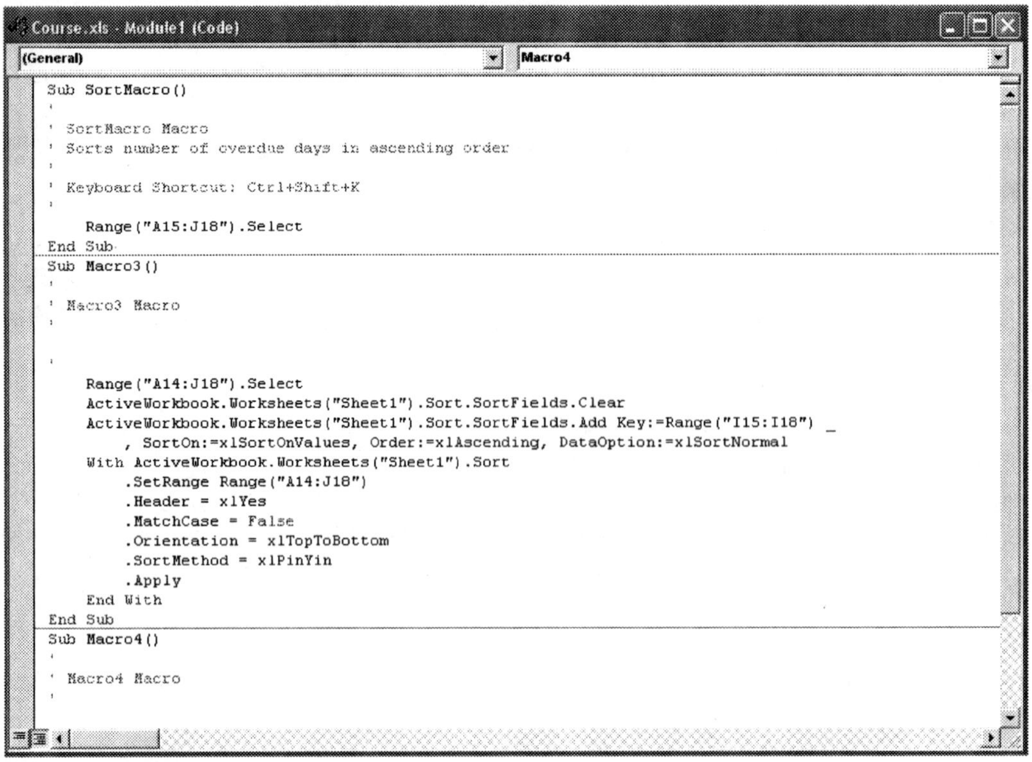

```
Sub SortMacro()
'
' SortMacro Macro
' Sorts number of overdue days in ascending order
'
' Keyboard Shortcut: Ctrl+Shift+K
'
    Range("A15:J18").Select
End Sub
Sub Macro3()
'
' Macro3 Macro
'

    Range("A14:J18").Select
    ActiveWorkbook.Worksheets("Sheet1").Sort.SortFields.Clear
    ActiveWorkbook.Worksheets("Sheet1").Sort.SortFields.Add Key:=Range("I15:I18") _
        , SortOn:=xlSortOnValues, Order:=xlAscending, DataOption:=xlSortNormal
    With ActiveWorkbook.Worksheets("Sheet1").Sort
        .SetRange Range("A14:J18")
        .Header = xlYes
        .MatchCase = False
        .Orientation = xlTopToBottom
        .SortMethod = xlPinYin
        .Apply
    End With
End Sub
Sub Macro4()
'
' Macro4 Macro
'
```

Settings button. Select *Macro Settings* in the left pane of the Trust Center window. The Macro settings you can choose from are:

- Disable all macros without notification
- Disable all macros with notification
- Disable all macros except digitally signed macros
- Enable all macros

To edit a macro in your worksheet, open the View tab, click *Macro* and then click *View Macros*. Select the macro you wish to work with in the list box, and then click *Edit* to display the editing window. (Notice that you can also delete a macro in this dialog box by selecting the *Delete* button.) In the editing window, make the desired changes, and then click the *Close* button at the right end of the blue Title bar.

Troubleshooting Macros

When troubleshooting macros, you will generally come across one of three different problems. First, if you click the *Refresh* button, a message may display telling you that your macro changes will be lost. (This message displays if you have edited a macro in the Visual Basic Editor and have changed the copy of your workbook in the Microsoft Script Editor.) In such cases, click *No* in the message box, switch to the Visual Basic Editor, and export any modules you have changed. Then in your workbook in Microsoft Script Editor, click *Refresh* on the Refresh toolbar. Finally, click *Yes* and then import the desired modules to restore the changes to your macro.

Second, while recording a macro, you may accidentally record an undesired action. To delete that action, open the Visual Basic Editor, remove the unwanted steps, and then click the *Close* button. Alternately, you can delete the defective macro and re-record it with the correct steps.

Third, a recorded macro may display an error message in some situations, but not in others. (For example, a macro that looks for a certain column header will run properly if the column header is displayed, but it may malfunction if the header is not displayed, thereby prompting the error message.) In these inconsistent situations, write down the number of the error message. Open Visual Basic Help, search for *error messages*, and find information about the message number you received.

Spreadsheet Case 13
Chef's Garden

Problem:	Develop a faster method of data analysis
Management skills:	Support management decision making
	Prepare ad hoc reports
Excel skill:	Creating and Using Pivot Tables
File:	CHEFSGARDEN_Q.XLSX

Chef's Garden, an importer of organic fruits and vegetables, was formed only one year ago by New Jersey investors Jerri Vitigliano and Harriet Peat. With more and more Americans concerned about eating a healthy diet that includes plenty of vegetables and fruits, grocery stores that emphasize health foods and organic foods have experienced rapid growth. Good food is not inexpensive, and upscale grocery chains like Trader Joe's and Whole Foods charge premium prices for their products. Although it is less well known than its competitors, Chef's Garden has also grown beyond its founders' expectations.

As is often the case with quick success in business, Chef's Garden is having severe growing pains. They are frequently out of stock of the most in-demand items in one city, but are overstocked with the same item in another city. Because of the perishable nature of their products, it is impossible to reship the items to where they are needed.

Fortunately, their business manager, Max Uphoff, has kept very accurate weekly sales records over the last year. Vitigliano and Peat realize that this data could help them better predict the areas and timing of future product demand.

They frequently ask Uphoff what he considers "off the wall" questions, and he spends hours rearranging his spreadsheets and using the data commands to give them the reports they want. However, every day they want more information and different reports, and as a result, Uphoff can't concentrate on his regular work of paying bills and salaries!

He has recently taken an advanced Excel course and learned about pivot tables. Uphoff thinks these may be the answer to his problem. Using a pivot table, he can quickly and easily rearrange the data to provide the answer to "today's question"!

Using the file CHEFSGARDEN_Q.xlsx, create a pivot table that would answer some of the questions posed by Uphoff's managers.

Tasks

There are four tasks in this case. Each of these tasks can be solved with a pivot table. Do not make four separate pivot tables. Pivot tables consume considerable memory, and it is not necessary. Instead, rearrange the fields in the table to get the answer you need, format your table using one of the Autoformats, and then print it out. Write a short paragraph to support your reports.

1. During what month are peaches most in demand in Princeton?

2. Who is the least productive salesperson? From the information provided by the pivot table, can you suggest any reasons for this person's poor performance?

3. Sales to restaurants entail more labor than sales to other venues. Is it worthwhile to continue marketing to restaurants? (**Hint:** To have the total show as % of column, select *Field Settings/Options/Show Data/% of Column Total*.)

4. Chef's Garden may be growing too fast and be spread over too wide a geographic area. Vitigliano and Peat want Uphoff to choose a city where closing down or decreasing marketing would have the least negative impact on the company's revenues. What city should he choose?

Excel Tutorial for Spreadsheet Case 13: Pivot Tables

This case asks you to use Excel for more than the routine tasks of entering and formatting data and using formulae and functions to calculate answers. In this case, you are being asked to look at existing data to discover correlations and predict trends.

Excel's data management commands provide some of this functionality, but often several commands and combinations of commands are needed to look at and compare the data you want to analyze. To look closely at one segment of data, like the first month of the year, you would first need to select and extract it with a filter, perhaps sort it and then perform calculations. This process would need to be repeated for each different segment of data, i.e., for each month. Perhaps you want to look at the data by quarters and not by months? Or by product type? Or by salesperson? For each different analysis, you would need to rearrange your data and repeat the commands and calculations.

Solve it!

Excel's Pivot Table command accomplishes the same results as many of the data commands more easily and without the need to disturb your original data. It allows you to summarize and analyze your data in alternative perspectives merely by dragging and dropping names. A pivot table can be used on data from large external data bases, or from Microsoft Access, as well as on one or multiple ranges from an Excel spreadsheet.

For this tutorial, you will use the student data file COURSE_DEMOGRAPHICS.xlsx. This file is automatically downloaded when you download files from the Web site www.MySolveit.Com. You will use this file to create a Pivot Table, and then to answer a number of questions. Once you complete this tutorial, you will have learned the skills needed to perform the tasks in this case.

The COURSE_DEMOGRAPHICS.xlsx student data file is a list of students in Professor Lydia Gillespie's biology class at the University of Torrington. The file contains data regarding each student's name, major, sex, attendance, and grade information.

Excel data used in a Pivot Table must be in the form of an Excel database or list, where: (1) each column has a label, (2) there are no blank rows or columns, and (3) there are no totals in the list. See the Tutorial for Case 10 for a review of Excel database requirements and functions.

Professor Lydia Gillespie has several questions about her students:

- Did the men miss more classes than the women?
- Were the students from Springfield absent more often than others?
- Is it true that women get better grades?
- Does the student's birth month correlate to his or her grades?

Use the Excel student data COURSE_DEMOGRAPHICS.xlsx downloaded with your student files to create a pivot table to answer these questions. Before you create a pivot table, it is a good idea to give a range name to the list data. Here we have named cells A7:K106 as tblSTUDENT.

A pivot table consists of 4 areas:

- *Data* items are what you want to measure.
- *Columns* are usually the fields in which you are looking for a trend.
- *Rows* are usually the fields by which you want to categorize.
- *Pages* are often used for major categories.

In order to create a pivot table you must use the Pivot Table Wizard.

Creating a PivotTable

To create a Pivot Table:

1. Select the top left cell of data in your table, in this case, cell A8. This allows Excel to recognize the beginning of your data set.

2. Open the Insert tab on the Ribbon, and in the Tables group, click *PivotTable*. This opens the Create PivotTable dialog box.

3. In the PivotTable dialog box, Excel automatically recognizes the data table to use (the range from A7:K106). Select *New Worksheet* for where you want the PivotTable report to be placed (Figure 3-20) and click *OK*.

   Excel opens a new worksheet, Sheet1 with a blank PivotTable Report ready for you to configure. On the Ribbon, two PivotTable Tools tabs display with commands for working with PivotTables: Options and Design.

4. In the PivotTable Task pane on the right of the worksheet, drag the *CITY* field from the Field List down to the *Row Labels* box below.

5. Drag the *SEX* field to the *Column Labels* box.

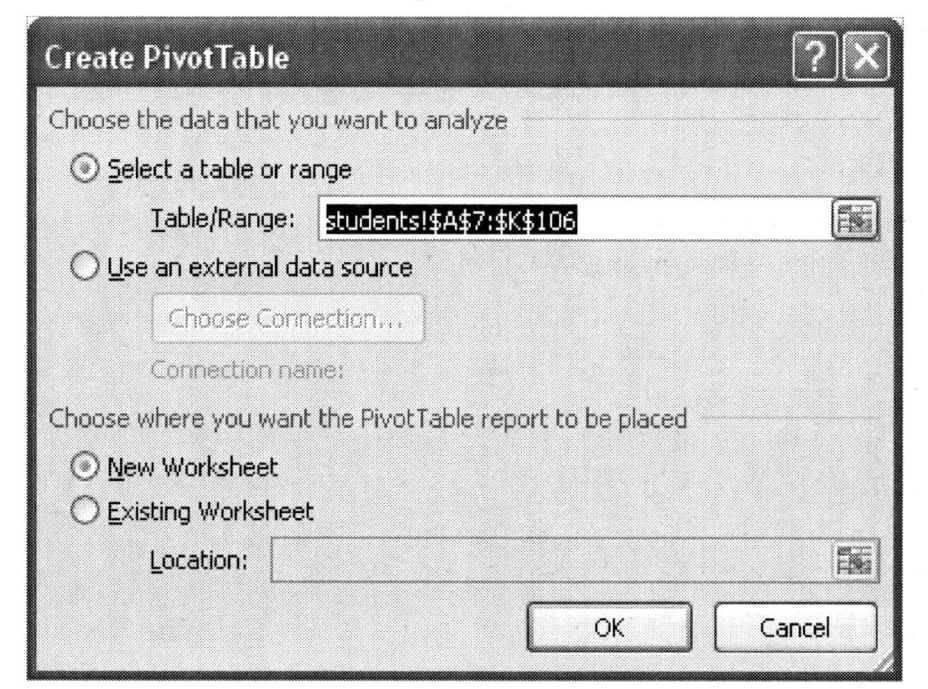

Figure 3-20

108 *Solve it!*

6. Drag the field *DAYS ABSENT* to the *Values* box. Your worksheet should resemble Figure 3-21.

Voila! You have created your first Pivot Table!

Examining Your Pivot Table

One of the most common problems people have with pivot tables is figuring out what to put where to get the answers they need. The pivot table you just created answers two of Professor Gillespies' questions: "Did the men miss more classes than the women?" and "Were the students from Springfield absent more frequently than those from other cities?"

To answer both of these questions, it was necessary to use the fields for SEX and for CITY. The data being analyzed was DAYS ABSENT. Examine Figure 3-21. What are the answers?

Note that the pivot table is showing the raw number of days absent for students from each city and of each gender. This could be misleading if there were more

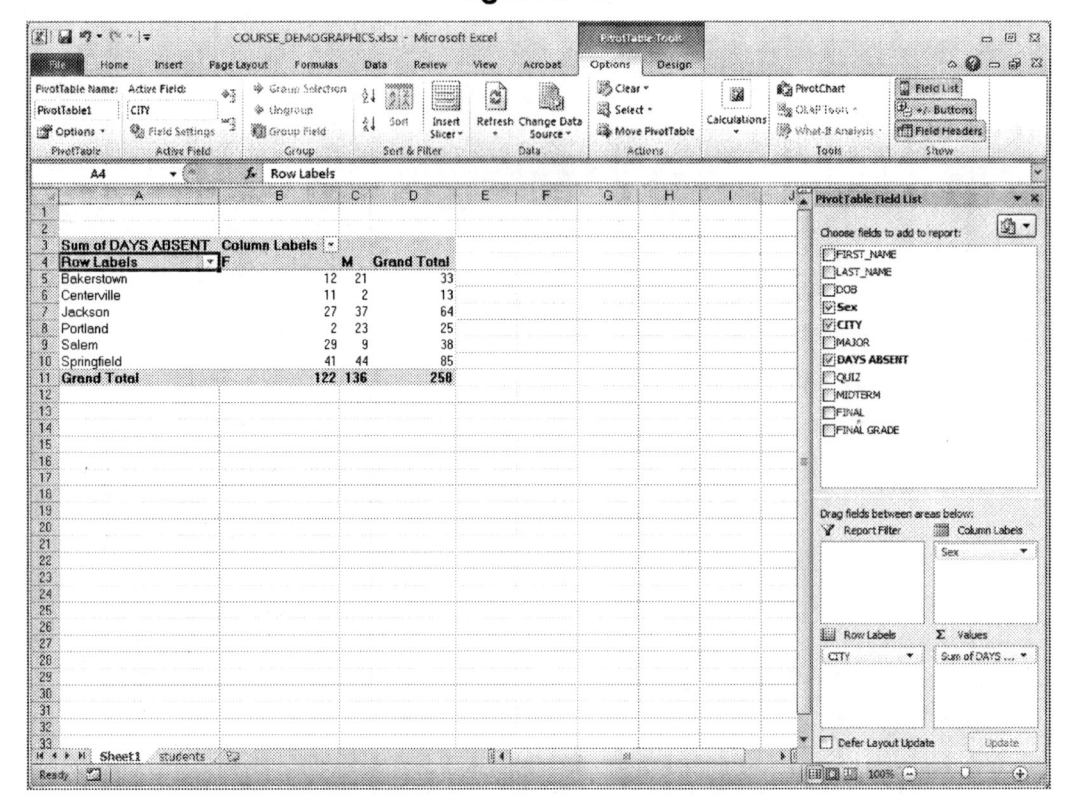

Figure 3-21

Sum of DAYS ABSENT	Column Labels		
Row Labels	F	M	Grand Total
Bakerstown	12	21	33
Centerville	11	2	13
Jackson	27	37	64
Portland	2	23	25
Salem	29	9	38
Springfield	41	44	85
Grand Total	122	136	258

men than women, or if there were a different number of students from each city (as there are). It would be more useful to obtain an average of the days absent rather than their sum. Below, we will see how easy it is to change the function in the data area from sum to average.

The pivot table is located on a new sheet in your workbook, with the PivotTable Task pane at the right. The Task pane and the PivotTable Tools tabs on the Ribbon remain visible as long as the PivotTable in the worksheet is active. If you click away from the PivotTable, the PivotTable tabs and the Pivot Table task pane close. You can easily reopen these by clicking within the Pivot Table on your worksheet.

Filters

Any field in the Row or Column area can be filtered to display only the categories you select, and the data totals will reflect only those categories. To filter the data so that only two cities are showing, click the list arrow above the CITY column on the table. Deselect *Select All*, select both *Centerville* and *Springfield* and click *OK*. Look at the Totals (Figure 3-22). Reselect *Show All* for CITY and notice the changed totals.

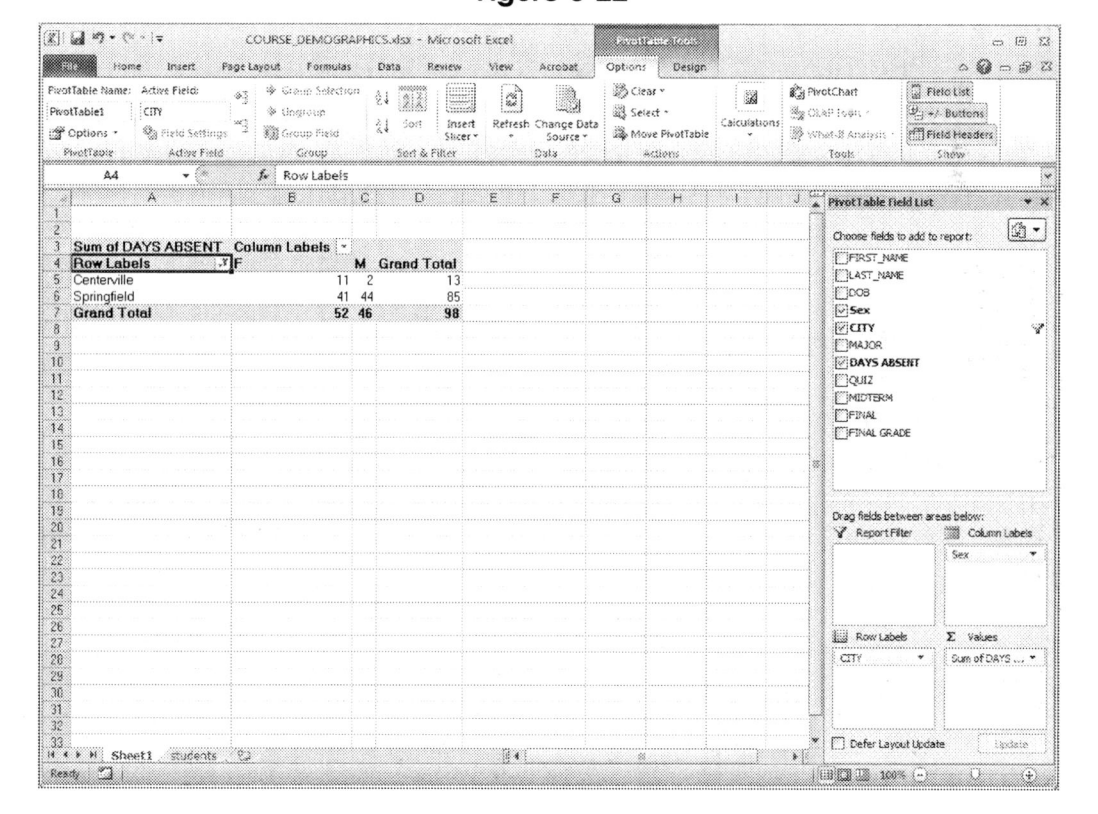

Figure 3-22

Add/Delete/Rearrange Fields in a Row or Column

To add or delete a field, just drag it to or from the Field List. You can add sub-rows or sub-columns by adding a second field beneath or to the left of another field.

To rearrange fields, simply drag and drop them to the desired location. Move *SEX* to the Row Labels box and *CITY* to the Column Labels box. Your pivot table should now look like Figure 3-23.

Change the Field in the Data Area

To change the field in the data area, drag the new field from the PivotTable Field List into the Values box and then remove the original field. To remove a field from one of the boxes at the bottom of the PivotTable Field List pane, simply drag it back to the list of fields at the top. You can also deselect the field's check box in the field list.

To answer Professor Gillespie's second two questions, you must analyze the Final Grades. Drag the *FINAL GRADE* field to the Values box and remove the field *DAYS ABSENT* field. To do so, you can drag it away from the box or click the field's down-arrow and select *Remove*. Return the CITY field to the Row Labels box and the SEX field to the Column Labels box.

Change the Type of Calculation in the Data Area

The default calculation for fields in the data area is Sum. However, Professor Gillespie wants to see the average of the Final Grade for each category. To change the type of calculation, first select any cell in the data area of the Pivot Table. On the PivotTable Tools: Options tab of the Ribbon, in the Active Field group, click *Field Settings*. This opens the Value Field Settings dialog box. On the Summarize by tab, select *Average* in the *Summarize value field by* list box. Click *OK* to close the Value Field Settings dialog box.

Format Data Cells

To remove the multiple decimal positions that appear for Average Grades, select any cell in the data area and click the *Field Settings* button on the Ribbon again. Click the *Number Format* button to open the Format Cells dialog box. In the left pane, click *Number*, and in the right pane, select *0* decimal places. Click *OK* twice to close the Format Cell dialog box and the Value Field Settings dialog box. Examine Figure 3-24.

Do women in this table get better grades?

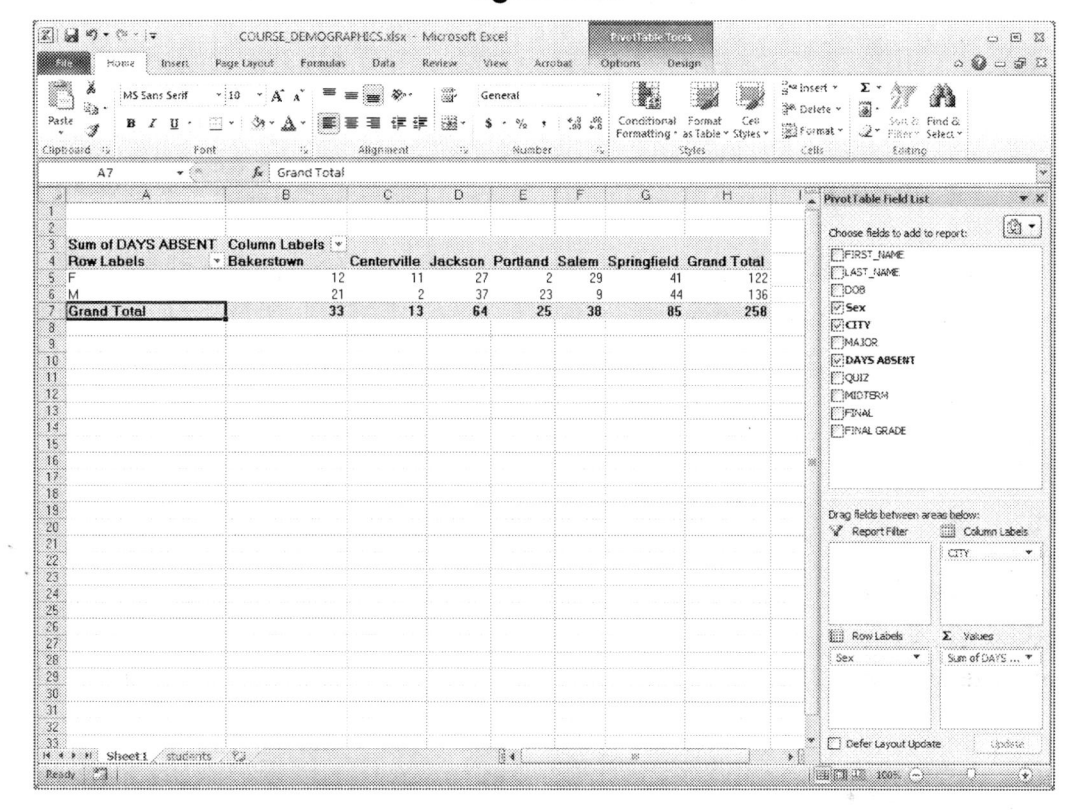

Figure 3-23

Report Filters

Unlike the Row and Column areas, you use the Report Filters area to display only a subset of the PivotTable data. It is a very helpful tool when analyzing large amounts of data. Essentially, the ReportFilter makes the pivot table a 3-dimensional cube of information. Drag the field *MAJOR* into the *Report Filter* box on the PivotTable task pane. On the pivot table, click the arrow to the right of (ALL) and select *MATH* in the drop-down menu to see the only Math majors.

Grouping Data

One of the most powerful features of a pivot table is its ability to consolidate large amounts of data. Data can be grouped by categories you create, or for date or time data, by standard units of measurement such as months or hours. To group data, click on the field in the pivot table that you would like to see grouped. On the

Figure 3-24

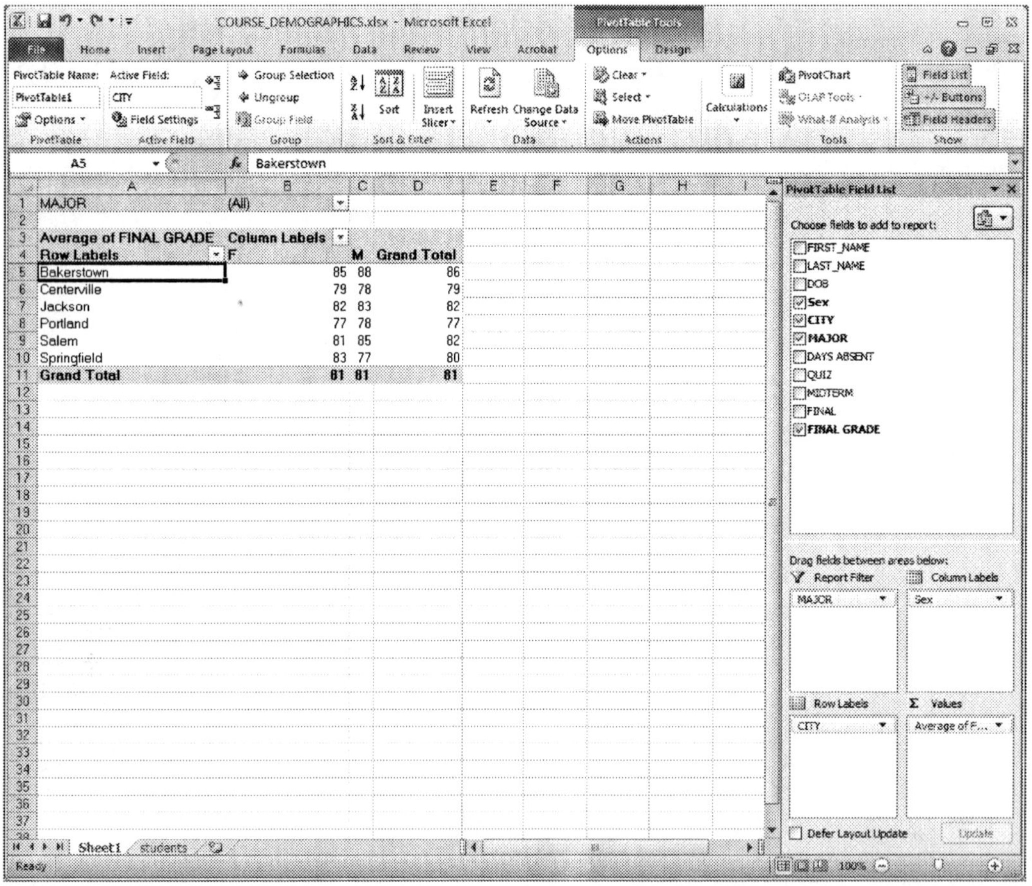

PivotTable Tools: Options tab, in the Group group, click *Group Selection*. In the Grouping dialog box that opens, select the parameters you wish and click *OK*.

Does a student's birth month correlate with his or her grades? Replace the *City* field in the *Row Labels* box with the *DOB* field, and group the DOB field by months to find out. See Figure 3-25.

Refreshing the Pivot Table

When changes are made in the original data, they are not immediately reflected in the table. To update the Pivot Table with the latest data, click the *Refresh* button on the PivotTable Tools: Options tab on the Ribbon, in the Data group.

Pivot Table Formatted Reports

Excel provides over 20 table and report formats to enhance your pivot table. To select one, open the PivotTable Tools: Design tab and select one of the many styles in the PivotTable Styles gallery. You can also change the layout of the table, including how to present subtotals, grand totals, whether the layout should be in compact, outline, or tabular form, and whether to include blank lines by using the commands in the Layout group. The PivotTable Style Options group allows you to select whether or not to show row and column headers, and whether columns or rows should be banded (alternately shaded). Select a Table Style that you feel enhances the Student pivot table and print it. If you want to return your Pivot Table to its original view, select *None*, which is the first Style thumbnail in the PivotTable Styles gallery.

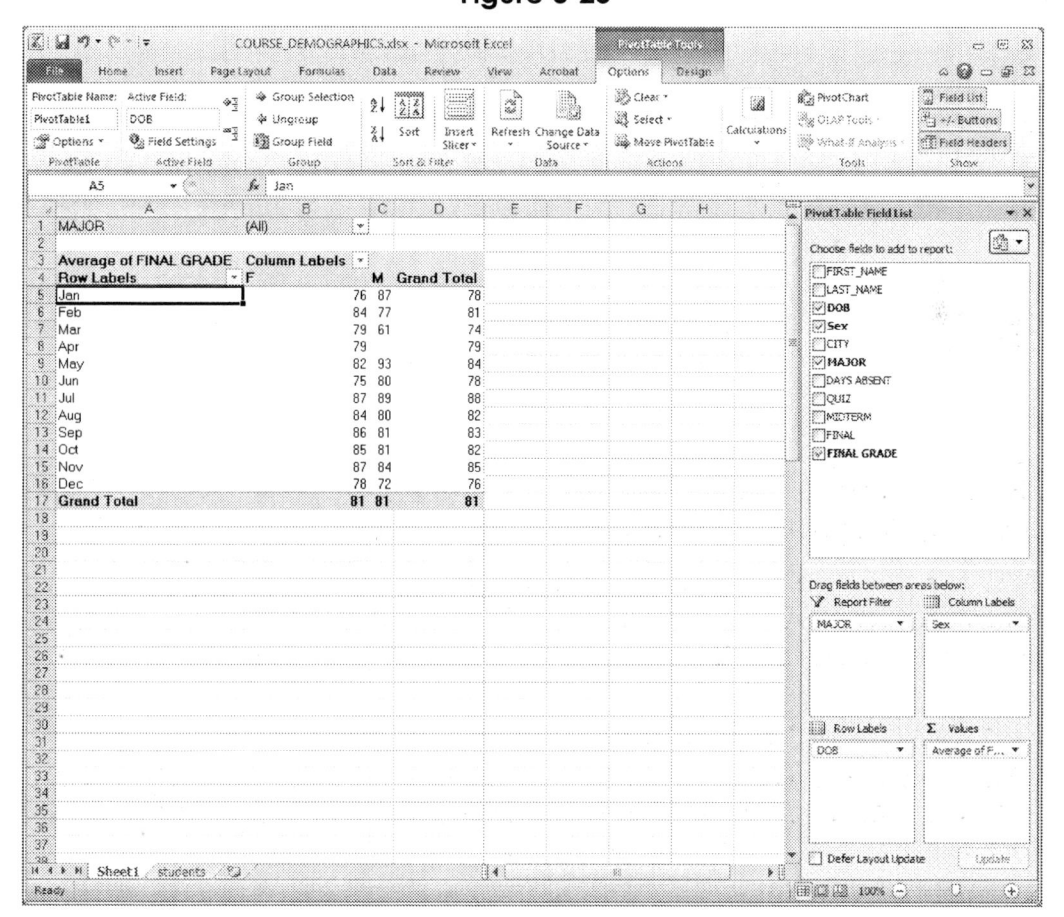

Figure 3-25

Solve it!

Now that you are comfortable with the basic concept of Pivot Tables, take a few minutes to answer some questions of your own about these students.

1. What major has the most women? What major has the most men?
2. From what city do the best performing students come?
3. Do you think that the PivotTable Styles help to clarify the data, or do they just make it "pretty?" Why?

If you make a mistake, remember that the *Undo* button on the *Quick Access* toolbar can reverse your actions and restore the screen to its original state.

4

Introduction to Database Software

This chapter describes the elements of a computerized database and how to use database software. The name "database" sounds formidable, but you use databases every day.

Some examples of common manual databases are telephone books, address books, and recipe collections. Digital databases we use every day are lists of songs on our iPods or other MP3 players, the home pages of Web sites like Youtube.com and Yahoo.com, and of course search engines like Google. In fact, the entire World Wide Web is a collective database with somewhere over 10 billion pages.

In the business world, some common manual databases are a list of customers and customer addresses, a list of suppliers, a list of products sold and their respective prices, a list of products in inventory, and a filing cabinet that contains invoices arranged in numerical or date order. For the most part, with the exception of very small businesses, these manual databases have been converted to digital databases.

What is a Database?

These examples of common databases can help provide an initial definition of a database as any organized list or file of information about people, places, or things (see Figure 4-1).

For spreadsheet software, the central metaphor is that of a matrix where quantitative information is organized in rows and columns, but in a database, the central metaphor is that of a list or file where information is organized in rows (records) and columns.

Any problem in the real world that can be expressed as a problem of lists or files is potentially amenable to solution by a computerized database.

There are three basic types of databases: hierarchical, network, and relational. It is recommended that you consult a textbook for a detailed description of the various kinds of databases. Here we will describe only *relational databases*.

A simple example of a database file is a customer file:

Record #	Field 1 Last Name	Field 2 First Name	Field 3 Address
1			
2			
3			
4			

As you can see, in a database file all the information you have on an entry is called a *record*. Each record is composed of a number of *fields* that constitute the information stored on each entry. A collection of records is called a *file*. Below you will learn how to create a computerized database file, but modern database packages like Access offer much more than just computerized files.

What is a Database Management System?

A database management system (DBMS) is a software package that, at a minimum, allows the user to create several different database files *and* relate information in one file to information in another file. Second, a modern DBMS provides a number of related tools needed to develop complete information systems.

One important advantage of *relational* database management systems over a manual filing cabinet is the ability to easily combine specific pieces of information (*fields*) from several different database files into a new file.

Figure 4-1

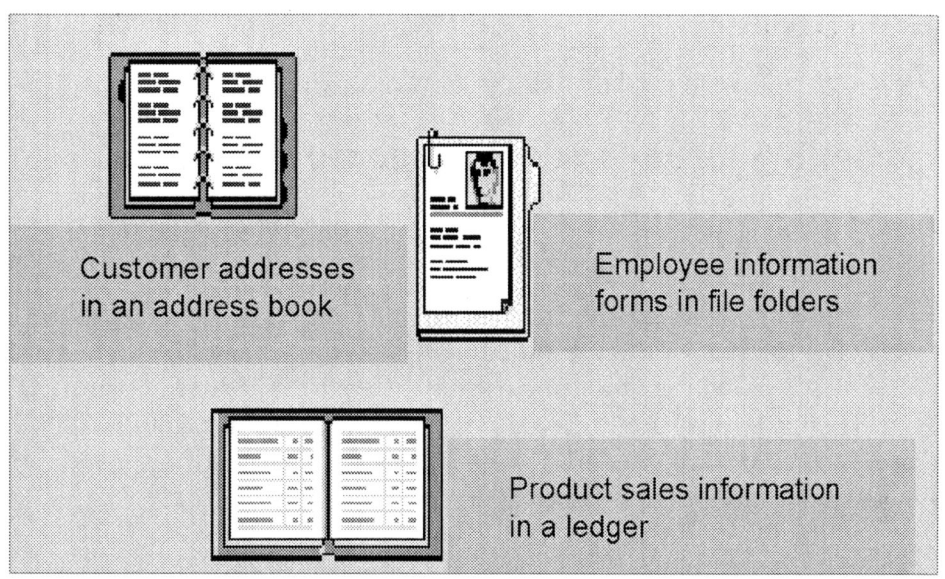

Customer addresses in an address book

Employee information forms in file folders

Product sales information in a ledger

For instance, what if you wanted to determine a daily inventory that was calculated by deducting daily sales of all products from a beginning inventory?

Here, you would want to find out from the invoice file at the end of each day exactly which items were sold. You would then want to go to the inventory file and debit the existing inventory. In a truly sophisticated system, you might want to go into a third file that contained the names and addresses of your suppliers, and then generate a purchase order and mailing label for those products where inventory was low.

In a manual record system stored in the traditional filing cabinet, a lengthy search process would be required to solve this problem. In a contemporary relational database management system, the job can be done in seconds.

A second feature of a relational DBMS is a set of powerful tools that can be used to develop a complete information management system. Included here are facilities to create and store memos, notes, data entry screens (called forms in Access), reports, labels, and programs. These features are controlled through a powerful fourth generation language or menus that require little or no programming knowledge.

Briefly, a contemporary DBMS for the PC is a system development tool that permits the user to create complete management systems suitable for a small business or an office within a large business organization.

Comparative Advantages of Database Packages

Once students learn a relational database package, they often find it more powerful and useful than spreadsheet packages, yet the programs have very different strengths (and weaknesses).

Spreadsheet programs are very good at manipulating quantitative data, but they are poor at storing and manipulating lists or extracting parts of files from a larger data set. They generally are quite poor at combining information from several different files, and they typically have very limited macro or programming languages, although recent releases of popular spreadsheets have improved.

Database packages are very good at creating and manipulating lists of information, especially text information. Contemporary relational database packages have very friendly, easy-to-learn, menu-driven command systems that permit the novice to accomplish many, if not all, of the program's functions.

In addition, relational database packages are accompanied by powerful fourth-generation languages that are easy to learn and permit intermediate users to build complete information systems suitable for a small business or an office within a larger business.

Database software is comparatively weak at manipulating quantitative data. This gap, however, is closing with the development of more sophisticated reporting tools.

To operate a contemporary business, both kinds of packages are needed. Data can be exchanged between the packages so that the most appropriate software is used.

Introducing Microsoft Access for Windows

Microsoft Access 2010 is an integral part of Microsoft's Office 2010 suite of applications. An Access database is represented as a collection of objects. One database file (a file with an MDB or ACCDB extension) contains all the tables, queries, forms, reports, and other objects associated with a particular database. A brief description of these objects, the relationships between them within the

Figure 4-2

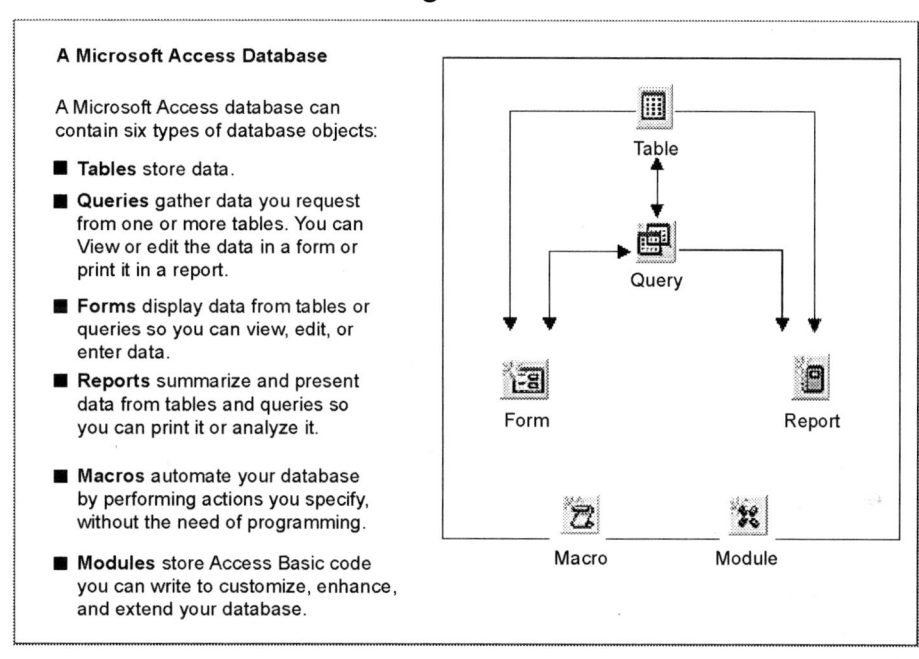

A Microsoft Access Database

A Microsoft Access database can contain six types of database objects:

- **Tables** store data.
- **Queries** gather data you request from one or more tables. You can View or edit the data in a form or print it in a report.
- **Forms** display data from tables or queries so you can view, edit, or enter data.
- **Reports** summarize and present data from tables and queries so you can print it or analyze it.
- **Macros** automate your database by performing actions you specify, without the need of programming.
- **Modules** store Access Basic code you can write to customize, enhance, and extend your database.

database envelope, and the graphical buttons that identify them is shown in Figure 4-2.

Access 2010 object names are not limited to eight characters as was true in older PC databases. Access object names (and field names in tables) can be up to 64 characters in length, and can include spaces as well as a mixture of upper and lowercase letters. Access is also not case sensitive, and it will locate data within a field (as long as the spelling is correct!) regardless of the case originally used to enter it.

The Ribbon

In Office 2010, the Ribbon replaces the Menu bar, Standard toolbar, and other toolbars used in Office versions prior to 2007 to access to commands and settings. The Ribbon runs across the top of the screen, and commands are grouped into separate tabs, according to the general type of work being performed.

The Home tab contains the most commonly accessed buttons and functions. The Create tab contains commands for creating new tables, forms, reports, queries, and macros. The External Data tab includes commands for importing, exporting, and collecting external data and for working with a SharePoint server (a Microsoft Office networking application). On the Database Tools tab are commands for managing your database, such as working with macros and analyzing performance.

A number of Ribbon tabs are contextual: they only appear when you are working with an object that requires them. For example, the three Report Layout Tools tabs (Format, Arrange, and Page Setup) are hidden until you begin working with a report. Similarly, some Office or Access add-in programs may have their own tab that is present only when the add-in is enabled. For example, if your version of Office has the Adobe Acrobat add-in installed for working with PDFs, your Office programs will include an Acrobat tab on the Ribbon.

Many of the commands on the Ribbon are presented as buttons to click; others with arrows lead to a drop-down list of related commands and options. Some commands are check boxes that you select to enable or disable certain settings; others may include a text box to enter data or instructions. If you are uncertain what a button's function is, you can hover the mouse pointer over it and a ScreenTip will appear to name and describe the button and give its keyboard shortcut, if any.

Another new feature in Office 2010 is the File tab on the Ribbon, which replaces the Microsoft Office button in Office 2007. The File tab, like the File menu in earlier versions of Microsoft Office, contains commands and settings for working with the application or with a document as a whole. For example, the commands for Opening, Printing, Saving, and Closing a file are found on the File tab. The File tab is referred to as the Backstage view and it is what you see when you open Access from the Start menu.

To the right of the Access application icon in the upper left hand corner of the application window is the Quick Access toolbar: by default it contains the *Save*, *Undo*, and *Redo* button commands, but you can add or remove commands as you please by clicking the arrow to the right of the toolbar.

Get Help At Any Time!

Access 2010 includes two other interactive help tools: an extensive context-sensitive help system (press **[F1]** or click the icon with the question mark at the top right of the window at any time to launch Access Help), and various wizards that offer help in creating Access objects, such as tables, queries, forms, reports, and macros. Unlike the main help system, which you must search or browse to find answers to questions, wizards ask you relevant questions and actually create a customized version of the object in question according to your responses. A summary of Access wizards used in this edition of *Solve it!* is presented in Figure 4-3.

Other Access Wizards include the Input Mask Wizard, the Lookup Wizard, the Simple Query Wizard, the Label Wizard, the Chart Wizard, the Table Analyzer Wizard, the Database Documenter Wizard, the Import Spreadsheet Wizard, the Import Text Wizard, the Link Text Wizard, the Find Unmatched Query Wizard, the Find Duplicates Query Wizard, the Crosstab Query Wizard, the PivotTable Wizard, the Database Splitter Wizard, and the User-Level Security Wizard.

Access Setup Requirements

To use Access 2010 (Microsoft Office Professional 2010) you will need:

- A personal computer with 500 MHz or faster processor
- Available hard-disk space usage will vary depending on configuration and operating system (3 GB recommended for Office 2010 Professional).
- 256 MB of RAM
- Operating Systems: Microsoft Windows XP with service pack 3 (SP3) or higher, Windows Server 2003 with SP2, or later
- 1024X768 or higher resolution monitor

Figure 4-3

Query Wizard	Helps users construct complex queries for common database management tasks, such as the merging two tables or performing cross tabulations.
Form Wizard	A tool for creating forms in a variety of predefined formats and presentation styles.
Report Wizard	A tool for creating reports in a variety of predefined formats and presentation styles.
Macro Wizard	A tool used for creating or editing a macro from within an event procedure in a form or report.
Control Wizards	Creates code behind command buttons, option groups, and list and combo boxes used in forms or reports.

Terminology and Conventions Used in the Access Tutorials:

- *Double-click* means to press the left mouse button twice in rapid succession.
- *Click* means to press the left mouse button once only.
- *Right-click* means to click the right mouse button once.
- New terms, new file names, key concepts, commands and menu choices, and action words appear in *italics*.
- New object names are shown in bold (e.g., **MyContacts**).

Getting Started—Access 2010 for Windows

To Start Access 2010

1. From Windows, click the *Start* button at bottom left of the screen, and then point to *Programs* (or *All Programs* in Windows XP and Windows 7).

2. Within the Programs or All Programs menu, point to (or click) *Microsoft Office 2010*, and then select the *Microsoft Office Access 2010* option. This action will start the Access program. The application opens on the File tab with an Available Templates window that allows you to create a new blank database or choose a database template. The top half of the Available Templates window includes the *Blank database* button and buttons for templates that are included with the program. The bottom half provides links to database templates on Office.com. The File menu in the left pane includes a list of recently opened databases and commands to open an existing database, save objects and databases, print database objects, save and publish a database, open the Help and Info tabs, install add-ins, set database options, and exit the program.

Creating a Database in Access 2010

Now that you've started the program, let's create a database. Throughout Chapter 5 we will be using a practice database table called **FRIENDS** in the tutorial sessions to illustrate the various features of Access. A copy of this practice table is included in the student data files you have downloaded from the MySolveIt.com Web site). But let's build this database from scratch to show you how easy it is to work with Access.

1. With Access 2010 started on the File tab on the Ribbon, the *Blank* database button should be preselected in the Available Templates window.

2. On the right side of the screen in the Blank database section, above the Create button, enter **Contacts.accdb** in the *File Name* text box to name the database. Click the Folder icon to specify the file location where the new database should be stored. (Note that versions earlier than Access 2007 use a different file format, with the extension .mdb. Access 2010 can open, work with, and save files using the .mdb extension as well as the .accdb file format. However, earlier versions of Access will not be able to work with .accdb files.) For convenience, save the new database in the same directory where you are storing your other *Solve it!* Student Files. Now click *Create* to create and save the database.

3. After you create the database, Access opens a new, blank table for you to begin adding records to the database. It also displays the Fields tab on the Ribbon which contains commands for working with tables and populating them with data (Figure 4-4).

On the left of the Access window is the Navigation Pane, which allows you to navigate to different Access objects by locating and clicking the name of the object. You can specify which types of objects are shown and how they are grouped in the Navigation pane by setting the options in the Navigation

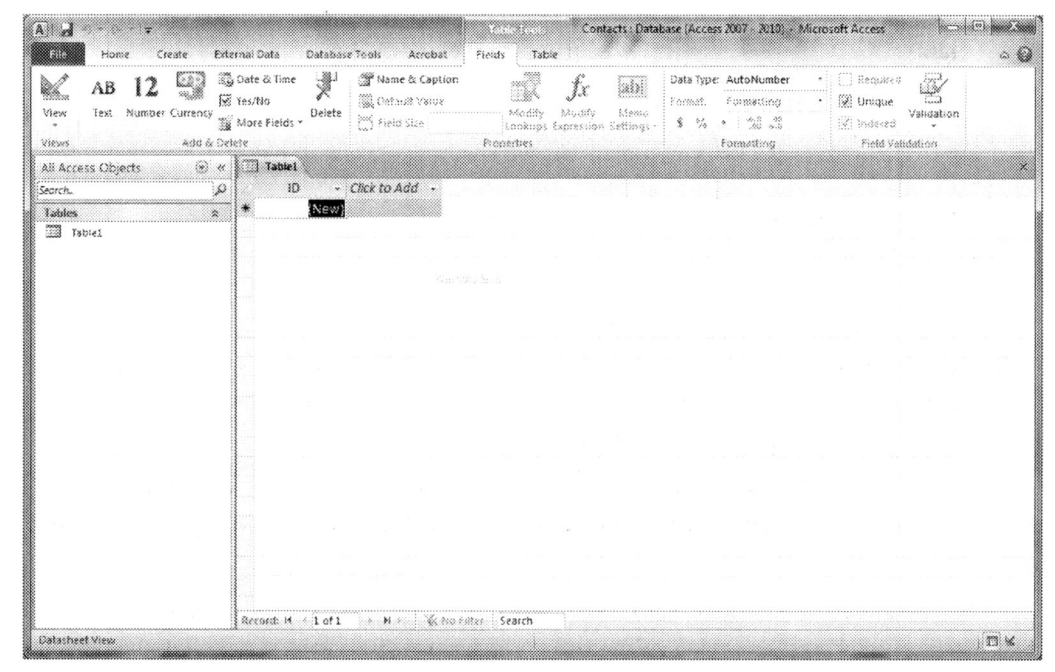

Figure 4-4

Pane menu. To open the menu, click the down arrow at the top of the pane. In the Navigate to Category section, you can specify how the objects displayed in the pane are grouped. Click *Object Type*. In the Filter by Group section, you can limit the objects that are viewed to certain categories. Click *All Access Objects* in this section. For now, only Table1 shows, because currently it is the only object in the database.

You can collapse the Navigation Pane by clicking the Shutter Bar *Open/Close* button – the button with two arrows to the left of the Navigation Pane Title. To open the Navigation Pane you can click either on the Shutter Bar *Open/Close* button or click directly on the shutter bar itself. The shutter bar is the narrow, vertical bar between the Navigation Pane and the main window. When the Navigation Pane is collapsed, it says Navigation Pane.

Creating Tables in Access

Access has automatically created the blank Table1 object to begin building a database because all the basic information stored in a database is stored as records in a table. A database table is a matrix of rows and columns, just like a spreadsheet. Each row in an Access table is a *record*, and each column is a *field* that describes some unique information about the records.

For instance, a telephone book is a familiar table:

Last Name	First Name	Address	Phone Number
Bell	Robert	52 Galley Road	737-3423
Bellini	Andrew	9 Francis Drive	736-9005
Bellis	Aldo	241 Albany Road	528-2007
Belotti	John	32 Forest Ave	736-9340

Each row contains the information on a unique record—in this case a person. Each column contains important information about all the records—in this case last name, first name, address, and phone number. These columns are called fields in the language of databases.

Now let's create the basic table for our practice Contacts database. In Access you can work with Tables in two different ways:

- **Design View:** In this view, you work with field names and properties.

Introduction to Database Software   125

This view is useful for creating and modifying the table itself.

- *Datasheet View:* In this view, data is presented similar to a spreadsheet matrix; it is useful for entering and editing data.

Let's use the Design View because it will give you a better understanding of how tables are built and used. You can return later and practice using the Datasheet View for creating tables.

1. On the Fields tab on the Ribbon, click the arrow at the bottom of the View button (in the Views group) to open the View menu and then click Design View. You will be prompted to name the table; enter MyContacts as the table name. The table opens in Design view along with the Table Tools: Design tab on the Ribbon (Figure 4-5). The name of the table in the Navigation pane is changed to MyContacts.

   Design View allows you to determine what fields you want in your database. In the Contacts database you will want to keep track of all of your professional and business contacts. Here's a list of fifteen basic fields you would want in a contacts file:

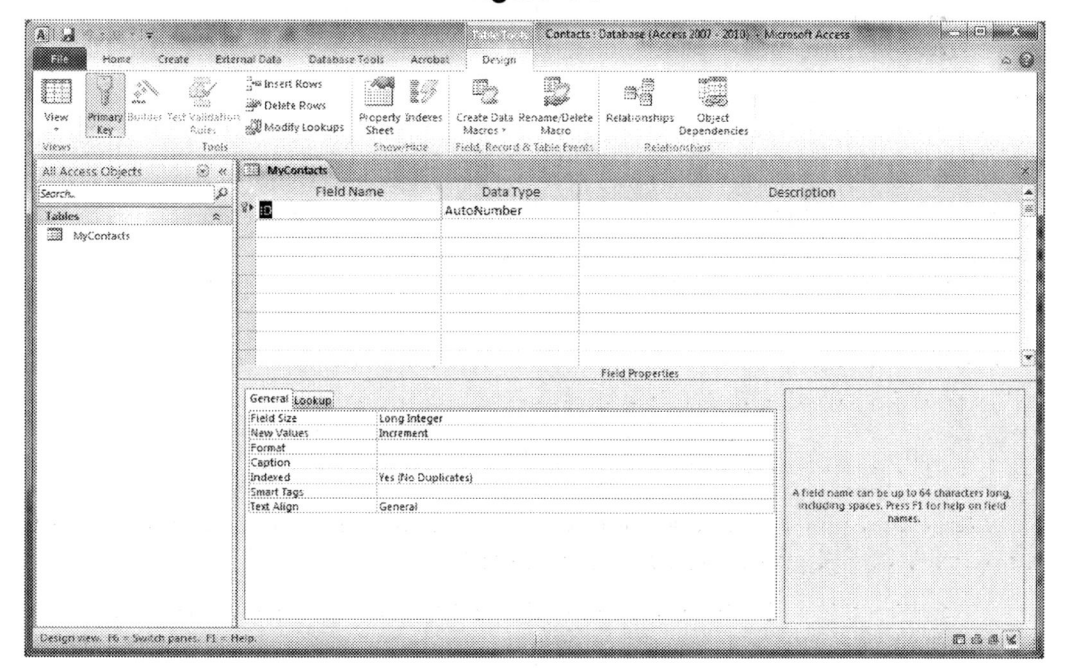

Figure 4-5

CUSTOMER_ID	CITY	Fax
LAST_NAME	State	Last_Meeting_Date
FIRST_NAME	Zip	Notes
Company	Business	Professional
Street	Mobile	Personal

2. Access has automatically created the first field for you, ID, which can be used as a "primary key" to uniquely identify any record in your table. Primary keys will be discussed later in this chapter. Rename this field CUSTOMER_ID, to match the first field in our list above. Then, press [Tab] to move the insertion point into the second column, Data Type. Access has automatically chosen to create an AutoNumber field. Since this is the correct data type so that customers will be automatically assigned a unique consecutive record number as they are entered into the database, press tab again twice to create a second field.

3. In the second row, under Field Name, enter the second field from the table above, LAST_NAME, then press [Tab]. The cursor moves to the Data Type column. Even a simple personal contacts database has many different types of data, from text for names, to dates and binary yes/no data (personal versus professional contact). There are eleven different data types in Access 2010 (see Figure 4-6).

You can see these different data types by clicking the down arrow in the Data Type column. The Data Type drop down list begins with Text—alphanumeric characters. In this case—for the LAST_NAME field—you will want to keep the Text data type that Access has selected. For other fields, you will use other data types. For example, for the NOTES field you would select *Memo* as the data type, and for the LAST_MEETING_DATE field you would select the *Date/Time* data type. For the PROFESSIONAL and PERSONAL fields, which will be used to indicate whether the contact is a professional and/or a personal contact, use the *Yes/No* data type.

Contrary to what you might think at first, telephone numbers and zip codes are usually created as Text data types simply because there are no calculations that will be performed with these numbers. When finished, your table will use five data types: AutoNumber (CUSTOMER_ID), Date/Time (LAST_MEETING_DATE), Memo (NOTES) and Yes/No (PROFESSIONAL, PERSONAL), and Text (all other fields).

Figure 4-6

Text	Use for text, combinations of text and numbers (such as an address), or numbers on which you don't intend to perform calculations (such as phone numbers or part numbers).
Memo	Use for longer text, such as notes and comments.
Number	Use for data on which you might want to perform calculations, unless it's money.
Date/Time	Use for dates and times.
Currency	Use for large numbers requiring rapid calculation, or numbers that require highly accurate rounding, such as money.
AutoNumber	Use to automatically assign consecutive or unique values, such as invoice numbers.
Yes/No	Use for true/false, yes/no, or on/off values.
OLE Object	Use for inserting other OLE compatible files or objects, such as pictures or Excel spreadsheets.
Hyperlink	Use to store text or combinations of text and numbers as a hyperlink address; This is typically used for connection to data stored on the public World Wide Web or a firm's internal Intranet.
Attachment	Use to attach one or more files to a record; takes up less file space than OLE Object.
Calculated	Use to create a field that combines, or concatenates, two or more existing fields in the table.
Lookup Wizard	Use to create a field that allows the selection of a value from another Access table or from a list of values.

4. Now that you have created the Last_Name field with the text data type, press [Tab] to move the cursor to the Description column. Here you can enter a description of the field, but this is not required. The description appears in the status bar when using an Access database. For now, leave this area blank.

5. The Field Properties area in the lower half of the Table Design View window allows you to set the properties for each field and to control the kinds of data entered into the database for each field. For instance, you might want to restrict the length of the Last Name field to 30 characters; prevent the entry of text data in a date field; or force users to enter data in some required fields before accepting any of their data. For now, accept the default values.

6. Use your mouse to place the cursor in the third row of the Field Name column, and enter the third field name: FIRST_NAME and select its data type (Text). Repeat this process for the remaining thirteen fields defined in the personal contacts table above. Your MyContacts table should look like the table in Figure 4-7.

7. When you are finished entering all the fields in the Contacts database, close the Design view window by clicking on the *Close Window* button ⊠ to the far right of the MyContacts tab. When you are prompted to save changes to the design of the MyContacts table, click *Yes*.

   Congratulations! You have defined your first table in a database!

Adding Records to the Contacts Database

Now that you have created the **Contacts** database, add records to the MyContacts table for three of your closest professional or personal contacts.

Double-click the **MyContacts** table in the Navigation pane to open it in Datasheet View with the fields displayed across the top of the table. The cursor prompts you to enter data into the first field. Since the first field is CUSTOMER_ID, which will be auto-numbered, press [Tab] to move to the second field, LAST_NAME, and begin to enter your first record. When you are finished filling all fields for the first record, press ENTER. Repeat for two more contacts.

Modifying a Database and Changing Tables

You can re-enter Design view and change a database table at any time.

1. On the Home tab of the Ribbon, click the *Design View* button in the Views group. This button changes from Design View to Datasheet View, depending on which view you are in at the moment, allowing you to toggle quickly between the two views. Alternatively, you can click the small *Design View* icon at the far right of the bottom Status bar of the Access window.

2. Add a new field MIDDLE_NAME to the list of fields between LAST_NAME and FIRST_NAME. Place your cursor in the FIRST_NAME row. On the

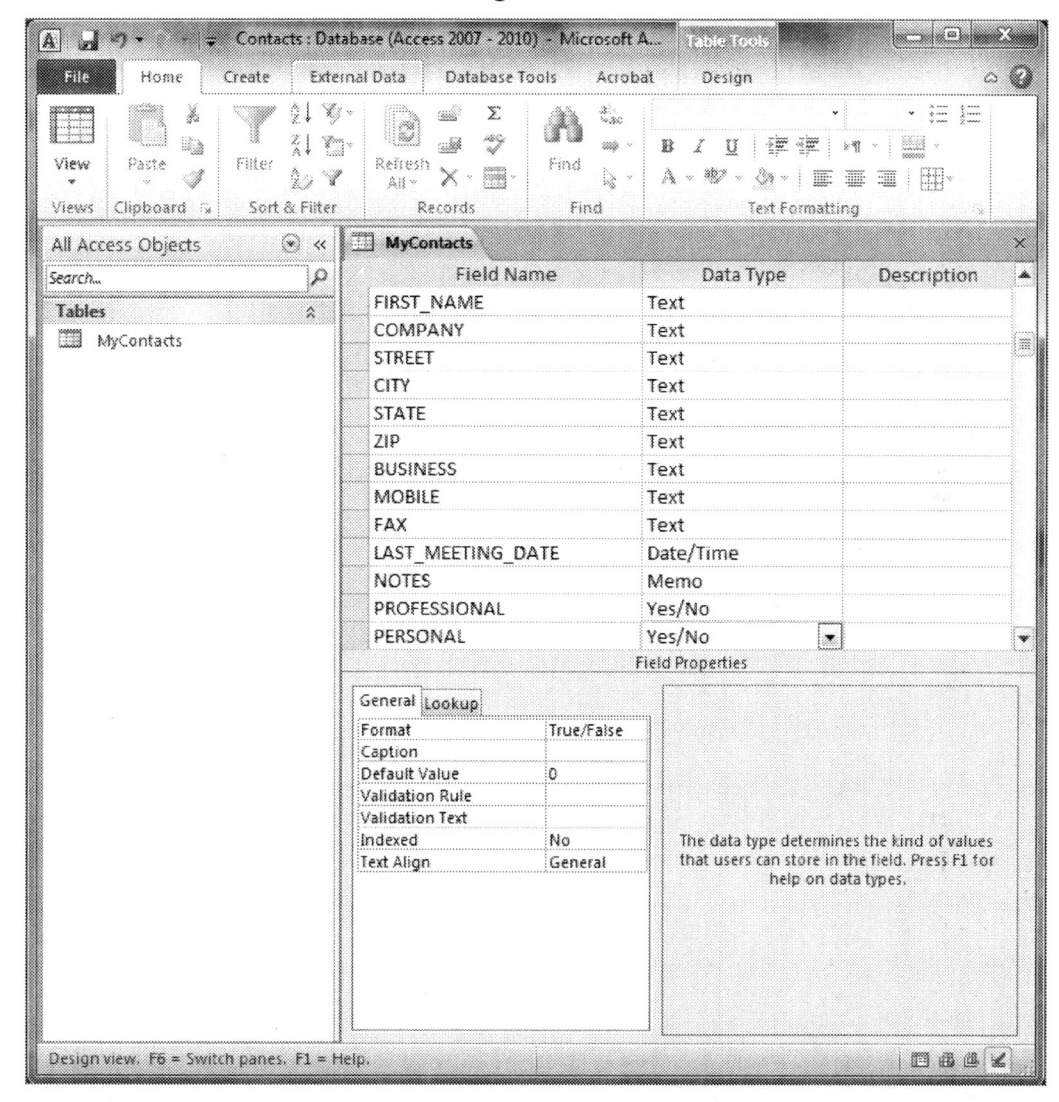

Figure 4-7

Design tab of the Ribbon, in the Tools group, click *Insert Rows*. This will add a row above the currently selected row. Now enter MIDDLE_NAME as the field.

3. You can also delete fields in Design View. On the Table Tools: Design tab with the row selected, click the *Delete Rows* button or right-click a row and select *Delete Rows* on the shortcut menu.

Primary Keys

Access uses a unique tag called a primary key to identify each record in a table. As a license plate is unique to car, or a fingerprint is unique to an individual, the primary key should uniquely identify each record. While tables can be created without declaring any field as primary, Access discourages this by prompting you to define a primary key every time you create a table.

Why are primary keys so important? Mainly because primary key fields are used to create relationships between tables. Why would you want to have multiple tables? In a simple database like **Contacts**, a single table is sufficient for the basic purpose of keeping track of friends. But in the business world, matters are more complex, and a single table is rarely sufficient to capture all the information required to support a business.

For instance, consider a typical business that uses a sales force to sell products to customers. In order to keep track of customers, their orders, the parts they ordered, sales people, and shipping information, you probably will want to have at least five different tables in your sales database—one for each of the entities you want to keep track of. You will want one table for customers, another for orders, and others for order details, employees (sales people) and shippers (see Figure 4-8). And you want to be able to pull information from each of these tables in a flexible manner in order to answer important business questions.

In Figure 4-8 the primary keys for each table have been selected. The primary keys are used to build relationships between the various tables in a database so complex queries can be answered. For instance, if you want to know what sales person made a sale to a specific customer, and when was it shipped, you would have to draw information from the following tables: customers, orders, employees, and shippers.

Not all fields are good candidates for primary keys. For instance, if you chose the Last Name field as a primary key, your table could not contain two records with the last name "Jones." Because many large databases have persons with duplicate last names, Last Name is not a good choice as a unique identifier of people. Telephone numbers are often unique, but sometimes two people share a single phone number.

Some number fields make good primary keys. For example, an employee ID number would uniquely identify each record in an Employee table. Similar unique numbers include a product number (SKU or stocking unit number), an order number, or employee ID number. In our case we are using the unique

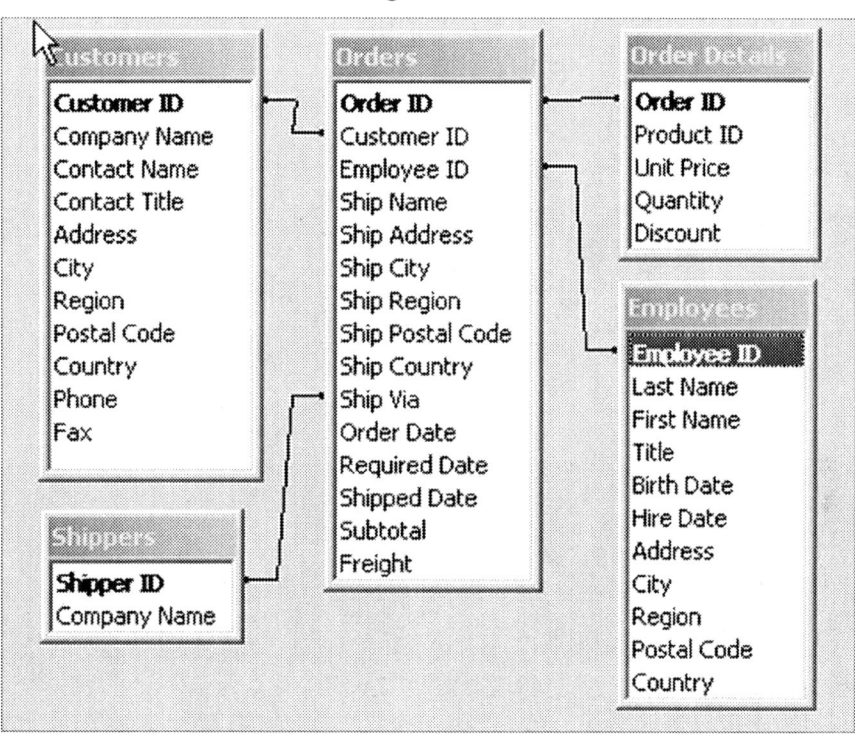

Figure 4-8

Customers	Orders	Order Details
Customer ID	**Order ID**	**Order ID**
Company Name	Customer ID	Product ID
Contact Name	Employee ID	Unit Price
Contact Title	Ship Name	Quantity
Address	Ship Address	Discount
City	Ship City	
Region	Ship Region	**Employees**
Postal Code	Ship Postal Code	**Employee ID**
Country	Ship Country	Last Name
Phone	Ship Via	First Name
Fax	Order Date	Title
	Required Date	Birth Date
Shippers	Shipped Date	Hire Date
Shipper ID	Subtotal	Address
Company Name	Freight	City
		Region
		Postal Code
		Country

CUSTOMER_ID number created for each contact. But what if we wished to use another field as primary key?

Let's look at how to assign a primary key.

1. Open the MyContacts table in Design View.

2. Place the cursor in the first field CUSTOMER_ID. This is a unique number for each contact. Notice that a key symbol appears to the left of the field, indicating that this is a primary key field. On the Design tab, the *Primary Key* button in the Tools group is also highlighted.

3. Click the *Primary Key* button on the Ribbon. This action removes the Primary Key status of the current field, and the key symbol beside the CUSTOMER_ID field disappears.

4. Place the cursor in the second field, LAST_NAME and click *Primary Key* again. This assigns LAST_NAME as the primary key of the table.

5. You do not need to un-assign a field as primary key before you reassign another. To reassign CUSTOMER_ID as the primary key place your cursor in the CUSTOMER_ID field and press the *Primary Key* button to change the primary key of the table.

Exiting Access

You now have enough information to complete the database cases in Chapter 5. To exit Access, click the File tab and then click *Exit* on the File menu in the left pane or click the *Close* button on the far right of the Access application title bar, to close the program. When you are prompted, save the changes to your Contacts database.

5

Database Management Software Cases

Database Case 1
Chesapeake Electronics

Problem:	Create and modify a sales support system.
Management Skill:	Organize
Access Skill:	Data Table Setup Data Input and Editing Selecting Data Subsets Printing
Data Table:	CHESAPEAKE

Samantha Suzuki had always been competitive. As long as she could remember, there was always something to strive for: getting better grades, achieving faster times in her long distance running, and outdoing her three sisters. It thus gave her great satisfaction to learn last week that she had been selected as "Salesperson of the Year." She had sold more circuit breakers, fuses, and gas discharge tubes last year than any of the other 196 sales staff at Chesapeake.

Chesapeake Electronics was founded in Maryland in 1939 two years before the United States entered World War II. The founders recognized the growing need for a variety of electronic measuring and testing equipment. Chesapeake's primary customers were manufacturers in the northeastern United States. The family-owned business grew solidly throughout the years, and by 2012, the company was the leading supplier of circuit breakers and fuses in the country.

Recent advances in computer-controlled machinery, along with robotics and flexible manufacturing systems, provided a strong growth period for Chesapeake. The new machines required large quantities of high quality fuses. These expensive machine tools were used on a 24/7 basis. To minimize downtime and maintain high quality, fuses were changed frequently, often before wearing out.

Although very profitable, the electronic components industry had become very competitive. Chesapeake Electronics had many competitors who undercut them on particular items, but only Raytheon had as large a range of products. Chesapeake Electronics follows a high product quality and premium pricing strategy based on excellent customer service. Their competitive advantage lies in three areas:

- A comprehensive product range
- A hard-working and knowledgeable sales force
- Guaranteed overnight delivery for stock items

Suzuki has been very successful in presenting Chesapeake Electronics to her customers as a provider of a full range of electronics supplies. Rather than approach new companies, she has concentrated on increasing the average purchase of existing clients.

In the four years Samantha Suzuki has been with Chesapeake Electronics, her rise to success has been rapid. It seemed that only yesterday she had started out as a trainee sales representative with old Philip "Killer" Kendall. Kendall preached that there were only two important things in sales: *"Get close to the customer and know the products inside-out."*

Suzuki kept her client information in a large notebook ledger. The data was stored alphabetically by the client's company name. She had acquired more than 250 companies in her Midwestern territory of Iowa, Kansas, Oklahoma, Missouri, and Nebraska.

Within each company, she called on an average of four different groups of people in purchasing, engineering, production, and the workshop. She had nearly 920 names as well as details on the products they ordered and plenty of other useful information. Suzuki often asked about her clients' wives or husbands by name, and she always knew the pattern of their last few orders. If the orders were decreasing, she asked why and found out if one of her competitors had more fully met any of her client's needs.

As her client base expanded, Suzuki's ledger became impossibly heavy. She was also constantly trying to find information that was in the ledger but was not easily accessible. For example, last month a new low-cost gas discharge tube had been introduced. Suzuki wanted to know which of her clients had ordered the product it superseded so she could write or call on all those clients and demonstrate the new product. Locating that information in her ledger would have taken a week of searching, so she relied on her memory, but she felt sure that she had overlooked some major users.

Suzuki had tried asking Chesapeake's overworked Information Systems department to get the information for her from past invoices, but the IS Manager replied, *"We'd love to, but we can't even finish our own work. Besides, I don't think it's possible. You'd be better off putting it on a laptop computer and using a database package like Access. It will be much more flexible than our system. It's also cheaper and portable."*

One of the perks of winning the "Salesperson of the Year" award was a new ideas budget of $35,000, which Suzuki has decided to devote to her new Sales Support System. Suzuki has purchased a laptop with Microsoft Office 2010 that includes Access. She wants you to help her build prepare a prototype database that could take the place of her manual system.

Suzuki wants all of the important data to be entered into the database so she can look up information in many different ways, even while she's on the road. At night in her hotel room, she can update the database after visiting clients throughout the day. Suzuki feels certain the new system will enable her to keep improving her performance and maybe even win her the "Salesperson of the Year" award a second time.

The important fields for the prototype system are:

Company Name	First Name	Product Group
Address	Last Name	Spouse Name
City	Department	Order Pattern
State	Title	CompanyID
Zip	Last Order Date	

Chesapeake Electronics' products are classified into three major groups: gas discharge tubes (G), fuses (F), and circuit breakers (C). Within each group, there are up to 99 subgroups, i.e. S01 to S99. Order patterns are coded as: increasing (I),

136   Solve it!

decreasing (D), or stable (S). Each client company is assigned a 5-digit identification number.

A portion of Suzuki's database has been started for you in the table CHESAPEAKE in SOLVEIT_CH5.ACCDB database. Create a new Access database and import this object now.

Tasks

There are seven tasks in this case:

1. Complete the table structure to include the information desired by Suzuki.
2. (a) Enter data for the new fields to complete the existing records. (b) Enter data for three new clients into the data table.
3. Alisha Crowley, the Production Manager for Crowley Mechanics in Kansas City, Missouri, has retired and was replaced by Juan Sanchez. Juan's wife's name is Melissa, and he will now be known as the Production Director. Update the data in the table to reflect these changes.
4. Print a listing of the entire table.
5. Print all of the records in the table, but only include the following fields: Company, City, Client First and Last Names, and Last Order Date.
6. Suzuki is traveling to Kansas City to meet Juan Sanchez at Crowley Mechanics and wants to know her other clients in Kansas City. Create a query, and then print a listing of all clients based in Kansas City. The list should only include these fields: Company, Client First and Last Names, and Title.
7.* After using the client database for three months, Suzuki reports tremendous savings in time and she is able to do her job more efficiently. She has found, however, that the database does not handle customers that buy from more than one product group. For example, General Electric purchases products from the G10, F20, F35, F40, F30, C50, and C70 product groups. Find a way to incorporate this extra information into the database.

Time Estimates (excluding tasks marked with *)
Expert: 30 minutes
Intermediate: 1 hour
Novice: 1.5 hours

Tutorial for Case 1 Using Access 2010

To learn and practice the skills for this case, and many of the following cases, you will need to use the practice database table FRIENDS, which is one of the tables in the SOLVEIT_CH5.ACCDB database that you downloaded with your Student Files.

> **Access Help:** You can use Microsoft Access Help at any time by clicking the *Help* button at the top right of the Access window or pressing F1 on the keyboard.

To start Access:

1. Click *Start* to open the Start menu. Point to *All Programs* (or *Programs*), and then click *Microsoft Office* on the All Programs menu. If you are having difficulties, ask your instructor for assistance.

2. Click *Microsoft Access 2010* on the Microsoft Office submenu to launch the Access program.

3. Click the File tab on the Ribbon. On the File menu in the left pane, click the *Open* command. Use the Open dialog box to navigate to the SOLVEIT_CH5 database, which you downloaded from the Solve It! Web site. Once you find the database, double-click the file to open the database. You may see a security warning below the Ribbon that alerts you that some content has been disabled. If so, click the *Enable Content* button to allow the content.

4. Double-click the FRIENDS table in the Navigation Pane to open the table in Datasheet View, the default view.

> **Note:** To import a table from a separate Access database, click the External Data tab on the Ribbon, and in the Import & Link group, click Access. In the Get External Data – Access Database wizard, click Browse and navigate to the database file from which you are importing the table. In the File Open dialog box, select the database from which you wish to import objects and click Open. In the Get External Data wizard, make sure the Import tables, etc. option button is selected and click OK. In the Import Objects dialog box, select the table you want to import on the Tables tab and click OK. The imported object will display in the Navigation Pane.

Access displays table data in columns and rows, similar to a spreadsheet. Each row in an Access table represents a *record*, and each column represents a *field*. For example, in Figure 5-1, there are 20 records in the FRIENDS table, and the *Current Record* box, at the bottom of the table's window, displays 1 of 20 indicating that record 1 is currently selected. Above the rows of records are the *field selectors*, which contain the field names for each column. Fields describe various categories of information (e.g.: Last_Name, First_Name) that make up each record. To the left of each record are the *record selectors*, which are used to select a particular record. A record is highlighted in blue to indicate that it is currently selected, and the record selector is highlighted in orange. As you make changes to a record, a pencil icon displays in the record selector. An asterisk appears in the record selector of the next new blank record into which you can enter data.

Tables can be displayed in two ways. Figure 5-1 shows the default Datasheet View, represented by the Datasheet View button on the status bar . Datasheets are used to display, edit, and delete records, as well as to print tables. Later in this tutorial, we will also be using Design View, represented by the status bar button . Design View is used for adding, editing, and deleting fields, as well as for defining field properties and indexes.

Navigating Within a Datasheet

Use your [Tab] key or click with your mouse to move to a particular column within a record. Use the horizontal or vertical scroll bars to practice viewing records and

Figure 5-1

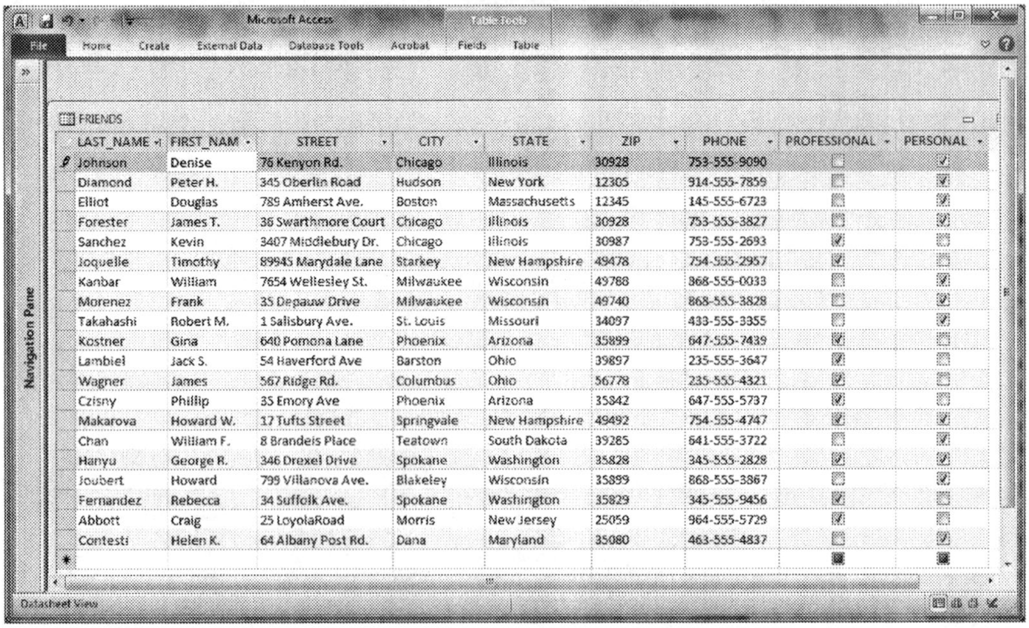

fields in the datasheet. Use the *Specific Record* box and the navigation buttons shown in Figure 5-2 to move to a specific record in the datasheet.

Figure 5-2

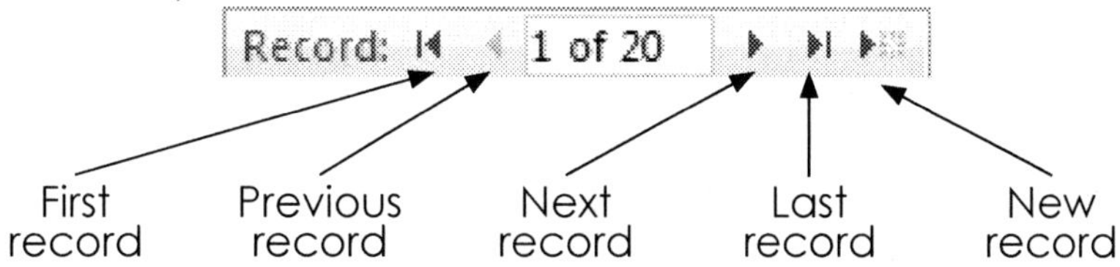

Record: |◄ ◄ 1 of 20 ► ►| ►*

First record | Previous record | Next record | Last record | New record

Resizing Columns and Rows in an Access Datasheet

To resize a column (field), position your mouse on the right edge of a column at the field selector level, (e.g.: Last_Name). When a horizontal resize pointer ✛ displays, as shown in Figure 5-3, drag horizontally until the column is the desired size. You can also double-click the right edge of any column heading to automatically resize the width to display all data in the column. You can also right-click a selected column and click the *Field Width* command to open the Column Width dialog box. (Alternatively, on the Home tab, in the Records group, click *More* and then click *Field Width* on the drop-down menu.) Click *Best Fit* to size the column so that all data in the column displays, or enter a specific width in the *Column Width* box and click *OK*.

Record rows can be resized by positioning the mouse pointer between any two record selectors at the left side of the datasheet. When a vertical resize pointer ✛ displays, drag up or down until the rows are the desired size. **Warning:** *Unlike column resizing, this will resize all of the rows.*

Saving Datasheet Layout Changes

Open the File tab on the Ribbon and click the *Save* command, or click 💾 on the Quick Access toolbar.

Figure 5-3

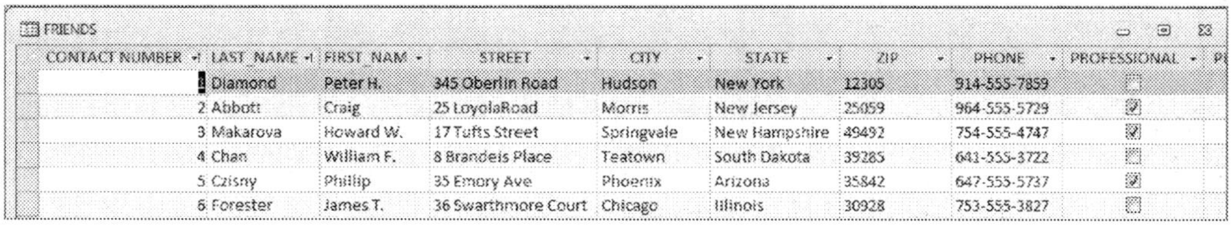

CONTACT NUMBER	LAST_NAME	FIRST_NAM	STREET	CITY	STATE	ZIP	PHONE	PROFESSIONAL
1	Diamond	Peter H.	345 Oberlin Road	Hudson	New York	12305	914-555-7859	
2	Abbott	Craig	25 LoyolaRoad	Morris	New Jersey	25059	964-555-5729	
3	Makarova	Howard W.	17 Tufts Street	Springvale	New Hampshire	49492	754-555-4747	☑
4	Chan	William F.	8 Brandeis Place	Teatown	South Dakota	39285	641-555-3722	
5	Czisny	Phillip	35 Emory Ave	Phoenix	Arizona	35842	647-555-5737	☑
6	Forester	James T.	36 Swarthmore Court	Chicago	Illinois	30928	753-555-3827	

Printing a Datasheet

With the table open in Datasheet View, open the File tab on the Ribbon. On the File menu in the left pane, click the *Print* command. Three options display in the main window: Quick Print, Print, and Print Preview. Click *Quick Print* to send the object directly to the default printer without making any changes. Click *Print* to open the Print dialog box and make changes to the printing options. If you have selected only certain records for printing, click the *Selected Records* option button in the *Print Range* section of the dialog box and then click *OK*. You can also choose the number of copies to print in the *Copies* section.

How to Change the Structure of an Access Table

Table Design View is used for establishing and modifying the field structure of a table. To switch to Design View, click the *Design View* button on the right side of the status bar, or, on the Home tab, in the View group, click the *Design View* button if it is available. (This button typically toggles between Datasheet View and Design View.) If it is not, you can click the arrow on the bottom half of the *View* button to open the View menu and click *Design View*.

As you move around the Design View window (see Figure 5-4), a help box on the right side of the Field Properties pane, in the bottom half of the window, describes

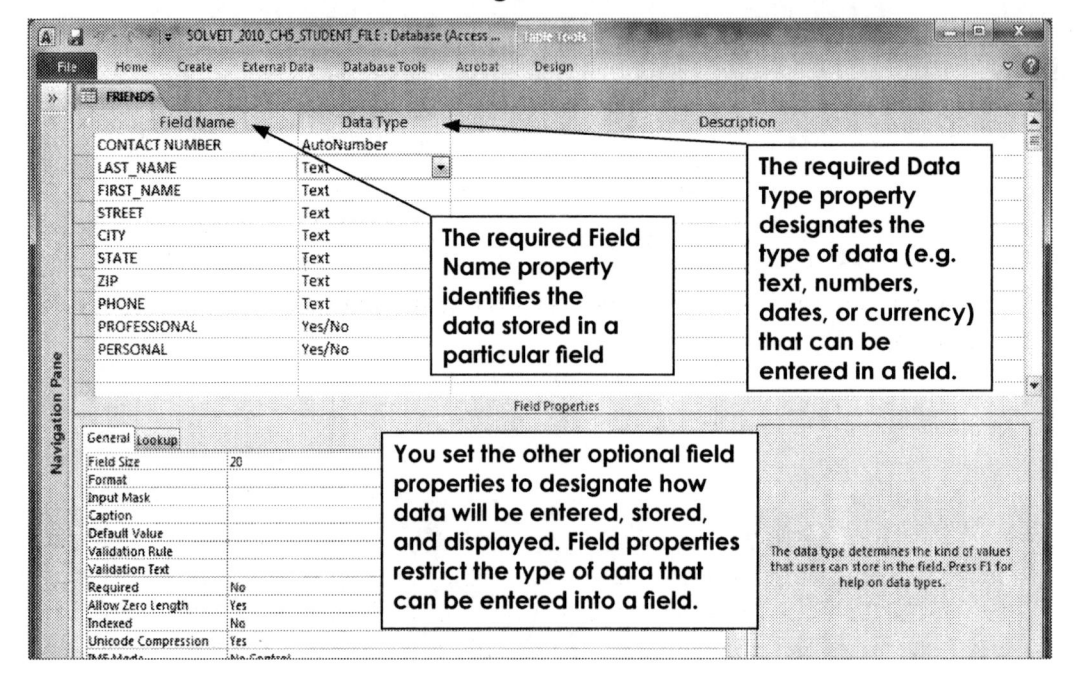

Figure 5-4

the purpose of the currently selected property. For example, the required Data Type property is used to determine the kinds of values that can be entered and stored in a field. Let's add a new field called TITLE to the table to store titles, such as *Mrs., Ms., Mr.,* and *Dr.*

1. Add the Title field before the Last_Name field. Position your mouse pointer over the row selector for the LAST_NAME field, and then click once to select the field. On the Table Tools: Design tab, in the Tools group, click *Insert Rows* to insert a blank row above the Last_Name field.

2. Click in the blank *Field Name* column and type *TITLE*.

3. Click in the blank *Data Type* column to choose the kind of data the field will accept. In this case, the default Text data type is the one we need. Notice the list arrow on the right end of the cell. Clicking the list arrow opens a list of the other available data types. Review the Access data types section in Chapter 4 for an explanation of each data type.

4. Click in the *Field Size* cell in the Field Properties pane. The default width for text fields is 255 characters. Since the field will contain only abbreviated terms, change the field size to 5 characters.

5. Click the File tab on the Ribbon and select *Save*, or click on the Quick Access toolbar to save the changes.

6. On the Table Tools: Design tab on the Ribbon, click the top half of the *View* button or click on the status bar to return to Datasheet View.

How to Enter Records

Scroll down to the end of the record set to the row indicated by the New Record symbol (*) in the record selector. Click inside the first empty field of this row. Add one record to the FRIENDS table. Move between fields using the [Tab] key. Press [Tab] once more to move to the first field of the next record. Access will automatically save your data when you leave a record either by moving to another record or by closing the table.

How to Edit Existing Records

In Datasheet View, move to the empty *Title* field and add appropriate titles for each of the records in the FRIENDS table. For example, for the record Peter H. Diamond, click in the *Title* field and enter the title *Dr*. Notice that the pencil symbol appears in the record selector, indicating that the record is being edited. Press the down arrow key on the keyboard to move to the Title field for the next record. Add a title and continue down the column to add titles for the remaining records. As you move down the column, the pencil symbol will appear in each record you are editing and Access will automatically save the changes.

Closing a Table

The application window has *Minimize*, *Maximize*, and *Close* buttons at the top right of the Access window. A second *Close* button is located in the upper right corner of the object. Click × to close the table.

How to Display and Print Selected Fields: Building a Query 1:

A *query* is a question that you ask about certain data in a database, such as, "How many customers live in Melbourne?" or "What were our sales figures for last month?" Alternatively, you may just want to view selected fields of a database in a certain order. The Select Query window is a graphical query-by-example (QBE) tool. This means you can use the mouse to select and drag the fields you wish to view to the window. Then you can choose to view the data in a certain order or set criteria so that only records that meet those criteria will display (e.g. customers who live in Melbourne). In other words, you are defining an example of the records you wish to view.

Let's say that you want to display and print just three fields from the FRIENDS table: Last_Name, First_Name, and City. Here's how to create an Access query to do this:

1. Open the Create tab on the Ribbon. In the Queries group, click *Query Design*. Access opens a select query window with a design grid at the bottom. The Show Table dialog box also opens above the query window (see Figure 5-5).

2. In the Show Table dialog box, select the table you want to base the query on, in this case, *FRIENDS*, and then click *Add*. This adds a field list for the FRIENDS table to the query window. Click the *Close* button to close the Show Table dialog box. Notice that the contextual tab Query Tools: Design opens on the Ribbon because you are working with a select query.

3. Select the *Last_Name* field in the FRIENDS field list. Hold down the [Ctrl] key and select *First_Name* and then *City*. (The [Ctrl] key is handy to use when selecting nonadjacent fields for a query.) Release the [Ctrl] key.

4. Use the mouse to drag the selection to the design grid. Release the mouse button when the mouse pointer is in the first Field cell in the design grid. The three fields are added in order to the design grid as shown in Figure 5-6.

Database Management Software Cases   143

Figure 5-5

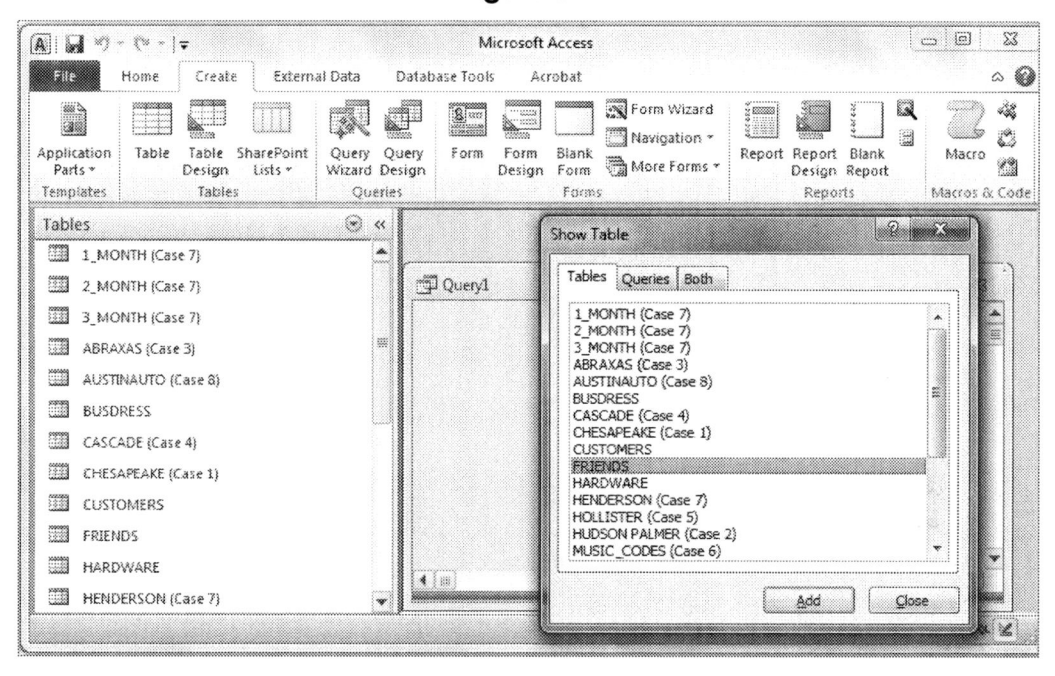

Figure 5-6

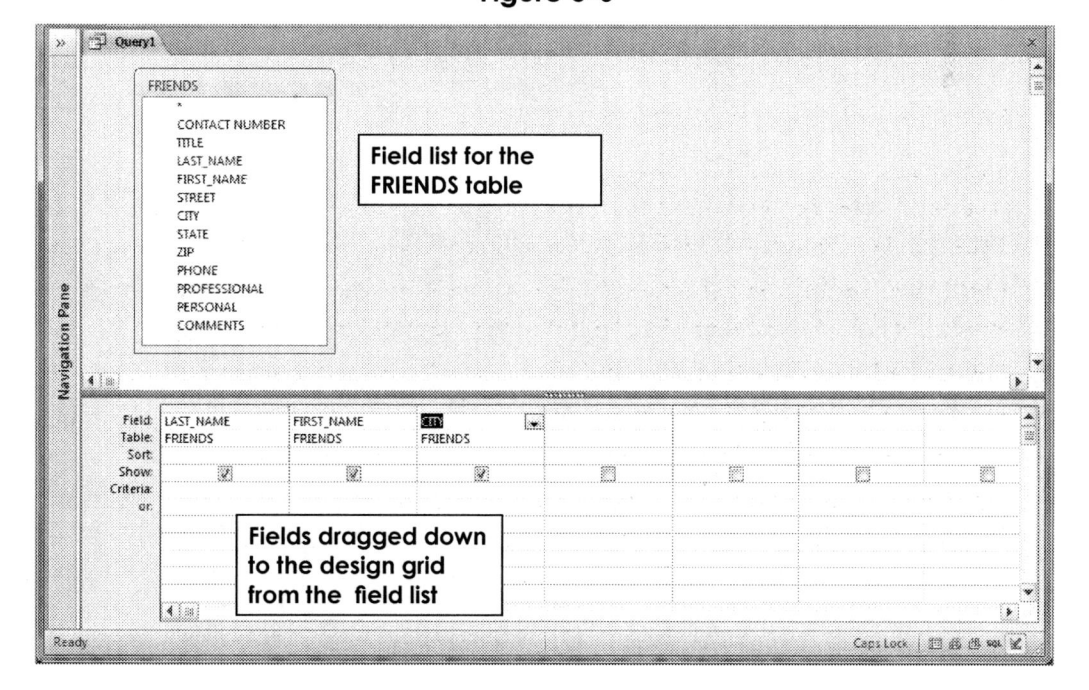

144   *Solve it!*

Figure 5-7

LAST_NAME	FIRST_NAM	CITY
Diamond	Peter H.	Hudson
Abbott	Craig	Morris
Makarova	Howard W.	Springvale
Chan	William F.	Teatown
Czisny	Phillip	Phoenix
Forester	James T.	Chicago
Morenez	Frank	Milwaukee
Hanyu	George R.	Spokane
Contesti	Helen K.	Dana
Lambiel	Jack S.	Barston
Takahashi	Robert M.	St. Louis
Johnson	Denise	Chicago
Wagner	James	Columbus
Joubert	Howard	Blakeley
Kostner	Gina	Phoenix
Joquelle	Timothy	Starkey
Kanbar	William	Milwaukee
Fernandez	Rebecca	Spokane
Elliot	Douglas	Boston
Sanchez	Kevin	Chicago

5. In the Results group on the Query Tools: Design tab, click the *Run* button to generate the query results set as shown in Figure 5-7.

6. Click the File tab on the Ribbon. On the File menu in the left pane, click the *Print* command. Click *Quick Print* to print the query.

7. The query should automatically reopen in the Query Design window. If not, click the Home tab to return to the Query Design window.

8. Click the *Save* button on the Quick Access toolbar, or click the File tab on the Ribbon and then *Save* to save the query. Type *Tute1Query1* in the *Query Name* text box in the *Save as* dialog box and click OK.

9. Click the bottom half of the *View* button and then click *SQL View* to view the Structured Query Language code generated by Access for the query. You can also open SQL view by clicking the SQL View button on the far right of the status bar at the bottom of the application window, next to the Design View icon.

    SELECT FRIENDS.LAST_NAME, FRIENDS.FIRST_NAME, FRIENDS.CITY FROM FRIENDS;

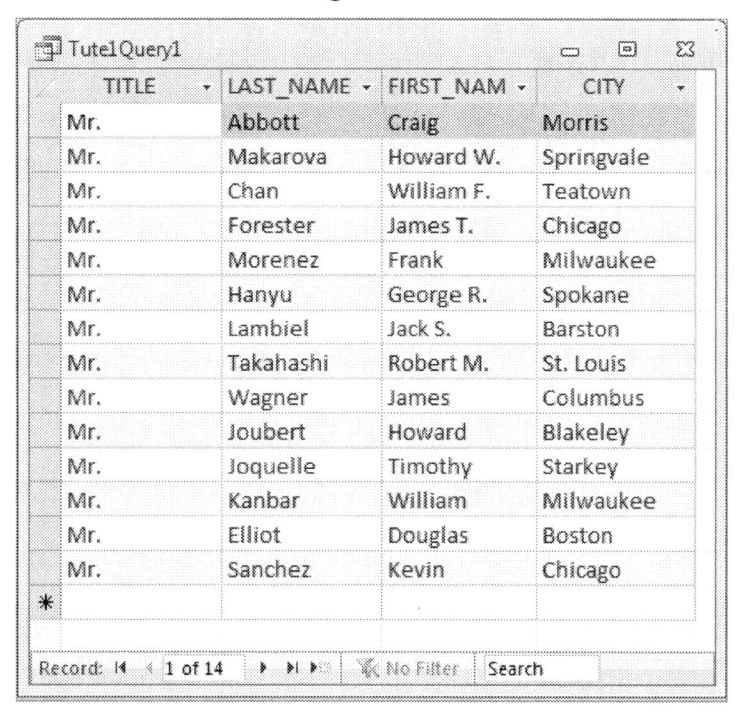

Figure 5-8

TITLE	LAST_NAME	FIRST_NAM	CITY
Mr.	Abbott	Craig	Morris
Mr.	Makarova	Howard W.	Springvale
Mr.	Chan	William F.	Teatown
Mr.	Forester	James T.	Chicago
Mr.	Morenez	Frank	Milwaukee
Mr.	Hanyu	George R.	Spokane
Mr.	Lambiel	Jack S.	Barston
Mr.	Takahashi	Robert M.	St. Louis
Mr.	Wagner	James	Columbus
Mr.	Joubert	Howard	Blakeley
Mr.	Joquelle	Timothy	Starkey
Mr.	Kanbar	William	Milwaukee
Mr.	Elliot	Douglas	Boston
Mr.	Sanchez	Kevin	Chicago

This code can be cut and pasted into an event procedure within a macro or a module and used as part of a larger program. Access provides a number of useful programming shortcuts. We will be looking at some of these in later cases. Return to Design View for Tute1Query1.

How to Display Selected Records: Building a Query 2

Now that you have constructed a simple query, let's go one step further and search the FRIENDS table for records that meet specific criteria. In this example, let's extract only those records that contain *Mr.* in the Title field.

1. Open Tute1Query1 in Design View. Select the *Title* field in the FRIENDS field list. Drag the selected field to the design grid and release the mouse button over the Last_Name field. Access automatically moves the fields to the right and inserts the Title field as the first field in the query.

2. In the *Criteria* cell for the Title field, type: *Mr.* On the Query Tools: Design tab on the Ribbon, in the Results group, click the *Run* button The query result set is displayed in Figure 5-8.

3. Click to return to Design View. Notice that Access has enclosed the

criteria in quotation marks, indicating that this is a text criterion. Access is not case sensitive, so entering *Mr.* in either lowercase or uppercase will produce the same search result.

4. Click the top half of the *View* button to return to Datasheet View.

5. Open the File tab and click *Save Object As* to open the Save As dialog box. Save the query as *Tute1Query2* and click *OK*.

6. To print the new query, click *Print*, and then click the *Quick Print* command.

7. Exit Access by clicking the *Exit* command or by clicking the *Close* button on the Microsoft Access Title bar.

Database Case 2

Marvin, Sanders, Holloman & Sandoval Certified Public Accountants

Problem:	Construct a Personnel Database
Management Skill:	Coordinate
Access Skills:	Table Setup
	Data Input
	Select Queries
	Report Design
	Printing
Data Table:	MARVIN_SANDERS

Marvin, Sanders, Holloman & Sandoval (Marvin Sanders for short) is a large CPA firm with offices in Akron, Toledo, and Youngstown, Ohio, specializing in corporate accounting. The Marvin Sanders Akron office employs more than 85 freelance and contract personnel, including systems consultants (SC), auditors (A), management consultants (MC), and tax researchers (TR). These people are hired on an as-needed basis on behalf of the many client corporations the firm represents.

Marvin Sanders has 38 Senior Accountants who are also the main partners in the firm. Each Senior Accountant has a staff of Junior Accountants. In addition, all Senior CPAs keep separate lists of contractors and freelancers with whom they have worked successfully in the past. Typically, these lists reside on personal files on each partner's computer. Whenever a client's case requires certain outside expertise, the partners open their personal files and select their favorite people.

The partner's remuneration is based in part on their performance—the more billable hours their Junior Accountants generate, the more money they make. Moreover, the more experienced and competent freelancers they know, the more likely they are to generate more billable hours. In this environment, there is a natural tendency to safeguard the names of good freelancers and contractors for one's own accounts. However, there is also the likelihood that by sharing this information, the firm's overall success would increase and everyone would benefit.

148 Solve it!

Raoul Marvin started the law firm 24 years ago with fellow Stanford University graduate Bradley Sanders. Raoul knows how the freelancing system works. The problem is that each Senior Accountant squirrels away the names of the people that he or she thinks are really excellent. When it comes to the talent pool, there is no sharing among Senior Accountants. Second-rate people may be used because the names of the first-rate people are only known by one or two partners. If a partner hires a poor freelancer and the client is not satisfied with the auditing or consulting services rendered, they may be inclined to look elsewhere for accounting services in the future, and thus the firm's profits and reputation suffer.

Marvin wants to establish some sort of centralized repository for this information. Too much time is wasted searching for people with particular skills or knowledge that may already be known to some of the partners. The central repository could also contain comments on the performance of the freelancer or contractor on prior occasions and other relevant data. Marvin would like some sort of scoring system so that freelancers and contractors could be rank-ordered. This would ensure that only the best people would be hired to work with the firm.

The partners are not happy with this idea. Sharing these resources with the other partners may mean that their favorite people will be unavailable when they need them most. On the other hand, a central repository might help them to find new resources with whom they were previously unfamiliar. Therefore, with somewhat mixed feelings, the partners have agreed to support the proposal to build a central repository of contractors. They have responded to a memo sent out by Marvin asking them to list the resources they would like to have stored in a central database.

The following fields were identified: First and Last Name, Skill, Hourly Rate, Number of Hours Employed for Each Quarter of 2012, Phone Number, Rating (Excellent, Good, OK, or Poor) and Initials of the Rater. Marvin reviewed the suggestions and added a field to store an additional free form text comment about each freelancer.

Parts of this database have been identified in the table MARVIN_SANDERS in the SOLVEIT_5 database. Create a new Access database and import this table now.

Tasks

There are eight tasks in this case:

1. Complete the design of the table to store the rating system devised by Marvin. Be sure to devise a way to limit the rating field to only 4 categories

and to record free-form text remarks from the attorneys. Fabricate and enter hours worked for the existing freelancers or contractors. Enter data for three new freelancers or contractors, such as auditors (A), management consultants (MC), tax researchers (TR), or systems consultants (SC). Enter data for at least the first three freelancers in the comments field. Use your initials for the partner who is contributing the remarks.

2. Devise a system for recording the numbers of hours worked each quarter by each contract worker so that excellent work can be rewarded with additional assignments and workers who are not satisfactory can be weeded out.

3. Create a query that shows the contractors sorted first by their skill, then by their rating, and then by their last name. Include the comment field and print the results of this query.

4. Create a query and then a report to list all the freelancers and contractors with the following fields: Last Name, Rating, and Total Number of Hours Worked in 2012. Print the report.

5. Create and print a report to show the Total Amount Earned (TOTAL_COMPENSATION) in 2012 by each contractor.

6. Produce and print a report to list all system consultants who charge more than $250.00/hour. Include in this report the total number of hours each freelancer worked for Marvin Sanders in 2012 and their total compensation. Print the report.

7.* There are several areas where this system can be enhanced and improved. (What will happen next quarter? What if two partners have the same initials?) Make a list of all of the improvements you would make, and then pick one and implement it in the database.

8.* Currently, with the comments in a Memo field, no analysis or data manipulation can be performed using the ratings of the freelancers. There may also be conflicting opinions on the merit of any one freelancer if they have worked for more than one partner. Devise a method to accommodate these differing opinions in such a way that meaningful analysis can be performed. Note that this may mean redesigning the database.

Time Estimates (excluding tasks marked with *)

Expert: 45 minutes
Intermediate: 1.25 hours
Novice: 2 hours

Tutorial for Database Case 2 Using Access 2010

In the previous case, you learned to use Table Design View to change the structure of a table by adding new fields and setting field properties and how to use Datasheet View to add and edit records. This case introduces the *memo* data type and *report design*. Start Access and open the FRIENDS table you used for the Case 1 tutorial to practice the skills you will need for this case.

Using Memo Fields

Memo fields are used in tables to store free-form text and notes. You use a memo field to store descriptive or narrative information and even large documents. A memo field in Access 2010 can hold up to 65,536 characters of text. Creating, entering, and saving data in an Access memo field is a very simple procedure. Because of their unstructured nature, memo fields cannot be indexed or sorted, but they can be searched. We will look at indexing, sorting, and searching in later cases.

1. Open the SOLVEIT_CH5 database. Double-click the FRIENDS table to open it in Datasheet View. Click the *Design View* button on the status bar or click *View* on the Home tab on the Ribbon.

2. Let's add a new field to the end of the existing table. The name for the new field will be COMMENTS and the data type will be *Memo*. (Review the tutorial for Case 1 if you are unsure how to add new fields and select data types.) Notice that the Field Size cell in the Field Properties pane does not appear when you select the memo data type. Save the changes to the table structure by clicking the *Save* button on the Quick Access toolbar or selecting *Save* on the File tab.

3. Return to Datasheet View by clicking the *Datasheet View* button or by clicking the *View* button on the Ribbon. Scroll or tab over to the new COMMENTS field and enter text for each record to describe their relationship (e.g. pediatrician, family physician, accountant, personal attorney, business contact, friend, family member, or a specific familial relationship). Press the down arrow key on the keyboard to move to each new record. (Remember that as you move to a new record, Access automatically saves the data.)

Printing Memo Fields

Memo fields can be printed like any other field in a table or query. To create a query that will select only certain fields in the table, including the memo field:

1. On the Create tab on the Ribbon, in the Queries group, click the *Query Design* button.

2. In the Show Table dialog box, select the FRIENDS table, click *Add,* and then click *Close*.

3. In the FRIENDS field list, select the Last_Name and Comments fields and drag them to the design grid. Release the mouse button when the pointer is over the first Field cell.

4. Click the *Run* button on the Query Tools: Design tab to display the data in the Last_Name and Comments fields (see Figure 5-9).

5. Click the File tab on the Ribbon. Click the *Print* command on the menu bar to open the Print dialog box and then click *OK* to print the query. Then click the *Close* button at the top right of the query window and click *Yes* when a warning dialog box asks if you want to save the changes to the design of Query 1. Save the query as Friends_Comments.

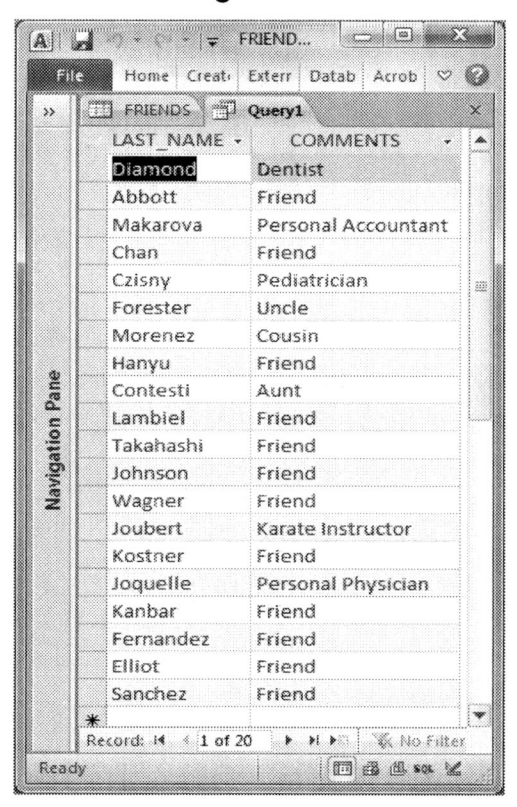

Figure 5-9

LAST_NAME	COMMENTS
Diamond	Dentist
Abbott	Friend
Makarova	Personal Accountant
Chan	Friend
Czisny	Pediatrician
Forester	Uncle
Morenez	Cousin
Hanyu	Friend
Contesti	Aunt
Lambiel	Friend
Takahashi	Friend
Johnson	Friend
Wagner	Friend
Joubert	Karate Instructor
Kostner	Friend
Joquelle	Personal Physician
Kanbar	Friend
Fernandez	Friend
Elliot	Friend
Sanchez	Friend

Creating Reports in Access

A more polished look can be achieved by creating an Access report. Reports are the database objects in Access specifically designed for printing. Reports can be based on tables and/or queries. They are used to provide subtotals and grand totals for numeric fields, and to produce summaries of information contained in the database, mailing labels, and presentation quality display of your data. Report Wizards speed up the creation, display, and printout by providing a series of dialog boxes to help you determine the data you want the report to contain.

The items on a report that contain the data for display and printing are called *controls*. Different types of controls are used to display data of the various data types. Controls are used to display data from fields, the labels that identify this data, the results of calculations, data or calculations for report headers and footers, which print at the top and bottom of every page of the report, and data or calculations for group footers, which identify a particular group of related data. Report controls can also be used to include graphs, pictures, and other Access objects.

1. On the Create tab on the Ribbon, in the Reports group, click Report Wizard to open the Report Wizard.

   The first Report Wizard dialog box opens. Here you can choose the fields that you want to display in the report and decide the order in which you want them to display. Notice that, because FRIENDS is the currently selected table in the Navigation Pane, Access has selected the FRIENDS table as the basis for the Available Fields list. Select four fields, Title, First_Name, Last_Name, and City, for inclusion in the report. With the Title field selected in the Available Fields box, click the Add Field button [>] to add it to the Selected Fields box (refer to Figure 5-10). Next, select the First_Name field in the Available Fields box and click [>] again to add it to the list of selected fields. Follow the same procedure to add the remaining two fields. (If you accidentally add the wrong field to the report, select the unwanted field and click the Remove Field button [<] to return it to the Available Fields box.) When you have finished, click *Next*.

2. The second of the six Report Wizard dialog boxes opens. Here you can add grouping levels for the data in your report based on one or more fields. Data can be grouped by City, for example, so that all contacts that live in a particular city will be grouped together in the report. Without adding any grouping levels, click *Next*.

3. In the third dialog box, you can impose a sort order on the data in the report based on one or more fields. Select *City* in the first sort order list box and then click *Next*.

4. In the fourth dialog box, you can choose the layout for the report. Option buttons are provided to choose either *Portrait* or *Landscape* orientation for the report and a *Columnar*, *Tabular*, or *Justified* layout. Select the *Tabular* layout if necessary, make sure the *Adjust the field width so all fields fit on a page* check box is selected, and click *Next*.

5. In the final dialog box, you can enter a title for your report. By default, Access enters the name of the table or query that serves as the record source for the report as the title name, which in this case is FRIENDS. Type *Friends_Report*.

6. Make sure the *Preview the report* option button is selected and click the *Finish* button. Access will generate the report and open it in Print Preview, with the Print Preview tab open on the Ribbon. Note that the records are displayed alphabetically by City according to the sort order selected in the Report Wizard. Click the *Print* button on the Print Preview tab to open the Print dialog box and then click *OK* to print the report. Close the report.

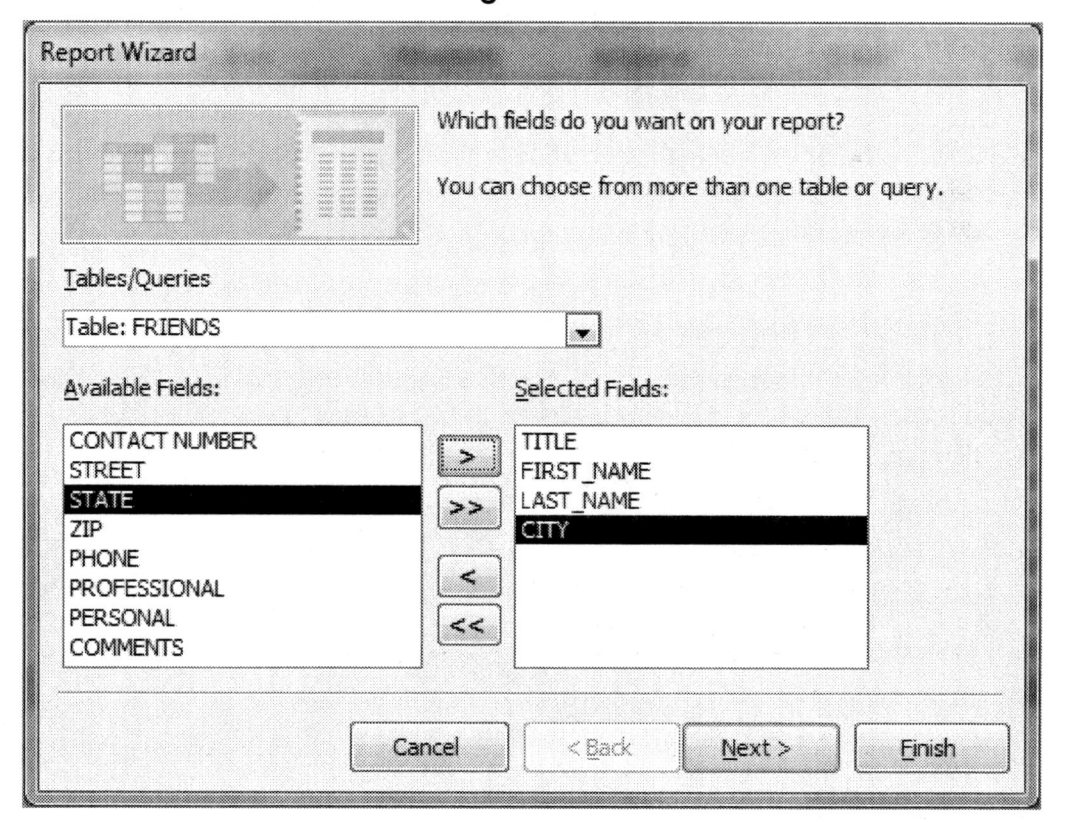

Figure 5-10

How to Use Reports to Display and Print Selected Fields

You can change the record source for an existing report, which will, in turn, change the records the report displays. For example, you can change the record source for the Friends_ Report to the second query created in the tutorial for Case 1 (e.g. *Tute1Query2*). This query filters out all records in the FRIENDS table that do not have the title MR.

1. In the Navigation Pane, double-click *Friends_Report*. (If the Navigation pane is not displaying all database objects, click the down arrow at the top right of the Navigation Pane and make sure that *Object Type* is selected in the Navigate To Category section and *All Access Objects in the Filter By Group section* of the menu)

2. On the status bar, click [icon] to open the Design View for the report (see Figure 5-11). Notice there are four Report Design Tools tabs on the Ribbon now: Design, Arrange, Format, and Page Setup.

   As Figure 5-11 shows, the Report Design View window is divided into sections. The **Report Header** prints once at the beginning of the report. It generally contains the report's title. The **Page Header** prints at the top of every page in the report and contains the labels or column headings. The **Detail** section contains the records that are being displayed in the report. The **Page Footer** prints at the bottom of each page and often contains calculated controls that display the current system date and time, along with the page number and total number of pages in the report. The **Report Footer**

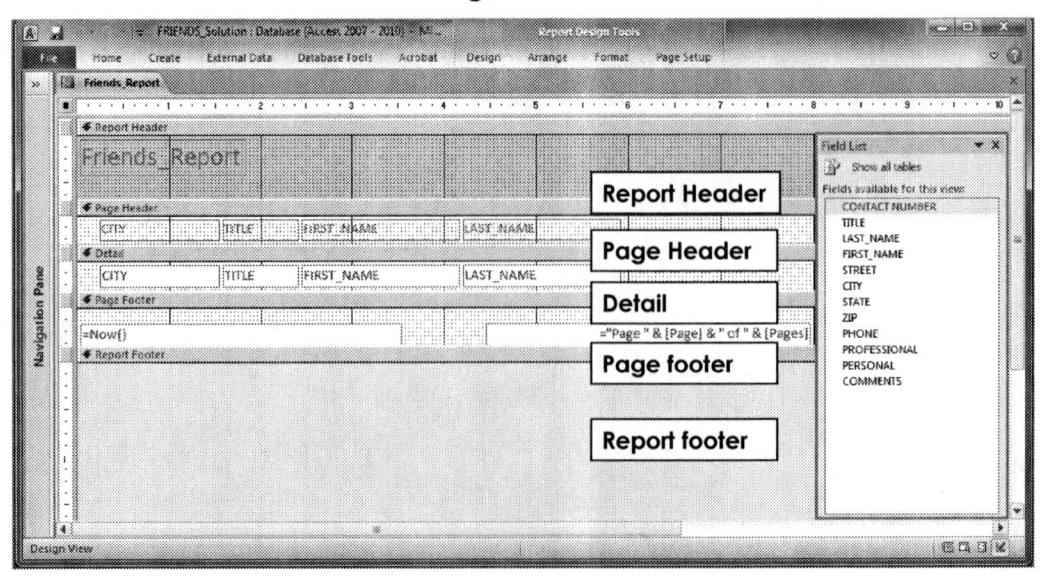

Figure 5-11

prints once at the end of the report. It often contains calculated controls that summarize or total the data contained in the report. Additionally, group headers will be automatically added to a report in which records are grouped based on like values. You can add group footers to include summary information about the group such as *Count*, *Sum*, or *Average*. We will look at report groups in a later tutorial.

3. On the Report Design Tools: Design tab, in the Tools section, click the *Property Sheet* button on to open the property sheet for the report. Report properties define the data source for the report, as well as its overall appearance.

4. Click the Data tab on the property sheet if necessary. Click in the *Record Source* property settings box and click the list arrow ▼ to open a list of the available data sources in the FRIENDS database. Select the second query you created in the Case 1 tutorial (Tute1Query2) to change the record source for the report (see Figure 5-12.)

5. Close the property sheet by clicking the × in the top right corner.

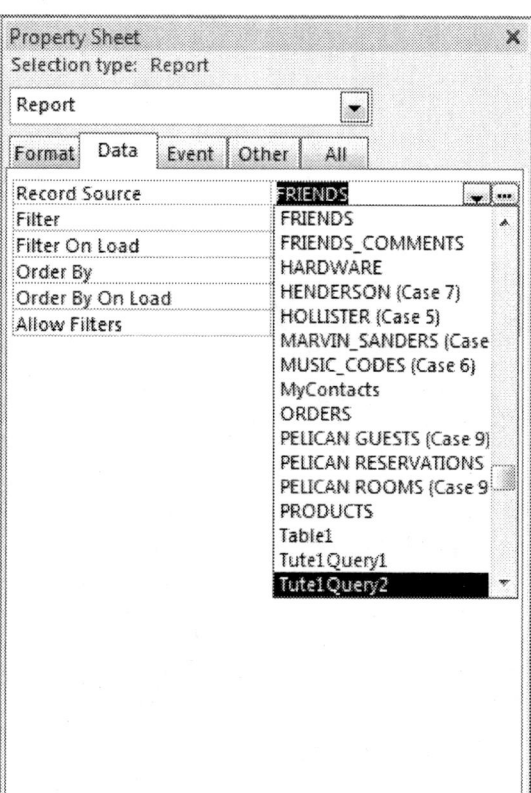

Figure 5-12

6. On the Report Design Tools: Design tab, in the Views group, click the arrow on the *Views* button and select *Print Preview* to view the new report. A reduced data set displays based upon the criteria set up in the query, but the sort order based on the City field remains.

7. On the Print Preview tab on the Ribbon, in the Print group, click the *Print* button to open the Print dialog box. Click *OK* to print the new report.

8. Click the *Close Print Preview* button to return to Design View. Click the File tab and then click *Save Object As* to open the Save As dialog box. Type *Tute2Report2* in the top text box and click *OK*. Close the report and the FRIENDS table.

Using Expressions in Reports

Calculated controls are used to display the results of expressions that can be built using Access functions, mathematical operators, raw values, and any values contained in the fields in the report. For example, the expression

= [UnitCost]*[Quantity]

multiplies the contents of the two fields with these names and displays a single value as the result. A *function* is a predefined formula that helps simplify the process of building expressions. For example, the function *Sum* will add all of the values specified. The *Now* function in the Page Footer section, shown in Figure 5-11, returns the current date as stored in your computer's system clock.

You can create calculated controls using expressions in one of three ways:

- By typing an expression directly into a text box control
- By entering an expression into the Control Source property for a control
- By using the Expression Builder to help you to create the expression

To learn and practice the skill of creating calculated controls using expressions, we will use the first method and the sample table COSMETICS provided in the SOLVEIT_CH5 database. First, create a new empty database with the name COSMETICS.ACCDB and then import the COSMETICS table from the SOLVEIT_CH5 database. (If you still have tables or reports open in the SOLVEIT_CH5 database, save and close them, and close the database.)

1. In the opened COSMETICS database, double-click the COSMETICS table to open it in Datasheet View. There are four fields: Invoice, Item, UnitCost, and Quantity.

2. Open the Create tab on the Ribbon. In the Reports group, click *Report Wizard* and use the Report Wizard to create a new report using the COSMETICS table as the record source. Include the fields Invoice, UnitCost, and Quantity. Sort the records by the Invoice field, use the Tabular layout and give the report the title *Calculating_Total_Cost*. Click *Finish*. The report is generated and opened in Print Preview.

3. On the Print Preview tab, click the *Close Print Preview* button to switch to Report Design View.

   To practice using expressions, we will create a field that calculates the total cost for an ordered cosmetics item by multiplying UnitCost by Quantity. Since this calculation, or expression, will use the values in two existing fields to calculate a new value, we must create a calculated control. A calculated control contains an expression and displays the result of that expression when the report is opened.

4. Open the Report Design Tools: Design tab on the Ribbon if necessary. Click the *Text Box* button in the Controls group. Click once with the Text Box pointer at the 6 ½ -inch mark on the horizontal ruler in the Detail section of the report. An unbound text box control and a label control to identify it are added to the report. The label text (*Text 9*) will vary depending on the number of controls on the report. Click the label control to select it and press the [Delete] key on the keyboard. You will add a label for the calculated control to the page header later.

5. Unbound controls are not linked to any existing field in the record source or sources for the report. They are used to display the results of *calculation*s, text, or graphics. Click inside the unbound text box to get a blinking insertion point (called an *I-beam*). Type =*UnitCost*Quantity*, making sure to begin the expression with an equals sign, and press the [Enter] key. Access automatically adds the correct syntax for you by enclosing each field in square brackets. Access is not case sensitive, so it does not matter if you enter your field names in upper or lowercase. You must, however, spell them correctly and use the correct spacing!

   > **Note:** If the field names contain spaces, you must enclose them in square brackets because Access will not recognize them as field names (e.g. [Time to Market]).

158 Solve it!

All expressions in Access must begin with an = sign. The asterisk is used to denote multiplication. A listing of other operators and functions used in Access is presented at the end of this tutorial.

6. You have now created a calculated control. The Detail section of your report should resemble Figure 5-13.

7. You will now add a label control to the page header to identify the calculated control. Click the *Label* button on the Ribbon. Click the Label pointer once in the Page Header section of the report at the 7-inch mark on the horizontal ruler. Type *TOTAL*.

8. Double-click the new calculated control in the Detail section to open the property sheet for the control. Click the Format tab. Click in the *Format* property settings box. Click the list arrow and select *Currency* on the list. Close the property sheet.

9. Select the calculated control in the Detail section. Hold down the [Shift] key and select the QUANTITY text box. On the Report Design Tools: *Arrange* tab in the *Sizing and Ordering* section, click the *Align* button and select *Top* to align the controls in the Details section along their top edge.

10. Click on the status bar to switch to Print Preview. Your report should look similar to Figure 5-14. Save the changes and close the report.

Calculations in Queries

A more rapid way of achieving the same result is to create a query that includes the calculated field you want to display in the report and then use the query as the record source for the report.

In the COSMETICS database, open the Create tab on the Ribbon and click *Query Design*. Add the field list for the COSMETICS table to the Select Query window and close the Show Table dialog box. Drag three fields—Invoice, UnitCost, and Quantity—to the design grid.

In the fourth Field cell, type *TOTAL: [UnitCost]*[Quantity]*. Your query window should look like Figure 5-15.

Figure 5-13

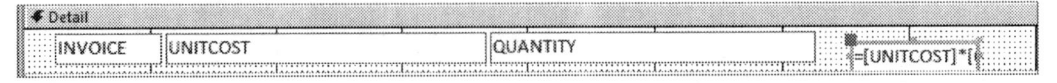

Database Management Software Cases

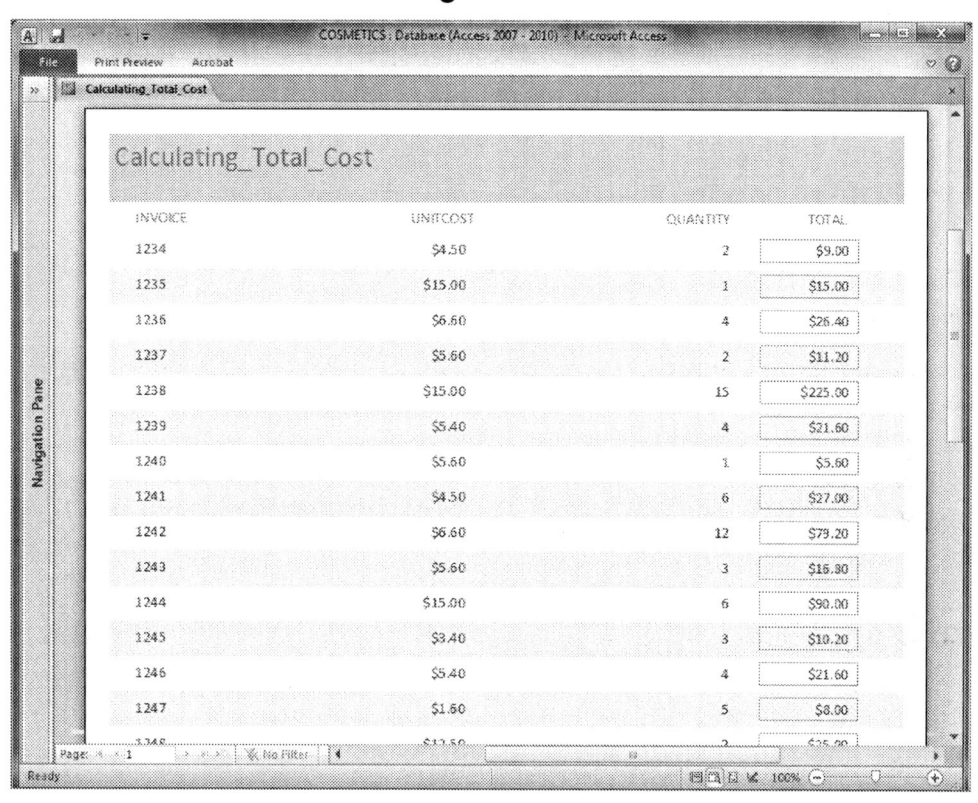

Figure 5-14

Figure 5-15

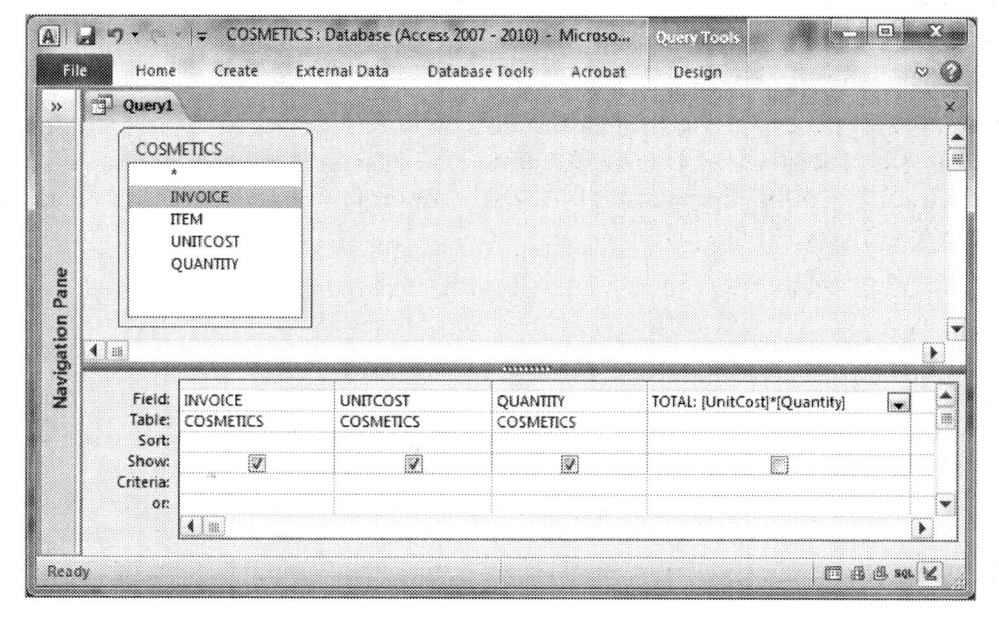

On the Query Tools: Design tab on the Ribbon, in the Show/Hide section, click the *Property Sheet* button to open the property sheet for the calculated field. On the General tab, click in the *Format* property settings box. Click the list arrow and select *Currency*. Close the property sheet.

Click Run on the Query Tools: Design tab (Results group) to run the query. Save the query as *CalculatingTotalCost*.

Use the Report Wizard to create a new report called *CalculatingTotalCost* using the query as the data source for the report. Sort the report in ascending order by Invoice number.

Expressions can play many roles in Access, and they can be used in virtually every type of database object. For example, you can use expressions in Table Design View to define default values for fields. In queries, expressions can be used to create calculated fields and criteria. The table below lists only those operators likely to be used in *Solve it!* For a more complete list, search the Access Help facility using the term *operators*.

Operators in Access

An *operator* in an expression describes the type of action the expression should perform or the way in which a comparison between two values should be carried out. Access has four kinds of operators: Arithmetic and Text, Comparison, Logical, and Miscellaneous. The table on the next page classifies, lists, and explains these operators. For a more complete list of operators, consult the Access Help facility.

Functions in Access

A *function* in Access performs a calculation on data and returns the result of that calculation. There are over 100 functions available in Access in eight different categories. The table on the next page lists only those likely to be used in *Solve it!* For a complete list, search the Help files using the keywords *functions* and *reference*.

The Access Form and Report Design Tools

The buttons displayed in the table on the following pages appear in the Controls group on the Report Design Tools: Design tab. You use them to create labels, text boxes, option buttons, etc. for forms, subforms, and other Access objects.

Access Operators

ARITHMETIC AND TEXT	^	Raise one number to the power of the other (exponentiation)
	*	Multiply two numbers
	/	Divide two numbers
	+	Add two numbers
	-	Subtract two numbers
	Mod	Divide two numbers and return the remainder
	&	Concatenate: join two strings of text
COMPARISON	< and <=	Less than; less than or equal to
	> and >=	Greater than; greater than or equal to
	= and <>	Equal to: not equal to
	Logical	
	And	Both comparisons are True
	Or	One comparison or the other is True
	Xor	One comparison or the other is True, but not both
	Not	The comparison is not True
MISCELLANEOUS	Like	Text matches a pattern (Use with wildcard symbols ? and *)
	Is	Comparison is True (e.g.: is Null)
	Is Not	Comparison is not True (e.g.: not Null)

Access Functions

DATE/TIME	Date	Returns current date
	Now	Returns current date and time
LOGICAL	IF	Tests and returns a value based on whether an argument is True or False
	Choose	Selects a value from a list based on the content of its argument
AGGREGATE	Avg	Average
	Count	Count how many
	Sum	Sum total

Access Form and Report Design Tools

ICON	NAME	DESCRIPTION
	Select Objects	Use to select a control, section, or form. Click this tool to unlock a control button that you have locked down.
	Control Wizards	Turns control wizards on or off; Use control wizards to help you create a list box, combo box, option group, command button, chart, subreport, or subform.
	Label	A control that displays descriptive text, such as a title, a caption, or instructions on a form or report; Access automatically attaches labels to the controls you create.
	Text Box	Use to display, enter, or edit data in either a form or report's underlying record source, display the results of a calculation, or accept input from a user.
	Option Group	Use along with check boxes, option buttons, or toggle buttons to display a set of alternative values. For example, you can use an option group to specify whether an order is shipped by air, sea, or land.
	Toggle Button	Use as a stand-alone control bound to a Yes/No field, an unbound control for accepting user input in a custom dialog box, or as part of an option group.
	Option Button	Use as a stand-alone control bound to a Yes/No field, an unbound control for accepting user input in a custom dialog box, or as part of an option group.
	Check Box	Use as a stand-alone control bound to a Yes/No field, an unbound control for accepting user input in a custom dialog box, or as part of an option group.
	Combo Box	Combines the features of a list box and a text box; You can type in the text box or select an entry in the list box to add a value to an underlying field.
	Chart	Adds a chart.
	List Box	Displays a scrollable list of values; In Form View, you can select from the list to enter a value into a new record or to change the value in an existing record.
	Command Button	Use to perform actions, such as finding a record, printing a record, or applying a form filter.

Access Form and Report Design Tools

ICON	NAME	DESCRIPTION
	Attachment	Use to insert an attachment file such as a Word document, Excel spreadsheet, or image file.
	Hyperlink	Adds a hyperlink.
	Image	Use to display a static picture on a form or report. Because a static picture is not an OLE object, you cannot edit the image inside Microsoft Access after you have added it to a form or report.
	Unbound Object Frame	Use to display an unbound OLE object, such as a Microsoft Excel spreadsheet, on a form or report. The object remains constant as you move from record to record.
	Bound Object Frame	Use to display OLE objects, such as a series of pictures, on a form or report. This control is for objects stored in a field in either the form or the report's underlying record source. A different object displays on the form or report as you move from record to record.
	Insert Page Break	Use to insert or remove a new page on a form, printed form, or report.
	Tab Control	Use to create a tabbed form with several pages or tabbed dialog box (such as the Access Options dialog box on the File tab). You can copy or add other controls onto a tab control. Right-click the Tab control in the design grid to modify the number of pages, the page order, the properties for the selected page, and the selected tab control properties.
	Subform/ Subreport	Use to display data from more than one table on a form or report.
	Line	Use to insert a line on a form or report to emphasize related or especially important information.
	Rectangle	Use to insert a rectangle for graphic effect, such as grouping a set of related controls on a form or for emphasizing important data on a report.
	ActiveX Control	Adds an ActiveX control (such as the Calendar control) to a form or report; ActiveX controls are stored as separate files.

Database Case 3
Remora Pianos

Problem:	Develop an automated Bill of Materials
Management Skill:	Plan
	Coordinate
Access Skills:	Creating Queries
	Sorting (tables, queries, reports)
Data Table:	REMORA

Emily Sanchez, Production Manager of Remora Pianos, walked out of the Chief Executive Officer's office muttering to herself. She had just left a meeting between Daisuke Chet, the CEO; Maria DeMarco, the Chief Financial Officer; and Simon Lester, the Purchasing Officer. They had more or less ordered her to computerize the Bill of Materials (BoM) and purchasing systems. She argued that such an instruction was easier given than implemented. They had finally compromised on automating a section of the factory's assembly facilities as a pilot project. The pilot project would provide an opportunity to improve the design of the new system and measure the benefits before moving to complete implementation in the entire factory.

Remora Pianos, based in Lincoln, Nebraska, had experienced steady sales for its range of high quality pianos until 2006 when less expensive imports of similar quality began to capture a significant market share. Costs had to be reduced, and senior management decided that increased production volume was needed before their pianos could regain competitiveness in such a capital-intensive industry. These increased volumes would provide economies of scale in materials purchases and enable a new, more efficient plant to be purchased. The increased volume would be obtained by entering the mid-priced piano market. Remora Piano's quality hardwood pianos would be particularly suitable in such a market. In addition, a range of new products including tuning tools and piano accessories was developed. The strategy proved fruitful. Remora Piano's instruments were acclaimed in magazines across the country. The strategy, along with a continuous improvement program initiated at the same time, reduced production costs, and gains occurred in both the household and business markets.

Management found that the increase in production rapidly outpaced the ability of the old manual, paper-based production control system. The result was poor market intelligence, an inability to implement activity-based costing, and reduced efficiency in production. For instance, supplies were being ordered and put in inventory, but there was no way to link the supplies to specific products. To understand the cost of building a particular piano, Remora needs to know the cost of all the supplies used in its production, down to the smallest screw and even the amount of glue used in construction. The old manual production system could not supply this information.

Emily considered the best ways to start the process. Even if her budget permitted a full-blown Materials Requirement Planning system, the jump would be too large for Remora. She decided that creating an in-house database system using Access would be the most suitable solution since DeMarco and Lester were not specific about what computer platform to use and future requirements were unclear. This approach would provide the necessary flexibility for incremental development and expansion. Because she had a poor understanding of databases, Sanchez called the School of Business at the University of Nebraska to seek help. The Placement Office at the university referred her to Camille Dennis, a first-year MBA student seeking a summer internship with a manufacturer. Dennis agreed to come on board as a consultant.

Although she had a liberal arts background, Dennis had minored in Information Technology in her undergraduate program and was keen to learn about production systems. Emily Sanchez explained what was required in the preliminary stages. Currently, the BoM for each product type was recorded on paper and used exclusively in the production area. Sanchez was sure that a BoM could be constructed for use by both the Production and Purchasing departments. Currently, the Purchasing department used a separate list of components, which often resulted in difficulties in attributing supply costs to particular product lines.

A BoM, Sanchez explained, was a list of materials, sub-parts, and quantities used in a finished product. Typically, the list would be arranged to represent the sequence of fabrication and assembly, highlighting manufacturing dependencies. For the pilot project, this would not be needed because of the relative simplicity of the production sequence.

Dennis decided to use the company's line of professional pianos for the pilot project, and run the new system in parallel with the existing system. In this way, Remora Piano could refine and cost out the system before committing to a complete implementation. This range had three products: two uprights, the Winston and the Charleston, and one petite grand, the Sterling. These three products were made of 22 different components, excluding glue.

The design for each product was very similar. The Winston and the Charleston had four maple legs supporting a spruce soundboard, a maple outer rim, and the cast iron plate (metal frame). The Sterling petite grand had just three maple legs and a spruce outer rim. The uprights required one type of jack, while the petite grand required another type. All three models used the same ivorite and ebony keys, whippens, hammers, hammer butts, dampers, and all other miscellaneous parts.

Remora Piano's designers decided to use a new line of carefully engineered composite parts rather than the hardwood parts used by their competitors. Each product has differing levels of exterior carved detail and finish.

Remora Piano manufactures the soundboards, pinblocks, rims, and legs as well as the composite whippens, hammers, and dampers. They purchase the high-tensile steel wire piano strings and the bridle wires from Chapin Piano String Mill. The bridle, which is a piece of tape about an eighth of an inch wide with a piece of leather glued to the end and a hole near the end for the point of the bridle wire, and the wool felt hammer coverings are manufactured by Taraway Tannery as are all of the other leather pieces. The keys come from Petaluma Plastics, and the cast iron plate, pedals, jack springs, tuning pins, whippen pins, and capstan screws from Shephard Hardware.

Dennis recorded each of the components as a record in an Access database table, with the number used for each product listed in separate fields. She also recorded the number of each component currently in inventory and the unit cost.

This partial Bill of Materials is supplied for you in the table REMORA in the SOLVEIT_CH5 database. Create a new Access database and import this file now.

Tasks

There are seven tasks in this case:

1. (a) Complete the supplied bill of materials by adding a field to represent inventory holdings (UNITS_IN_STOCK) of the materials, and fabricating the appropriate data.

    (b) Add new part codes, quantities used, and prices for Upright Catcher Leather ($4.95), Upright Butt Leather ($2.25), and Petite Grand Butt Leather ($3.95). Note that the part codes begin with a letter representing the first letter of the supplier's name: R for Remora, C for Chapin Wire & Cable, P for Petaluma Plastics, S for Shephard Hardware, and T for Taraway Tannery. The letter is followed by four numbers to complete the part codes.

    (c) Print out the completed table.

2. Managers in a number of functional areas have heard of Dennis's progress

and have requested information from the computerized BoM. Sales managers want to know the total dollar amount of the materials costs for each piano so they can more easily set appropriate prices. Accounting managers want to know the total dollar value of each component type in each piano. Sanchez wants an estimate of the investment in dollars in inventory holdings of the component types and a total dollar value of inventory holdings. Dennis is certain that these needs can be furnished within a single report.

(a) Create a report to satisfy these needs and (b) print this report.

3. Harney Corporation, a regular and valued customer, has ordered pianos for their new Provo convention center. They require 5 Winston uprights and 3 Sterling petite grands. CEO DeMarco and Lester from Purchasing want a detailed Materials Requirement report for this order, showing the number of each component required for each of the two products ordered, a total components required field, and the amount held in inventory. Create and print the report.

4. Simon Lester has heard rumors that Chapin Piano String Mill is having financial difficulties. DeMarco is worried by these rumors and the implications this may have for the Harney contract. Print out a listing of the components supplied by Chapin Piano String Mill, sorted by PART_CODE, to facilitate the investigation.

5. Engineering and Design wants a list of the components, sorted by value.

(a) Create a query and (b) print the result set.

6.* Suggest any improvements or additions to the Bill of Materials as it currently exists. Could the BoM be extended to encompass other aspects of Production Management or any other associated domains?

Time Estimates (excluding tasks marked with *):
Expert: 1.75 hours
Intermediate: 2.5 hours
Novice: 4 hours

Tutorial for Database Case 3 Using Access 2010

Creating Queries with Multiple Criteria
In the Tutorial for Case 1, we looked at creating queries to view and print certain fields in the FRIENDS table, as well as fields that met simple selection criteria. In

this tutorial, we will look at constructing more complex queries using logical operators.

1. Open the SOLVEIT_CH5 database. Double-click the FRIENDS table in the Navigation Pane to open it. Create a new query following the instructions given in the Tutorial for Case 1. Include the fields Last_Name, Zip, Professional, and Personal in the query.

2. The *Criteria* and *or* cells in the design grid allow for multiple conditions involving the logical operators "AND" and "OR". Conditions entered in the Criteria cell are "AND." Let's say you wanted a listing of all Personal friends with ZIP Codes greater than 35000. In the Criteria cell of the design grid, type *>35000* in the Zip field and enter *True* in the Personal field (see Figure 5-16).

3. Click the *Run* button on the Query Tools: Design tab to run the query. Results should show that there are four records in the FRIENDS table that match the criteria.

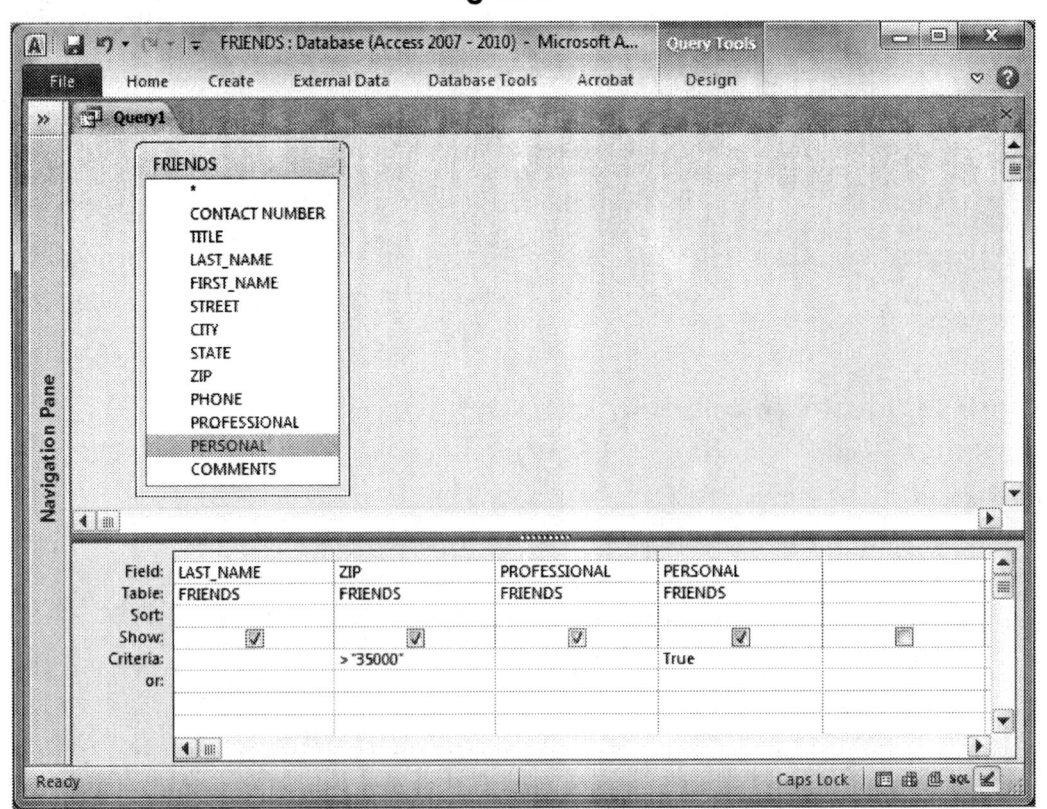

Figure 5-16

Database Management Software Cases   169

4. Click ![icon] to return to the Query Design View window.

5. Try using the OR operator by deleting *True* from the Criteria cell in the Personal field and entering it in the *or* cell on the next line down (see Figure 5-17). In this case, we are searching the table for people whose ZIP codes are greater than 35000 *or* people who are personal friends. Run the query again. This is a less stringent condition, and the resulting dynaset should show that there are seventeen records that match the chosen criteria. A "dynaset" is a sub-table in a database that results from a specific query.

6. Print each dynaset by clicking the File tab, *Print*, and then *Quick Print*. Save the queries as *Tute3Query1* and *Tute3Query2* and close them.

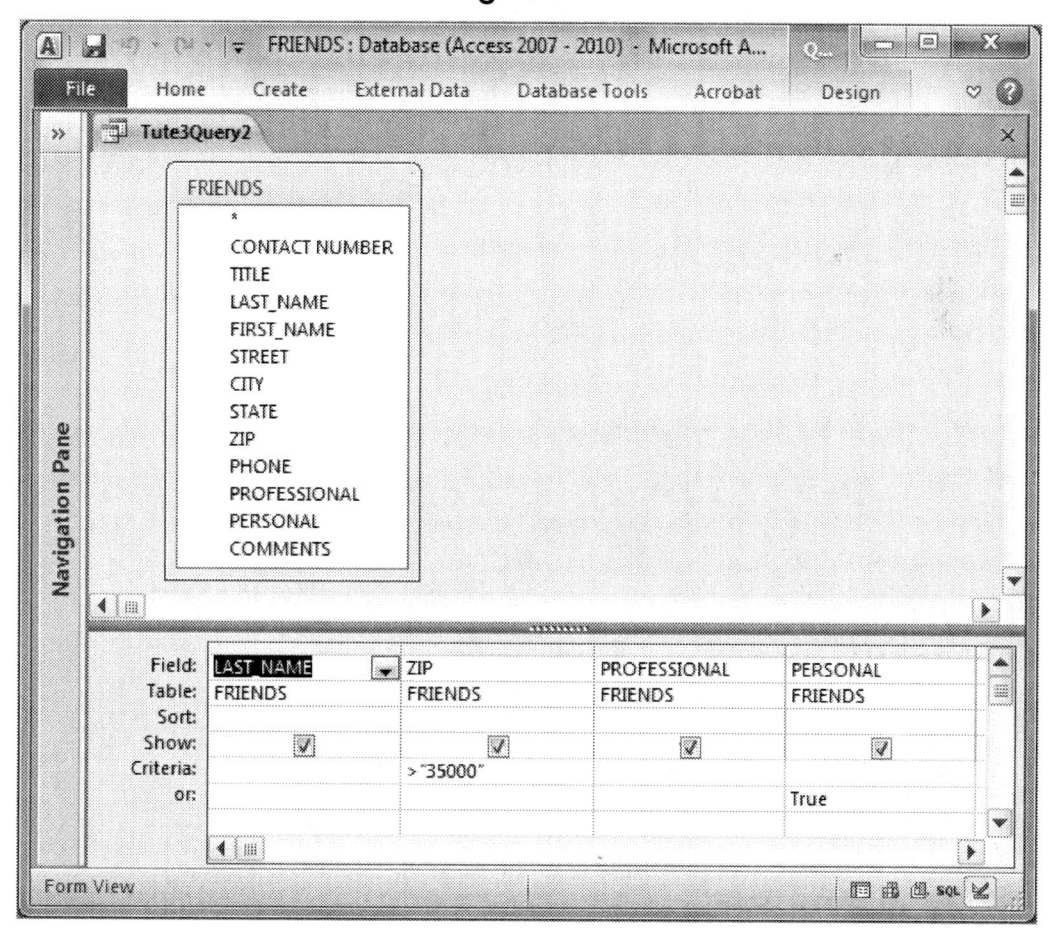

Figure 5-17

Sorting Tables in Access

It is often useful to sort a table by one or more fields. For instance, you may find it helpful to sort the records in your table alphabetically by Last Name, in chronological order, or by some numerical order. There are several ways of sorting data in Access. A quick sort on a single field in either ascending or descending order can be achieved in Datasheet View. You can also sort by multiple fields in either the Query Design View or in a Report.

To Sort on a Single Field

1. In the SolveIt_CH5 database, make sure the FRIENDS table is open in Datasheet View. Let's say you would like to sort the records alphabetically by last name. To do this, move the mouse to the Last_Name field selector so that the ⬇ arrow appears. Click to select the Last Name column (see Figure 5-18).

2. On the Home tab on the Ribbon, in the Sort & Filter group, click the *Sort Ascending* button A↓Z Ascending so Access will sort the records by last name in alphabetical order. Close the table, saving the change to the design when prompted. (Clicking the *Sort Descending* button will sort in reverse order.) ***Warning:*** *This is a dynamic sort and cannot be saved.*

Figure 5-18

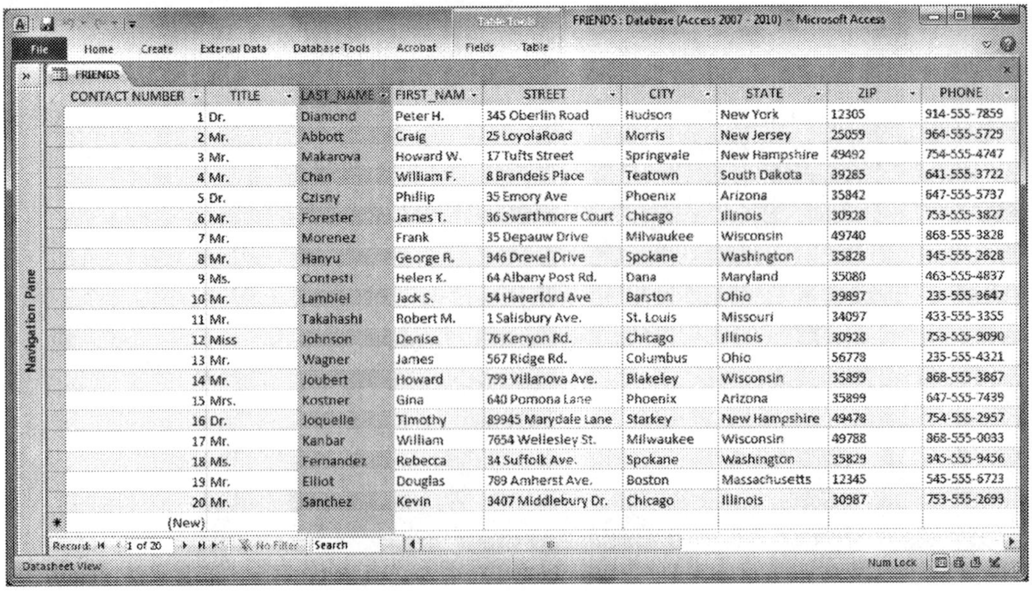

CONTACT NUMBER	TITLE	LAST_NAME	FIRST_NAM	STREET	CITY	STATE	ZIP	PHONE
1	Dr.	Diamond	Peter H.	345 Oberlin Road	Hudson	New York	12305	914-555-7859
2	Mr.	Abbott	Craig	25 LoyolaRoad	Morris	New Jersey	25059	964-555-5729
3	Mr.	Makarova	Howard W.	17 Tufts Street	Springvale	New Hampshire	49492	754-555-4747
4	Mr.	Chan	William F.	8 Brandeis Place	Teatown	South Dakota	39285	641-555-3722
5	Dr.	Czisny	Phillip	35 Emory Ave	Phoenix	Arizona	35842	647-555-5737
6	Mr.	Forester	James T.	36 Swarthmore Court	Chicago	Illinois	30928	753-555-3827
7	Mr.	Morenez	Frank	35 Depauw Drive	Milwaukee	Wisconsin	49740	868-555-3828
8	Mr.	Hanyu	George R.	346 Drexel Drive	Spokane	Washington	35828	345-555-2828
9	Ms.	Contesti	Helen K.	64 Albany Post Rd.	Dana	Maryland	35080	463-555-4837
10	Mr.	Lambiel	Jack S.	54 Haverford Ave	Barston	Ohio	39897	235-555-3647
11	Mr.	Takahashi	Robert M.	1 Salisbury Ave.	St. Louis	Missouri	34097	433-555-3355
12	Miss	Johnson	Denise	76 Kenyon Rd.	Chicago	Illinois	30928	753-555-9090
13	Mr.	Wagner	James	567 Ridge Rd.	Columbus	Ohio	56778	235-555-4321
14	Mr.	Joubert	Howard	799 Villanova Ave.	Blakeley	Wisconsin	35899	868-555-3867
15	Mrs.	Kostner	Gina	640 Pomona Lane	Phoenix	Arizona	35899	647-555-7439
16	Dr.	Joquelle	Timothy	89945 Marydale Lane	Starkey	New Hampshire	49478	754-555-2957
17	Mr.	Kanbar	William	7654 Wellesley St.	Milwaukee	Wisconsin	49788	868-555-0033
18	Ms.	Fernandez	Rebecca	34 Suffolk Ave.	Spokane	Washington	35829	345-555-9456
19	Mr.	Elliot	Douglas	789 Amherst Ave.	Boston	Massachusetts	12345	545-555-6723
20	Mr.	Sanchez	Kevin	3407 Middlebury Dr.	Chicago	Illinois	30987	753-555-2693
(New)								

Sorts within Sorts

You can sort by multiple fields in a query to achieve a sort within a sort. This is analogous to a telephone book, where entries are first alphabetized by last name and then by first name.

1. In the Navigation Pane, double-click *Tute1Query2* to open it in datasheet view. Then click the *View* button on the Home tab to toggle the query to Design View.

2. Let's sort by the Title field, and then, within this, by the Last_Name field in ascending order. Before we do this, first delete *Mr* from the *Criteria* cell in the TITLE field. Then click in the *Sort:* cell in the Title field and select *Ascending*. Repeat this action for the Last Name field. Your screen should now look like the one shown in Figure 5-19.

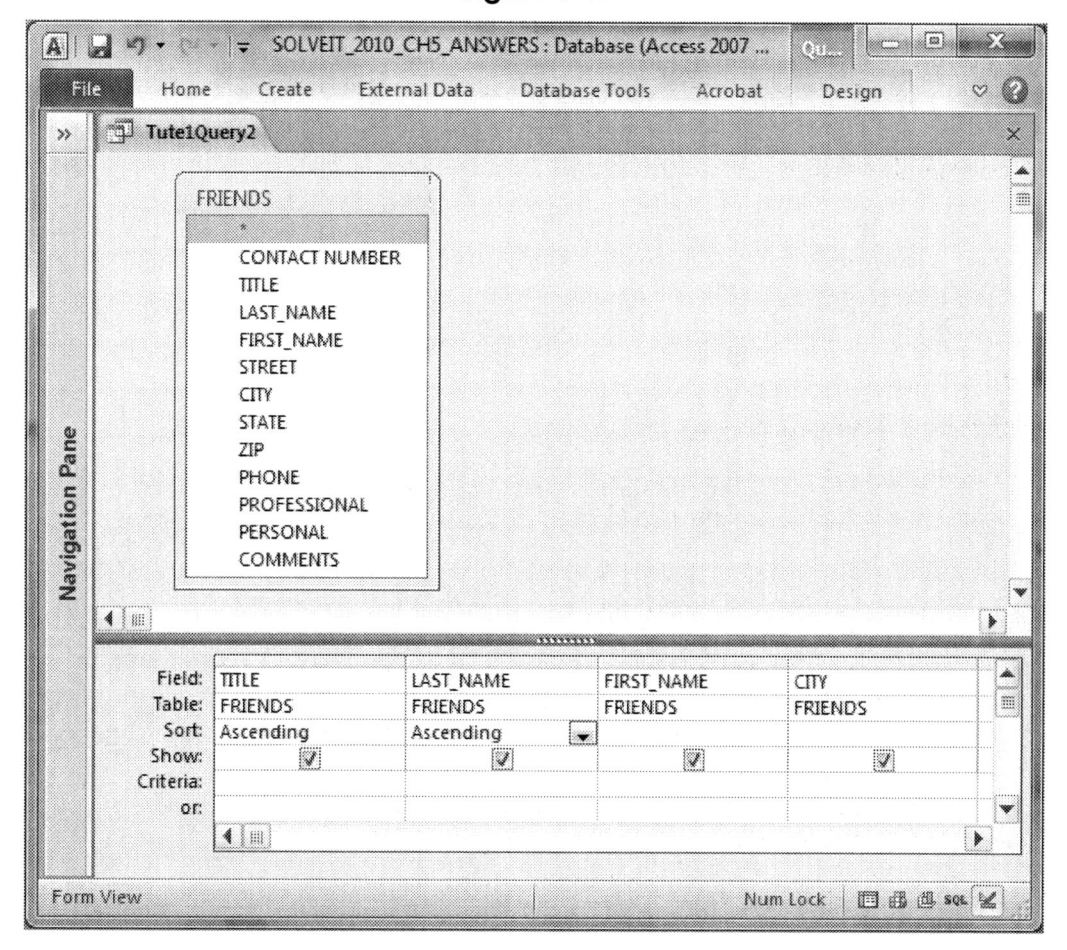

Figure 5-19

3. Click the *Run* button on the Query Tools: Design tab to view the results of your query. The records should be sorted first by Title (i.e. Dr. before Mr., Mr. before Ms. or Prof.), and then within each Title grouping, in ascending Last Name order.

4. Save your query with a new name. Click the File tab and select the *Save Object As* command. Type *Tute3Query3* in the top text box in the *Save As* dialog box and click *OK*. Close the query window when you are done.

Sorting Data in Reports

When you print a report, you usually want to ensure that the records are displayed in a particular order. For example, if you are printing a list of suppliers, you may wish to sort the records alphabetically by company name. When you are setting up the parameters for a new report using the Report Wizard, Access enables you to specify the sort order. If you change your mind after the report has been created, you can use the Group, Sort, & Total tool in Report Design View.

The Group, Sort, & Total tool allows you to sort by multiple fields and expressions, and you can sort on the same field or expression more than once. For example, in a five-character field, you could apply an ascending sort to the first three characters and a descending sort to the last two characters.

Let's repeat the query sort we just performed in Report Design View. (We could, of course, simply change the record source for the report to the query we just created to achieve the same results).

With the SolveIt_CH5 database open, double-click *Friends _Report* in the Navigation Pane to open the report created in the Tutorial for Case 2. Click to open the report in Design View.

5. On the Report Design Tools: Design tab, in the Grouping & Totals group, click the *Group & Sort* button to open the Group, Sort & Total pane.

6. In the first Sort by entry in the Group, Sort, & Total pane, click the list arrow beside *City* and change the field from *City* to *Title*.

7. Below the first entry, click *Add a Sort* to add a second entry to the pane. In the list box, select *Last_Name*. Note that the default sort order is ascending ("with A on top"), which is perfect for our needs. Your screen should now resemble Figure 5-20.

8. On the Home tab on the Ribbon, click the bottom half of the *View button* and then click *Print Preview* to see the effect the sort order has had on the report. Print your report.

Database Management Software Cases 173

9. Save the report as *Tute3Report1* by selecting the *Save Object As* command on the File tab. Close the *Tute3Report1* report.

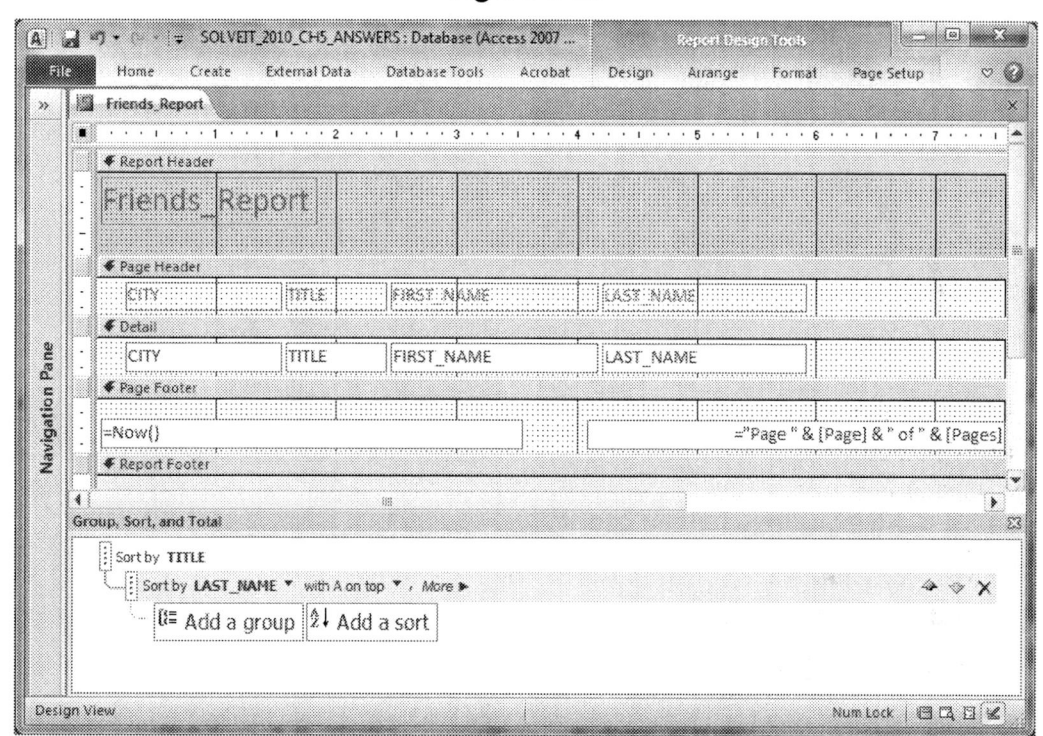

Figure 5-20

Database Case 4
U-Save Pharmacy

Problem:	Summarize and analyze data from a transaction processing system for government reporting requirements
Management Skills:	Organize Control
Access Skills:	Queries Sorting Data Reduction Reporting with Subtotals
Data Table:	U-SAVE

Danielle Duhamel, the owner and pharmacist of U-Save Pharmacy in Centralia, Missouri, was going through her daily mail when she came across a letter she had been expecting from the state government. The letter informed her of new regulations and reporting requirements for certain categories of drugs.

The Missouri state government had begun an initiative to restrict the growing use of addictive and dangerous drugs. One of the first steps involved is identifying the type and amount of these drugs sold by each pharmacy in the state. The state then intends to analyze this data and identify any regional trends.

The new regulations had been discussed at a recent meeting of Duhamel's local chapter of the Pharmacy Guild, the Missouri state professional body for pharmacists. Most pharmacists agree that implementing the new controls is a good idea, but the thought of yet another record-keeping chore is not attractive.

Three years ago, each member of the Pharmacy Guild had installed software to manage the pharmacy prescription process. When a customer wanted a prescription filled, the pharmacist entered his or her personal details (for all new customers), along with the drug and dosage requirements prescribed by the doctor. The system produced three outputs: a label to affix to the medication, a renewable prescription if required, and a detailed receipt for the customer for insurance purposes. For regular customers, the software could check whether new medication would interact adversely with any existing medication.

The letter from the government specified that usage information was required for only six classes of drugs: sedatives, stimulants, hallucinogenics, opiates, ephedrine products, and depressants. At any given time, U-Save Pharmacy stocked approximately 25 drugs in these target groups.

The government required each pharmacy to submit a quarterly summary report indicating the usage for each drug dispensed in the six target classes during this period. Total usage of these six classes was also required. The government would conduct random crosschecks with drug company delivery records to check the accuracy of the reporting. Severe penalties were specified for non-compliance.

The table below shows a sampling of the codes assigned to drug classes used by U-Save Pharmacy's prescription program. Use this to identify the drug codes of interest to the government.

DRUG_CODE	DRUG_CLASS
Z2	Steroids
Z3	Diuretics
Z4	Anti-hypertensives
Z5	Analgesics
Z6	Opiates
Z7	Stimulants
Z8	Hallucinogenics
F1	Anti-diarrhea
F2	Birth Control
F3	Sedatives
F4	Ephedrine Products
F5	Depressants
B3	Anti-inflammatories
B4	Anti-malarial
B5	Antibiotic
B6	Anti-depressives

PharmTek, the firm that provided the first computerized prescription system, had also attended the Pharmacy Guild's meeting. They said it would take many weeks to change the current system to meet the government's requirements. They quoted a very high fee and advised that a three-month delay would be necessary before conversion. They could, however, immediately deliver an add-on program that would convert each quarter's prescriptions into a generic data format, which could be readily used by various Windows-based database packages.

For a low cost alternative solution, PharmTek recommended that each pharmacist purchase a database package and use it with the conversion program to perform the government's usage analysis. The database package could serve other purposes as well. Many of the pharmacies stocked a range of gift lines, vitamins, and fashion accessories. Using a database to automate this side of the business was another attractive idea.

Duhamel felt confident that she could design her own database program to meet state government needs. The job could be performed on the pharmacy's personal computer on weekends when the store was closed. Duhamel estimated that she used only two or three of the drugs on the target list on any given day. She also believed that some of the information required by the government would be useful for her business. For example, it would be beneficial to know how much she sold of each company's drugs.

One problem still bothered Duhamel. Each drug company supplied medication in different tablet sizes. The strength of each tablet also varied in terms of milligram dosage. The government needed its usage statistics to be reported in milligrams (mgs). Fortunately, the pharmacy prescription system recorded both the number of tablets and their strength (in mgs) for each prescription. To satisfy the government's requirements, Duhamel only needed to multiply the number of tablets by strength to get total milligram usage.

Part of the table produced by the conversion program for a quarter's worth of prescriptions issued by U-Save Pharmacy has been created for you in the U-SAVE table in the SOLVEIT_CH5 database. Create a new empty database and import this table now.

Tasks

There are six tasks in this case:

1. Design a query to filter out all of the drugs **not** of interest to the state government. Print the datasheet.

2. Design and print a summary report to present to the state government each quarter. Include only the total drug usage and the sub-total usage for each of the state's targeted Drug Codes. It should be sorted by Drug Code and then

by Drug Name.

3. Duhamel would like to discover which drug companies produce the drugs she sells under each Drug Code. Design and produce a report that presents all the quarter's transactions grouped by Drug Code and Drug Class. Within each Drug Code, sort alphabetically by Supplier. Include all appropriate fields, including Drug Name and Supplier.

4. Duhamel has been frustrated by the slow delivery of supplies by Hospira. The Hospira sales representative is coming to visit next week and Duhamel will raise the subject. Duhamel would like to prepare for the visit by finding out how much of Hospira's products she actually uses. Create and print out a report of all prescriptions dispensed by U-Save Pharmacy that included a drug provided by Hospira. She would like this list in an outline grouped by Drug Class with sub-total usages included for each class.

5.* U-Save has extended their pharmacy system. The new system is compatible with several Windows-based database packages, including Access. The system is menu driven, and the pharmacist just selects the operation that is required. Menu options include "Enter a New Customer" and "Fill Prescription." The system has 4 main data files: customer, drug information, inventory, and transaction records.

The customer enters the store and gives the prescription to the pharmacist or shop assistant. The pharmacist goes to the computer and checks whether the customer is on file. If not, customer details are entered; otherwise, the customer's record is located by the system. Prescription details are then entered. A check automatically occurs to ensure that the new drug does not interact with any medication currently used by the customer.

The pharmacist then fills the prescription, the inventory level for that drug is adjusted downwards, a sticky label prints out, and a record is added to the transaction database. The transaction database is just a log of every prescription issued. A repeat script is printed if required, and a detailed customer receipt is printed for insurance purposes.

Draw a data flow diagram (first-level only) describing U-Save's new system. Include the major processes, data files, data flows, system outputs, and people involved in the system. Identify all the fields in each of the data files.

6.* At the end of each week, a number of management reports are produced. Suggest what you think these reports will be and what fields they are likely to contain.

178 Solve it!

Information on producing data flow diagrams is contained in most information systems texts. Our reference is: *Essentials of Management Information Systems: Managing the Digital Firm*, 13th Edition, K.C. Laudon & J.P. Laudon, 2012, Prentice Hall.

Time Estimates (excluding tasks marked with an *)
Expert: 1 hour
Intermediate: 1.5 hours
Novice: 2.5 hours

Tutorial for Database Case 4 Using Access 2010

How to Create Record Groups in Reports

For many reports, sorting the records isn't enough; you may also want to divide them into groups. A *group* is a collection of records that share a common characteristic, such as the same Product Number or the same ZIP Code. In Access, a group consists of a group header, a series of detail records, and a group footer.

Grouping enables you to separate records of groups visually, as well as display introductory and summary data for each group. For example, the report extract shown below groups sales by date and calculates the total amount of sales for each day.

Data Grouped by Date

Delivery Date:	Invoice No.	Company	Sale Amount
11-Nov			
	10423	Hungry Macs	$1,323.34
	10425	Barnacle Jill	$2,457.40
	10426	Blue Rooster	$161.18
	10428	Hot Chipps	$741.88
Total for 11-Nov			$4,683.80
14-Nov			
	10441	Chicken 'n' Chips	$1,074.20

Total summarises the Group   Sales sorted by Invoice No.

Let's produce a report with groups using the FRIENDS database and the *Friends_Report* created in the Tutorial for Case 2. We want to group the report by state to produce a listing of friends sorted alphabetically (ascending order) by state. For friends in the same state, we want to sort these alphabetically by Last Name. Before we can do this, we must make some modifications to the existing FRIENDS table.

Figure 5-21

CONTACT NUMBER	TITLE	LAST_NAME	FIRST_NAME	STREET	CITY	STATE	ZIP	PHONE	PROFESSIONAL
9	Ms.	Contesti	Helen K.	64 Albany Post Rd.	Dana	Maryland	22306	463-555-4337	
10	Mr.	Lambiel	Jack S.	54 Haverford Ave	Barston	Ohio	39897	235-555-3647	
11	Mr.	Takahashi	Robert M.	1 Salisbury Ave.	St. Louis	Missouri	34097	433-555-3355	
12	Miss	Johnson	Denise	76 Kenyon Rd.	Chicago	Illinois	30928	753-555-9090	
13	Mr.	Wagner	James	567 Ridge Rd.	Columbus	Ohio	56775	235-555-4321	
14	Mr.	Joubert	Howard	799 Villanova Ave.	Blakeley	Wisconsin	35899	868-555-3367	
15	Mrs.	Kostner	Gina	640 Pomona Lane	Phoenix	Arizona	85257	647-555-7439	
16	Dr.	Joquelle	Timothy	39945 Marydale Lane	Starkey	New Hampshire	09478	754-555-2957	
17	Mr.	Kanbar	William	7654 Wellesley St.	Milwaukee	Wisconsin	49788	868-555-0033	
18	Ms.	Marchel	Rebecca	34 Suffolk Ave.	Spokane	Washington	95829	345-555-9456	
19	Mr.	Elliot	Douglas	789 Amherst Ave.	Boston	Massachusetts	11345	545-555-6723	
20	Mr.	Sanchez	Kevin	3407 Middlebury Dr.	Chicago	Illinois	30937	753-555-2693	
21	Mr.	Buttle	Jeffrey	589 North St.	Bismarck	South Dakota	39299	841-555-1212	
22	Mr.	Rippon	Adam	6712 Twin Brook Lane	Crofton	Maryland	22866	410-555-7711	
23	Mr.	Fernandez	Javier	8912 Sunny Hill Ct.	St. Louis	Missouri	34098	433-555-3366	
24	Ms.	Phaneuf	Cynthia	67 Granite Reef Rd.	Ferndale	New York	12399	914-555-6677	
25	Mr.	Keegan	Messing	47 Turner Lane	Haverhill	Massachusetts	11499	545-555-9123	

1. Open the SOLVEIT_CH5 database. Double-click the FRIENDS table in the Navigation Pane. Add the five new records shown in Figure 5-21 to the table. To speed up this procedure, just enter the new records with the TITLE, LAST NAME, FIRST NAME, STREET, CITY, and STATE fields. Close the table.

2. Double-click *Friends_Report* in the Navigation Pane to open the report. Click the bottom half of the *View button* on the Ribbon and select *Design View* to work with the report in Design View.

3. On the Report Design Tools: Design tab on the Ribbon, click *Group & Sort* to open the Group, Sort, & Total pane.

4. Click the list arrow beside *City* in the first entry and change the primary sorting criterion from *City* to *Last_Name*.

5. Click *Add a Group* and select the *State field*.

6. Make sure the Group entry in the pane is selected (it will be enclosed in a box) and on the right of the pane click the *Move up* arrow once to move the *Group on State* entry up one level (Figure 5-22).

7. Close the Group, Sort, and Total pane by clicking the X in the top right-hand

Figure 5-22

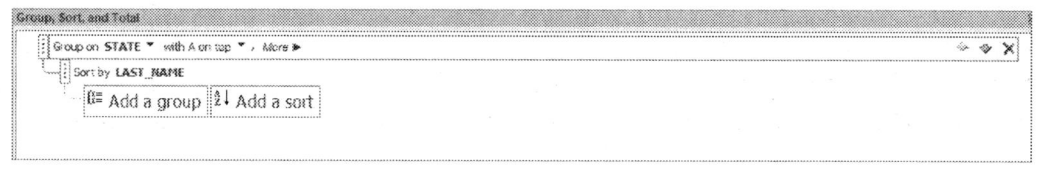

Group, Sort, and Total
Group on STATE ▼ with A on top ▼ , More ▶
Sort by LAST_NAME
Add a group   Add a sort

corner. In Report Design View, you should notice that a blank *State Header* area has been added to the layout.

8. On the Report Design Tools: Design tab, in the Tools group, click *Add Existing Fields* to open the Field List pane. Select the STATE field in the field list. Drag the STATE field to the State Header area and position it against the left margin. Two boxes—a label box and a text box—are inserted. Click the label to select it and press [Delete] on the keyboard. Drag the State text box to align its left edge with the left edges of the City fields above and below the State Header section. You can also select all three text boxes and use the *Align* command (Report Design Tools: Arrange tab/Sizing & Ordering group) to align them along their left edges.

9. Double-click the State text box to open its property sheet. Click the *Format* tab, if necessary. Scroll down the list of properties and change the *Font Size* property to *14* and the *Font Weight* property to *Bold*. Close the property sheet and resize the text box to suit the changes. Your screen should look similar to Figure 5-23.

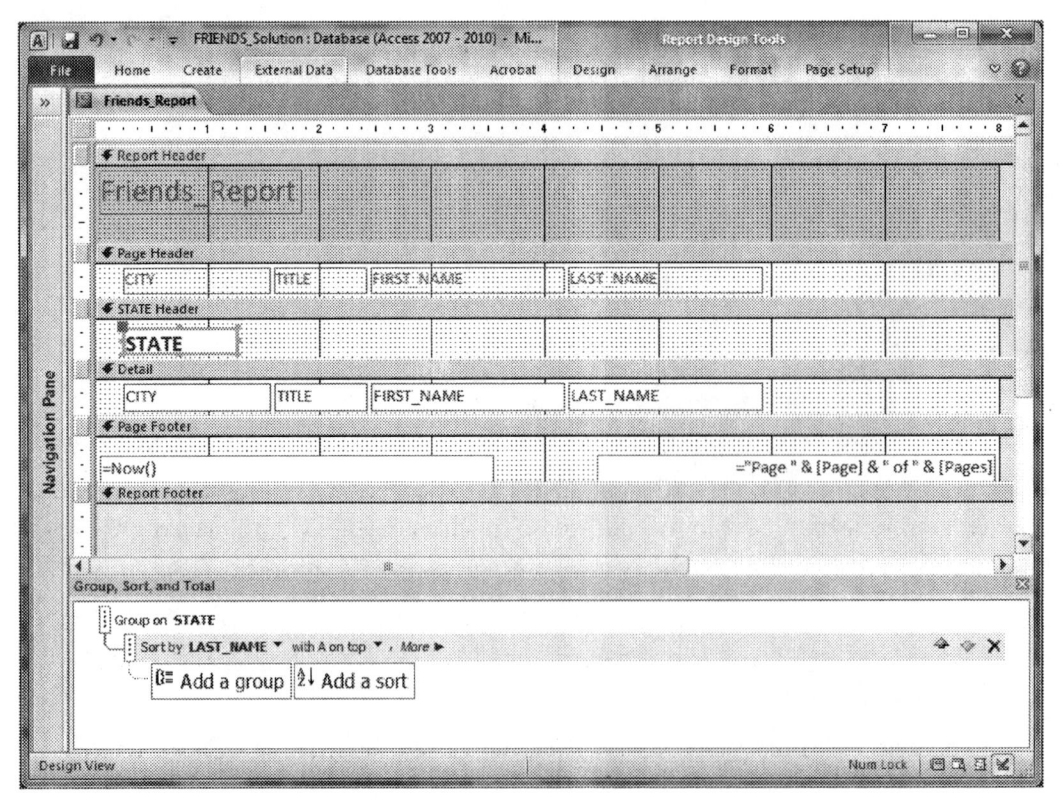

Figure 5-23

10. On the Ribbon, click the bottom half of the *View button* and select *Layout View* to see the effect the changes have had on the report. Increase the size of the State text box if necessary to accommodate the lengths of the state names. When you have completed the change, return to Print Preview. If your report appears in Landscape orientation, Click *Page Setup* on the Print Preview tab (in the Page Layout group) to open the Page Setup dialog box. On the Page tab, change the orientation to *Portrait*. (You can also click the *Portrait* button on the Print Preview tab.) Print the report.

Your report should display the FRIENDS records grouped alphabetically by state, and within each group, ordered alphabetically by last name.

11. Save the report as *Tute4Report1* by selecting the *Save Object As* command on the File tab. Click the *Close Print Preview* button on the Print Preview tab to return to Report Design View.

Calculating Group Summary Statistics

Under certain circumstances, you will want to ask questions about groups of data, such as "How many orders did we receive this month?" or "What's the average price of all the products in our Toothpaste category?" You can perform calculations on groups of records in reports or queries. The following table shows some of the types of *functions* (calculations) you can use with Access (refer also to the Access Tutorial for Case 2)

Use This Type of Calculation	To Find:
Sum	The total of values in a fiewwld
Avg	The average of values in a field
Min	The lowest value in a field
Max	The highest value in a field
Count	The number of values in a field (not including null values)

Let's use the *Count* function to count the number of friends we have in each state and display that number at the end of each group in our report.

1. In Report Design View, on the Report Desigwwn Tools: Design tab on the Ribbon in the Group & Sort group, click *Group & Sort* to reopen the Group, Sort, and Total pane.

2. Select the first Entry, *Group on STATE*, and click the *More* button to display

182 Solve it!

additional settings.

3. Click the list arrow beside *without a footer section* and change this setting to *with a footer section*. A blank *State Footer* section is added to the report design.

4. Click *Add Existing Fields* on the Ribbon, in the Tools group, to open the Field List pane. Drag the Last_Name field from the field list into the State Footer section. Delete the Last_Name label and drag the Last_Name text box to the right so that its left edge is at the 5" mark on the ruler. Double-click the Last_Name text box in the State Footer to open its property sheet. On the Data tab, edit the *Control Source* property to be:

   =COUNT([LAST_NAME])

   Be careful with the syntax here, as well as with the entering of parentheses and square brackets. When you use a function, you must enclose the expression on which it is being performed in parentheses. All field names must be enclosed in square brackets if they include spaces or special characters, so it is a good practice, as learned previously (Figure 5-24). Close the property sheet.

5. Click *View/Print Preview* to see the effect of this change on your report. Results should resemble Figure 5-25. Print your report.

6. Save the report as *Tute4Report2* by selecting the *Save Object As* command on the File tab.

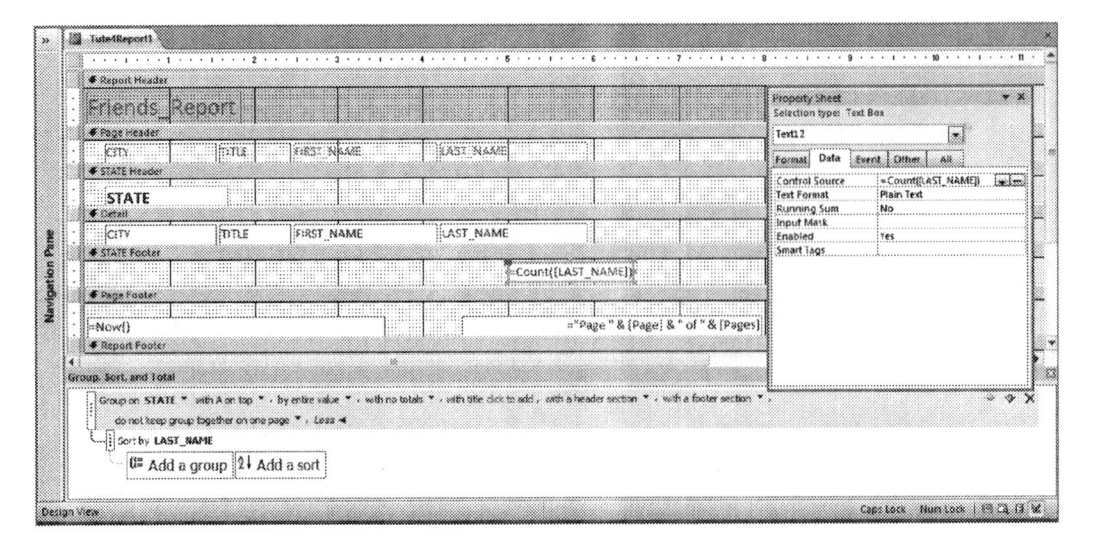

Figure 5-24

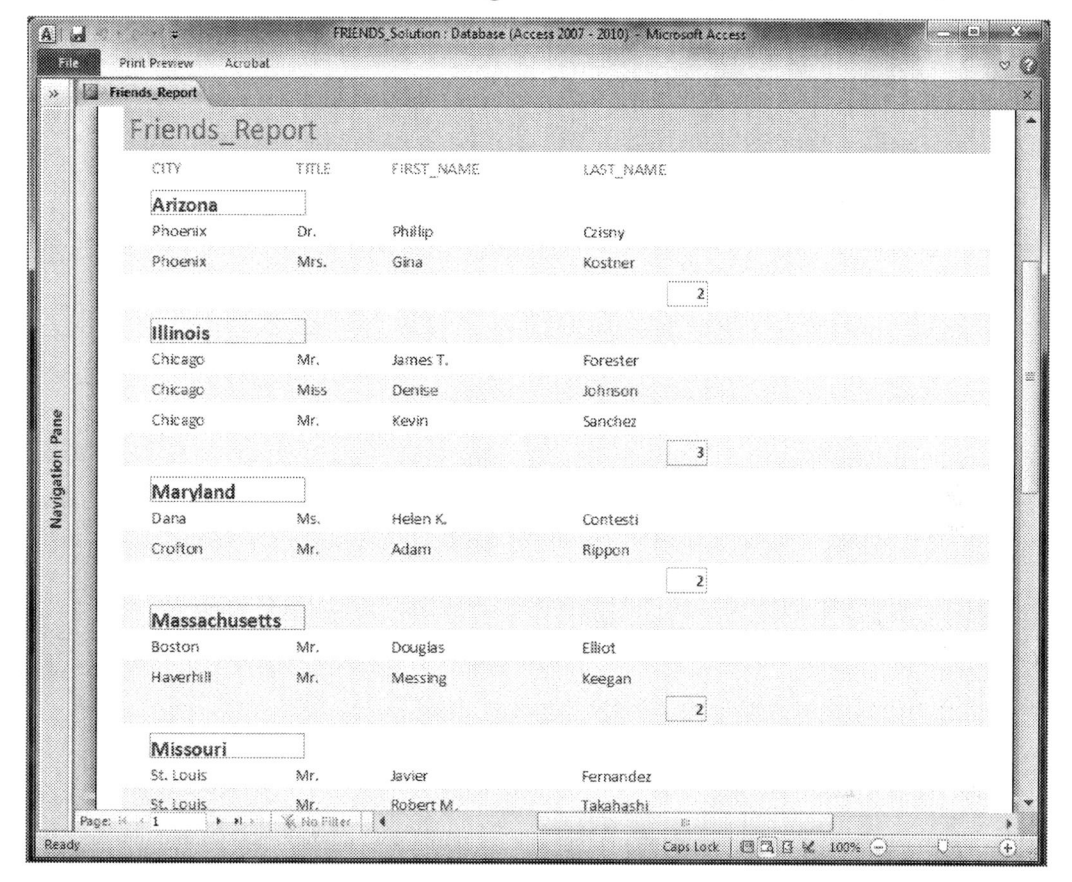

Figure 5-25

Deleting Records in Access

To delete a record in an Access table, highlight the record row intended for deletion, and then either press the [Delete] key or click the *Delete* button on the Home tab on the Ribbon, in the Records group. Access will ask you to confirm your action. Click the *OK* button to delete the record.

Database Case 5
Almeria University

Problem:	Develop an Admissions database
Education skills:	Coordinate
	Decide
Access Skills:	Queries
	Finding Records
	Sorting and Grouping
	Reporting
Data Table:	ALMERIA

The prestigious Graduate School of Engineering (GSE) at Almeria University began operations in the mid-1980s. Since that time, it has grown to become one of the most competitive and well respected schools of engineering in the United States. Almeria has a particularly strong faculty in the area of Structural Engineering.

Rebecca Faramond has been Dean of Admissions at the GSE for more than ten years, and she feels that it is time for a change in the way the applications are handled. She has promised herself and her boss, Alan Charbonneau, president of Almeria, that she will build a new admissions system. She could use your help.

The Office of Admissions gathers applications and supporting documentation from various sources. Each student submits a completed application form and an essay. Faculty members who have worked with the students at their undergraduate institution submit references. The undergraduate university also submits transcript verification forms and the College Board submits Graduate Record Exam (GRE) scores. Miscellaneous information regarding student ethnicity, age, and sex is also collected to meet various legal requirements and reporting standards.

The Alumni group has made it very clear that they want Admissions to treat the sons and daughters (but not more distant relatives) of alumni (legacy applicants) with special care.

All of this information is collected by the Admissions Office staff and summarized on an Admissions Sheet. The Admissions Sheet is the first piece of paper in the bulging folders kept on each student. The essays and outside faculty references are graded on a 1 to 5 scale (with 5 being the highest score) by faculty committees.

This procedure was developed in the mid-1990s when the school had 600 or so applicants for 200 openings. Today the school receives 5,500 applicants for approximately 500 openings. Although the Admissions Office (AO) staff has doubled in size to 8 full-time personnel, the workload is still heavy, and the process is breaking down as older, experienced staff retire and the number of applications increases.

The procedure for processing the Admissions Sheet is one source of the problems. Because the data arrive from different sources at different times, the AO clerks must go back to each student folder numerous times to enter and update the information.

Students, parents, faculty, institutions, and alumni frequently call to see if certain information has been received. Sometimes clerks pull the sheet to answer queries and then the sheet is misplaced. New sheets must be coded up in this case.

A number of data integrity problems have emerged. For instance, more and more students are claiming that their GRE scores are not correctly recorded. Changes from the University Board are submitted with growing frequency, but AO staff is often so pressed for time that these record changes are sometimes not made. Other data quality problems involve the undergraduate grade point average, address errors, and majors. The current system must be able to keep track of these changes.

The existing system does not appear to support the group decision-making process, which is at the heart of admissions. A small group of ten faculty members and three Admissions Officers make all the decisions on the Admissions Committee. Each member of the Admissions Committee who takes a look at the data wants it organized differently and feels frustrated when they are told that this is impossible. As a result, committee members spend too much time arguing over the decision criteria and weightings and too little time searching for appropriate candidates. For instance, some faculty are interested only in GPA and GRE scores, and they want to see the applicant pool sorted first by GPA and then by GRE. Other faculty members are more interested in GPA and references and do not even want to see the GRE scores.

Administrators want to ensure that within accepted academic criteria, alumni's children get special hearings. There is little opportunity to find those candidates who score high on all the criteria. All in all, the manual resorting of lists and list compilation is a tedious process characterized by long delays and mistakes.

All of these problems have produced a political dimension: no one is happy with the existing system and everyone blames the Admissions Office. As Dean of

Admissions, Faramond is now under attack from many sides. The AO staff is also unsatisfied, even a bit surly at times, because of the long hours they must spend each spring compiling lists, updating files, and meeting last minute deadlines.

Rather than rely on the Administrative Computing Center (which is already extended beyond capacity), Faramond has decided to build a PC-based admissions database using Access.

A sample of the admissions data table has been created for you in the ALMERIA table in the SOLVEIT_CH5 database. Create a new Access database and import the ALMERIA table now.

Tasks

There are five tasks in this case:

1. There are two main lists that the faculty requires:

    (a) A listing of all the applicants for professors on the Admissions Committee who want to see the applicants listed by decreasing GPA scores; students with the same GPA should be sorted by decreasing GRE scores.

    (b) A second listing showing the applicants sorted by decreasing GPA; students with the same GPA should be sorted by decreasing reference scores. Print out the results of both listings.

2. The AO clerks absolutely insist on having rapid access to students' complete records on the basis of Last Name only. That is, they want to type the last name of the student into a PC and have the complete record appear on the screen. Because so many people call in checking on student applicant files, this capability would save an enormous amount of time. Using the ALMERIA table, identify the Access sequence of commands that would enable the AO staff to do this.

3. Faramond wants a report or listing of just the applicants who are children of alumni. She will use this list as a crib sheet in committee deliberations. Whenever a candidate is settled on, she will check her list of legacy applicants to see if that person is on the list. If not, she will suggest an equally well-qualified alumni applicant. Thus, legacy applicants should be sorted by decreasing GPA. Students with the same GPA should be sorted by decreasing GRE scores.

4. A small group of professors is concerned that the Engineering school is exclusively admitting Math and Engineering majors. They would like to

ensure that students from Liberal Arts, Business, and Social Science backgrounds are considered as well. These non-traditional students tend to have better GPA scores than GRE scores (because of an alleged quantitative bias in the GRE test). They also tend to have better recommendations.

These faculty members would like a report that plays to the strengths of the non-traditional majors. Create a report that lists applicants by college major, showing name, GPA, and reference scores. Students with the same major should be sorted by GPA.

5. There is an ongoing dispute among Admissions Committee members about the comparative strengths of the various majors. Calculate the average scores by major on all quantitative variables and display the number of applicants from each major. Then compare the groups in a one-paragraph statement.

6.* There are number of ways this database system could be improved to better meet Almeria's needs. List the ways the system could be improved. Pick one of these improvements and implement it in the database.

Time Estimates (excluding tasks marked with *):

Expert: 1/2 hour
Intermediate: 1 hour
Novice: 1.5 hours

Tutorial for Database Case 5 Using Access 2010

Indexing in Access

If you often search a table or frequently need to sort records by a certain field, you can speed up these operations by assigning indexes to your fields. Access uses indexes in a table in the same way as you would use an index in a book: to find data, it looks up the location of the data in the index.

In Access, you create an index on a single field by setting the Index property. The table below lists the possible settings for Indexed properties.

Index Property Setting	Definition
No	Do not create an index for this field (the default)
Yes (duplicates OK)	Create an index for this field
Yes (no duplicates)	Create a unique index for this field

If you create a unique index, Access will not allow a value that already exists in that field to be entered in the same field for another record. Primary key fields (see the Chapter 4 Tutorial) are automatically indexed by Access to help speed up the execution of queries and other operations. Up to 32 indexes can be assigned to a single table or query, and each index can contain up to 10 fields. It is inadvisable to index a Memo field because the index would be extremely large, and fields with the OLE Object data type cannot be indexed.

You want an index only if it speeds up the execution of queries, searching, or sorting. A Last Name field is a good candidate for an index since the values stored in it vary greatly and it is often used to find specific records.

1. Open the SOLVEIT_CH5 database. Double-click the FRIENDS table in the Navigation Pane. Click the bottom half of the *View button* on the Home tab on the Ribbon and switch to Design View.

2. In the Field Name column, select the Last_Name field. In the Field Properties pane, click in the *Indexed* property settings box. Click the list arrow and select *Yes (Duplicates OK)* to set the index for the Last_Name field. Click the *Save* button on the Quick Access toolbar. Your Design View window should look like Figure 5-26.

3. To view and/or edit existing indexes, open the Indexes window by clicking the Indexes button on the Table Tools: Design tab in the Show/Hide group (see Figure 5-27).

4. Change indexes or index properties as needed. To delete an index, select the intended row in the *Indexes window* and press the [Delete] key. This removes only the index, not the field itself.

5. Close the Indexes window by clicking in the top right-hand corner.

Creating Multiple Field Indexes

If you often search or sort by two or more specific fields at the same time, you may need to create a multiple field index. For instance, if you often set criteria in the same query for Last_Name and First_Name fields, it makes sense to index both fields. When you sort a table by a multiple field index, Access sorts first by the first field listed in the Indexes window. If there are records with duplicate values in this field, Access then sorts by the second field listed.

Multiple field indexes are created in the Indexes Window by including a row for each field in the index, but including the Index Name in the first row only (see Figure 5-28). Access treats all rows as part of the same index until it reaches a

Database Management Software Cases   189

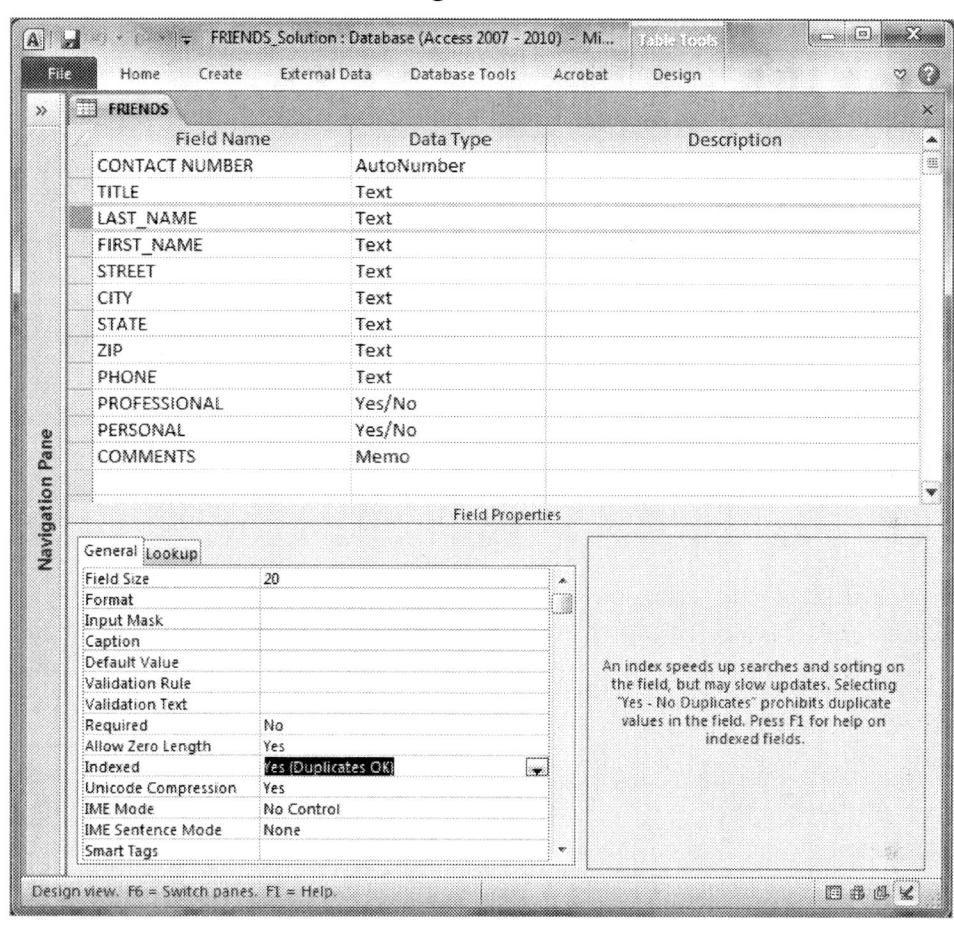

Figure 5-26

[Screenshot of Microsoft Access FRIENDS table in Design view showing the following fields:]

Field Name	Data Type
CONTACT NUMBER	AutoNumber
TITLE	Text
LAST_NAME	Text
FIRST_NAME	Text
STREET	Text
CITY	Text
STATE	Text
ZIP	Text
PHONE	Text
PROFESSIONAL	Yes/No
PERSONAL	Yes/No
COMMENTS	Memo

Field Properties (General tab):
- Field Size: 20
- Required: No
- Allow Zero Length: Yes
- Indexed: Yes (Duplicates OK)
- Unicode Compression: Yes
- IME Mode: No Control
- IME Sentence Mode: None

An index speeds up searches and sorting on the field, but may slow updates. Selecting "Yes - No Duplicates" prohibits duplicate values in the field. Press F1 for help on indexed fields.

Figure 5-27

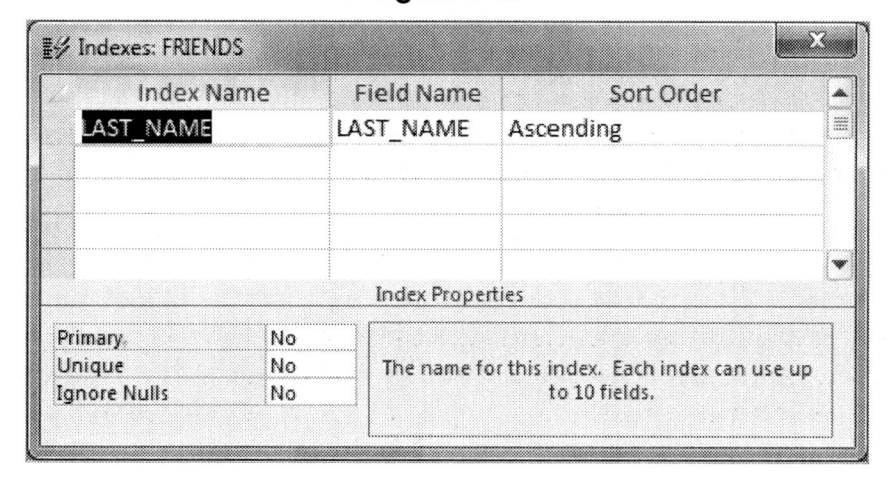

[Screenshot of Indexes: FRIENDS dialog]

Index Name	Field Name	Sort Order
LAST_NAME	LAST_NAME	Ascending

Index Properties:
- Primary: No
- Unique: No
- Ignore Nulls: No

The name for this index. Each index can use up to 10 fields.

Figure 5-28

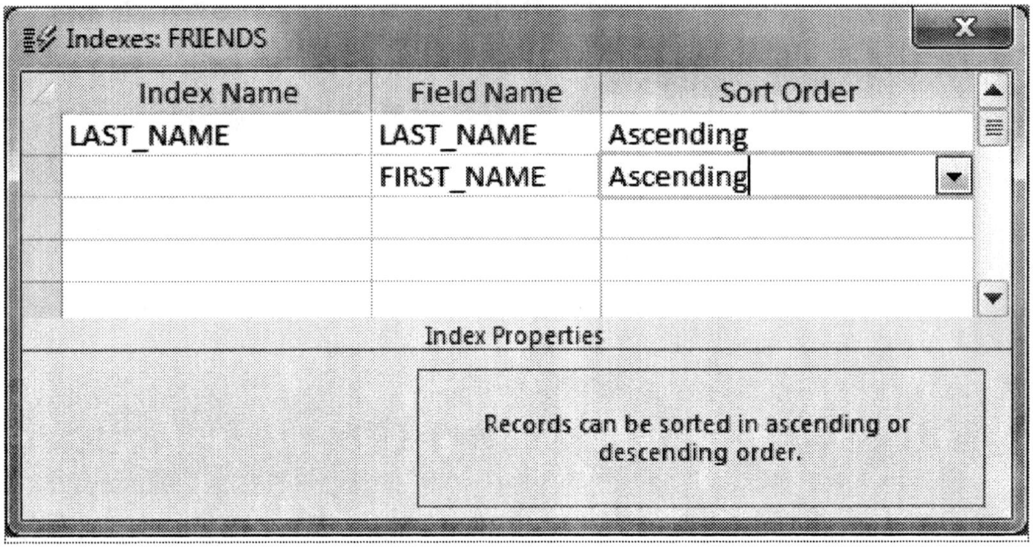

Index Name	Field Name	Sort Order
LAST_NAME	LAST_NAME	Ascending
	FIRST_NAME	Ascending

Index Properties

Records can be sorted in ascending or descending order.

different Index Name. To insert a new row between existing indexes, select the row *below* the location of the row to be inserted and then press the *Insert* key.

To create a multiple field index in the FRIENDS table:

1. Reopen the Indexes window. Click in the *Field Name* cell directly below the one containing the Last_Name field. Click the list arrow and select First_Name on the list. Ascending is automatically selected as the sort order.

2. Close the Indexes window. Save the changes. Close the FRIENDS table.

The Find Command

When you want to find a specific record or certain values within fields, you can use the *Find* command to go directly to a record. *Find* can be used with most Access objects. To use Find, click the *Find* button on the Home tab to open the Find and Replace dialog box (see Figure 5-29). The Find and Replace dialog box enables you to search and replace text within a field.

Type the text you want to locate into the *Find What* list box. For added flexibility, *Find* enables you to enter word stems and wildcard symbols. A question mark (?) stands for any single character in the same position as the question mark. The asterisk (*) stands for any number of characters in the same position as the asterisk. The pound sign or number sign (#) stands for a single numeric digit in the same position as the sign.

Choose between searching the current field or the current document; the whole field, any part of the field, or just the start of the field; and whether to search up, down, or the entire file (All). Practice using *Find* with your FRIENDS table.

Figure 5-29

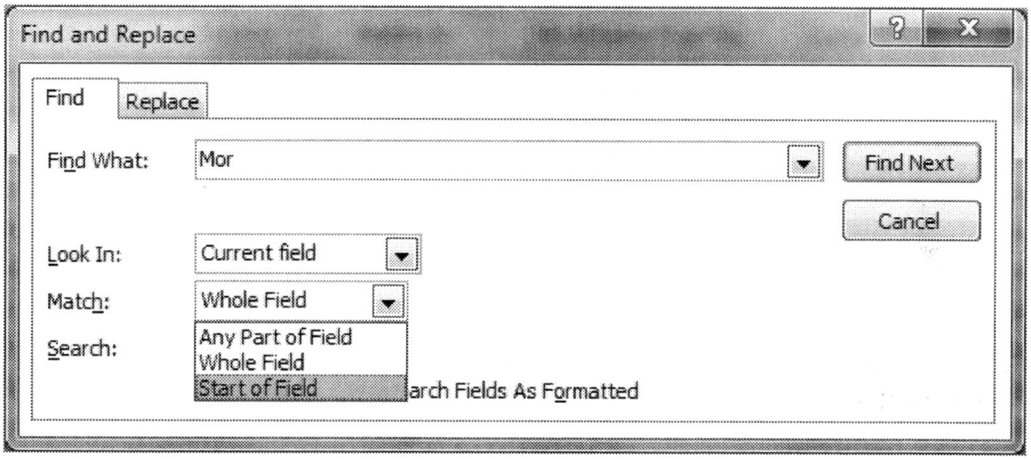

Database Case 6
SoundSpeed Audio I

Problem:	Develop a mailing list database
Management skills:	Organize Control
Access skills:	Database Design Queries Reports Linking Tables
Data Tables:	SOUNDSPEED_A SOUNDSPEED_B MUSIC CODES

SoundSpeed Audio is a medium-sized company based in Ann Arbor, Michigan. The business was established in the early 2000s by Valentina and Alessandra D'Argenio and grew out of a hobby the two sisters shared in music and electronic circuitry. The company has two distinct business divisions. The SoundSpeed Audio Lab side of the business designs, manufactures, and retails a range of audio equipment at the high end of the market. This business includes custom-built sound systems, the famous SoundSpeed Amp valve amplifier, which is eagerly sought by audiophiles around the world, and high performance ribbon speakers. This side of the business, managed by Valentina D'Argenio, is high margin and very successful.

Audio Lab's main customers are audio retailers, as well as music production houses, such as EMI, Warner Music, and Polygram Records. Every six months, SoundSpeed Audio Labs distributes a product catalog to its 3,500 customers.

Alessandra D'Argenio manages SoundSpeed Arcanum, the other division in the company. SoundSpeed Arcanum is a lucrative mail-order business that locates and purchases rare and hard-to-find sound recordings through contact agents around the world. Many of these items are sourced from the estates of deceased musical performers. Musical genres include classical, opera, jazz, rock, country and western, folk, soul, reggae, and ethnic (Asian and African). The business currently carries approximately 15,000 titles in this area, which are held in audio CD, vinyl record, tape, or video format, and they are sold to audio retailers and music production houses throughout the world. SoundSpeed Arcanum currently has approximately 12,000 customers on its mailing list and distributes a catalog of new and current offerings on a biannual basis.

The existing SoundSpeed Arcanum mailing list presents a problem for Alessandra D'Argenio. While the marketing side of Audio Lab has been handled by a PC-based database package for some years, Alessandra has been unsure of how to go about integrating the SoundSpeed Arcanum mailing list into this system, although she knows this could make good business sense. Alessandra suspects that at least 30% of the customers on her mailing list are also customers who regularly purchase from Audio Lab.

The SoundSpeed Arcanum mailing list has been steadily growing since the mid-2000s when this side of the business was formed. The mailing list was originally kept in an Excel spreadsheet that recorded customer mailing information and music interest details. This method soon became unwieldy as the list grew. In the late 2000s, SoundSpeed Arcanum outsourced the data management of its list to Next Step Computer Services. Next Step provides data entry and maintenance services, and produces mailing label printouts for SoundSpeed Arcanum whenever a catalog mailing is required.

Alessandra D'Argenio has several problems with outsourcing her mailing list. She recently received an invoice from Next Step requesting its usual quarterly payment of $3,500 for maintenance of her mailing list. Alessandra has been concerned about the escalating costs of using Next Step for some time, and she no longer believes their services are worthwhile. She also believes that outsourcing does not give her control over her own data.

The current mailing list is not stored in a database. In the 2000s, Next Step created the original list as a long sequential file that is organized alphabetically by customer last name. Alessandra is not happy with this structure, which she feels is inflexible and does not provide information vital to the management of her business. For example, she cannot easily obtain information about the music interests of her customers for targeted mailings. A simple query like *Print a list of all Australian customers with an interest in Opera* requires a special programming task by Next Step. This entails a lengthy delay before SoundSpeed Arcanum receives the information and incurs an additional charge for the company. More complex queries are simply impossible.

The structure of the current mailing list also complicates updating existing data or checking whether a customer is already on the list. Alessandra knows that a large portion of her mailing list is probably out of date. She has noticed that the number of return-to-sender envelopes SoundSpeed Arcanum receives has rapidly increased as customers relocate or contact names change. The present system makes it difficult to incorporate these changes. Meanwhile, SoundSpeed Arcanum is incurring a great deal of unnecessary mailing-associated expenses. Alessandra has also noticed that some of these returns have been sent to the same customer several times. This means that there is a level of data duplication in the mailing list. From current indications, she suspects the duplication may be as high as 15 percent.

Another inherent problem with the current system is that, if there are 45 customers at a large music company like Warner Music, the name and address of the company is repeated 45 times! If the name of the company were to change (as is common in the music business), the new name would have to be re-entered 45 times!

Alessandra is frustrated by the deficiencies of her current mailing list. Although SoundSpeed Arcanum is profitable, she suspects it could be more so if she had the right information when she wanted it and was able to do targeted mailings with ease. She has decided that the only way to get what she wants is to build a new mailing list system from the ground up. After consulting with her sister, Alessandra has purchased a computer and the same relational database package used by SoundSpeed Audio Lab. Once the new mailing system is working satisfactorily, she plans to dispense with Next Step's services. At a later stage, she will consider integrating her system with that of Audio Lab.

The existing mailing system has the right information, but it is not stored efficiently, nor is it easy to query. The existing system has the customer's name, primary music interest (MusIntA), secondary music interest (MusIntB), organization name, address, city, state, country, and ZIP code. The music interests of customers are coded using an internally developed schema.

To make storage and updating of the mailing list more efficient, Alessandra wants the data stored in two tables: one containing the names of the customers, and the other containing the name and addressing details of the company for which they work. Whenever a mailing list is required, the two tables could be joined and the results printed. Alessandra needs your assistance in developing this project.

The Access data tables in your SOLVEIT_CH5 database, SOUNDSPEED_A, and SOUNDSPEED_B, provide the overall design and sample data for the new mailing system. These tables form the basis of this case.

Tasks

There are six tasks in this case:

1. Link the two tables, SOUNDSPEED_A and SOUNDSPEED_B, on the Org field. It may be helpful to print out the structure of these tables first and then print the results of this join.

2. Create a report for marketing purposes that lists all customers separated into alphabetical organizational groups. The fields describing the music interests and addresses are not needed. Each group should contain one organization with the records sorted alphabetically by last name within these groups.

3. Design this report as a professional document. Include a title, group headings, a group footer with a calculated control to count the number of contacts in each organization, and any other useful features you think would be appropriate. Print the report.

4. Design a custom label with four lines of information that can be used as a mailing label.

5. SoundSpeed Arcanum has recently obtained some new Musical Theater and Movie Soundtrack sound recordings. Print a report of all USA customers with one of these two genres (i.e. 49 or 70) as either their primary or secondary music interest. Be careful with the Boolean logic in this problem.

6.* The current system uses codes (e.g. 39, 47) for data in the music interest fields. The user of the system and recipients of its reports must know what these codes mean. Devise a way to include the meaning for these codes into the database. You can create a new table for this and make up meanings for each of the music interest codes (or you can use the MUSIC_CODES (Case 6) table to make this easier.

Make sure that the method you devise does not include data redundancy. It would be poor database design to have the meanings for these codes repeated (redundantly) throughout the database. With your new table structure, produce a report of customers, their organizations, and their music interests that does not include codes.

Time Estimates (excluding tasks marked with *):

Expert: 45 minutes
Intermediate: 1.5 hours
Novice: 3 hours

Tutorial for Database Case 6 Using Access 2010

In this case, you will learn two important new skills: joining tables (creating relationships), and creating labels in reports.

Joining Tables

In many earlier database applications, joining tables is a procedure that requires you to generate programming code. Access allows you to do this simply on the Relationships tab, and then run the results of the join in a query (or a report). Access automatically generates the SQL (Structured Query Language) programming code for the procedure so that you can see the effect of your actions.

In order to join two tables, there must be a related field in both tables. While the field names need not be the same for the join to work, the two fields must contain matching data in the records. For this procedure, we will be using the FRIENDS database and a second practice table BUSDRESS. The latter contains the last names and business addresses of professional contacts in the FRIENDS database.

1. Open the SOLVEIT_CH5 database.

2. In the Navigation Pane, double-click the FRIENDS table to open it in Datasheet View. Click the down arrow button on the LAST_NAME field and select *Sort A to Z* to sort the list primarily by last name in ascending order. Click the down arrow button on the Professional field and select *Sort Selected to Cleared* to secondarily sort the professional contacts from the personal contacts and position them first in the table. Open the BUSDRESS table so that you can compare the two tables. Sort the last name field in ascending order. Note that both last name fields for the eleven professional contacts contain identical data (Figure 5-30). Remember that the field names themselves do not have to be the same. Close the two tables.

3. Open the Database Tools tab on the Ribbon. In the Relationships group, click the *Relationships* button to open the Relationships window. Drag the FRIENDS and BUSDRESS tables from the Navigation Pane to the Relationships window.

4. We will now create a relationship between the two tables. This will speed up the execution of the query we will create in a moment. Table relationships were last discussed in the tutorial for Chapter 4. Drag the BLAST_NAME field in the BUSDRESS table over to the LAST_NAME field in the FRIENDS table and release the mouse button. The Edit Relationships dialog box opens. Click the *Create* button. Access generates a dynamic link (line) between the two known as an *equi-join*. An equi-join selects all the records from both tables that have the same value in the selected field.

Database Management Software Cases 197

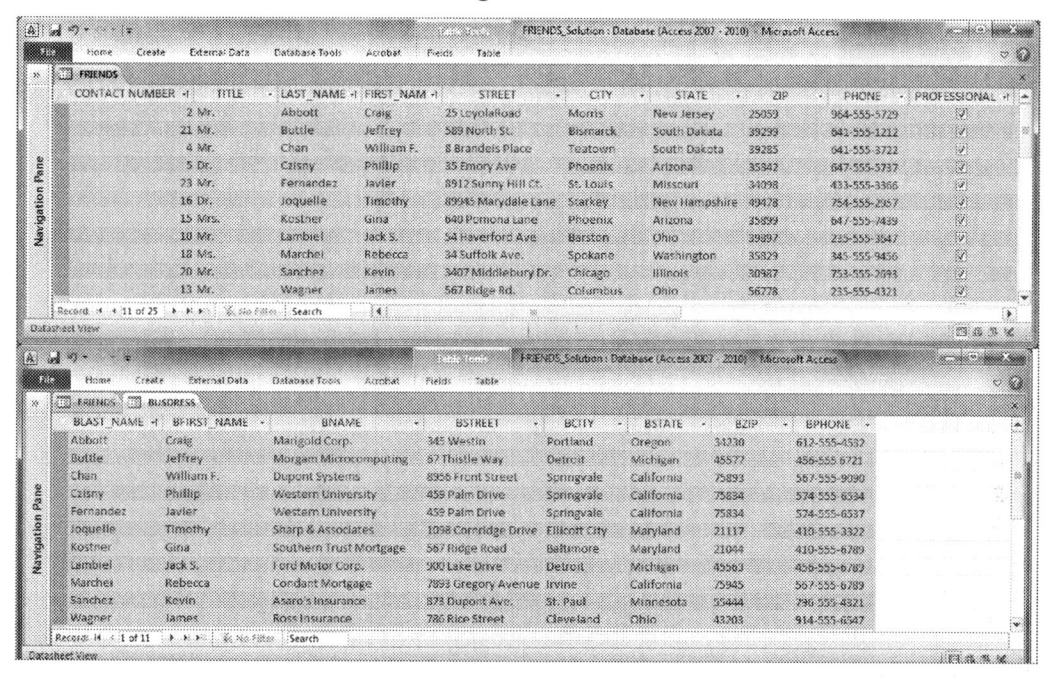

Figure 5-30

Figure 5-31

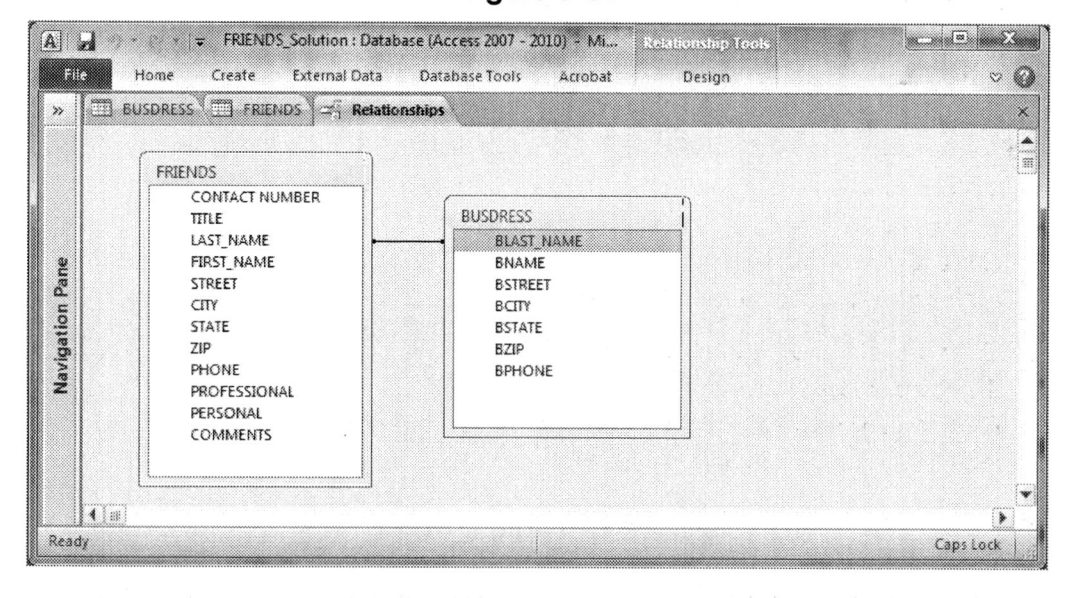

5. Your Relationships window should look similar to Figure 5-31.
6. Save the relationship by clicking the *Save* button on the Quick Access toolbar.
7. Close the Relationships window. You are now ready to create a query to

198   Solve it!

generate the effect of the joining action.

8. Open the Create tab on the Ribbon and click *Query Design*.

9. In the Show Table dialog box, select the BUSDRESS table and click *Add*. Repeat this action for the FRIENDS table. Click *Close*. Notice that Access has remembered the table relationship and has immediately established a join between the two last name fields.

10. Click the bottom half of the *View* button on the Ribbon and select *SQL View* to see the equivalent of this action in the Structured Query Language programming code:

    SELECT

    FROM BUSDRESS INNER JOIN FRIENDS ON BUSDRESS.BLAST_NAME = FRIENDS.LAST_NAME;

11. Click the bottom half of the *View* button and select *Design View* to return to Query Design View.

12. In the query design window, select and drag the following fields down to the Field row in the design grid.

From FRIENDS:	From BUSDRESS:
TITLE	BNAME
FIRST_NAME	BSTREET
LAST_NAME	BCITY
	BSTATE
	BZIP

13. Click in the *Sort* cell for the LAST_NAME field and choose *Ascending*. The design grid should now look similar to Figure 5-32.

14. Click the bottom half of the *View button* and select *SQL View* again to see the effect this action has had on the SQL programming code:

    SELECT FRIENDS.TITLE, FRIENDS.FIRST_NAME, FRIENDS.LAST_NAME, BUSDRESS.BNAME, BUSDRESS.BSTREET, BUSDRESS.BCITY, BUSDRESS.BSTATE, BUSDRESS.BZIP

    FROM BUSDRESS INNER JOIN FRIENDS ON BUSDRESS.BLAST_NAME = FRIENDS.LAST_NAME

ORDER BY FRIENDS.LAST_NAME;

15. Click the *Run button* and view the resulting dynaset. Access has matched and merged the business address data in the BUSDRESS table with the name data in the FRIENDS table to create a composite display containing non-duplicated data from both (see Figure 5-33).
16. Print the query if you wish or use it as the basis for a new report.
17. Save the query as *Tute6Query1* and then close it.

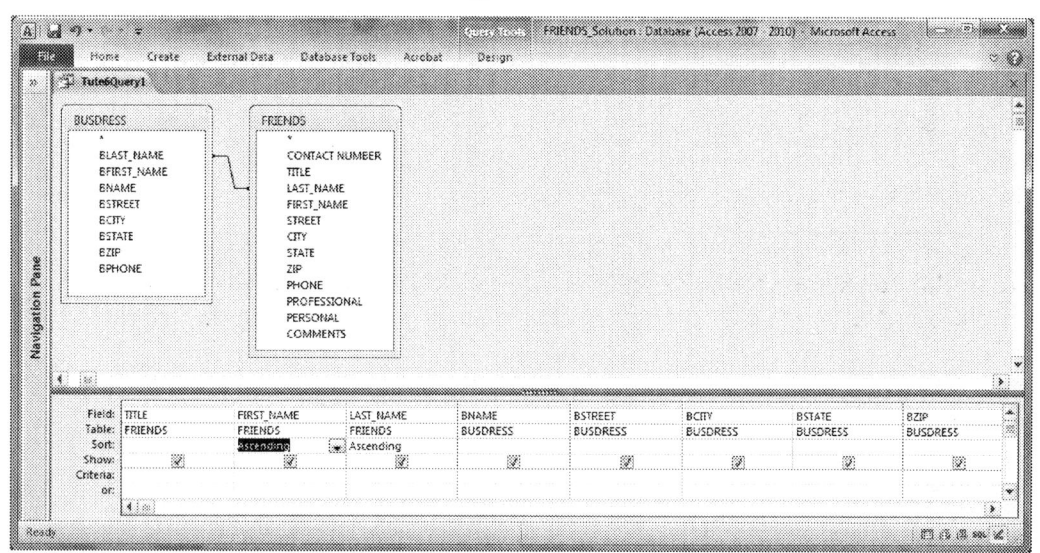

Figure 5-32

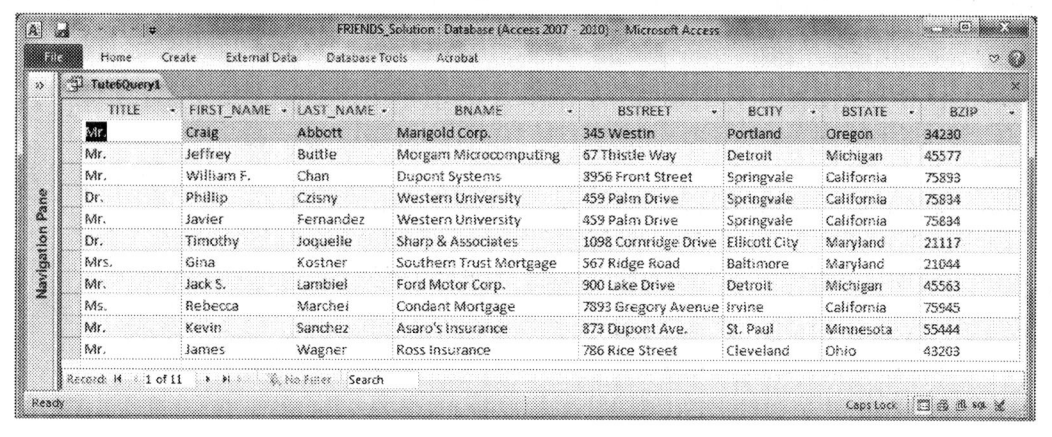

Figure 5-33

How to Create Labels in Access

A report designed to print names and addresses on labels is a common feature of most database applications. Access includes a Label Wizard which can be used to create mailing labels with sizes to match most common commercial adhesive labels. Let's use the table FRIENDS to create a simple three-line address label.

1. Open the Solveit_CH5 database. Select the FRIENDS table in the Navigation pane. Open the Create tab on the Ribbon and click *Labels* in the Reports group to open the Label Wizard.

2. In the first Wizard dialog box, accept the default label type and dimensions. Click the *Next* button.

3. On the second screen, select the font, font size, font weight, and text color you want for the label. Click the *Next* button.

4. Choose fields for your label:

    a. *First Line*

    Select TITLE, and click the Add Field button [>] to enter it onto the prototype label. Press [Space bar] on your keyboard.

    Repeat this action with the FIRST_NAME field. Press [Space bar].

    Select LAST_NAME and click [>]. Press [Enter].

    b. *Second Line*

    Select STREET and click [>]. Press [Enter].

    c. *Third Line*

    Select CITY and click [>]. Add a comma (,) and press the [Space bar].

    Repeat this action with the STATE field. Press the [Space bar].

    Select ZIP and click [>].

    The Label Wizard screen should now look like the one in Figure 5-34. Click the *Next* button.

5. In the next Label Wizard dialog box, select the LAST_NAME field to sort by. Click the *Next* button.

6. In the last Wizard dialog box, type in *Tute6Report1* as the name for your report. Click the *Finish* button. Access will generate your labels and display them in Print Preview.

7. Send your labels to print, close the report, and exit Access.

Figure 5-34

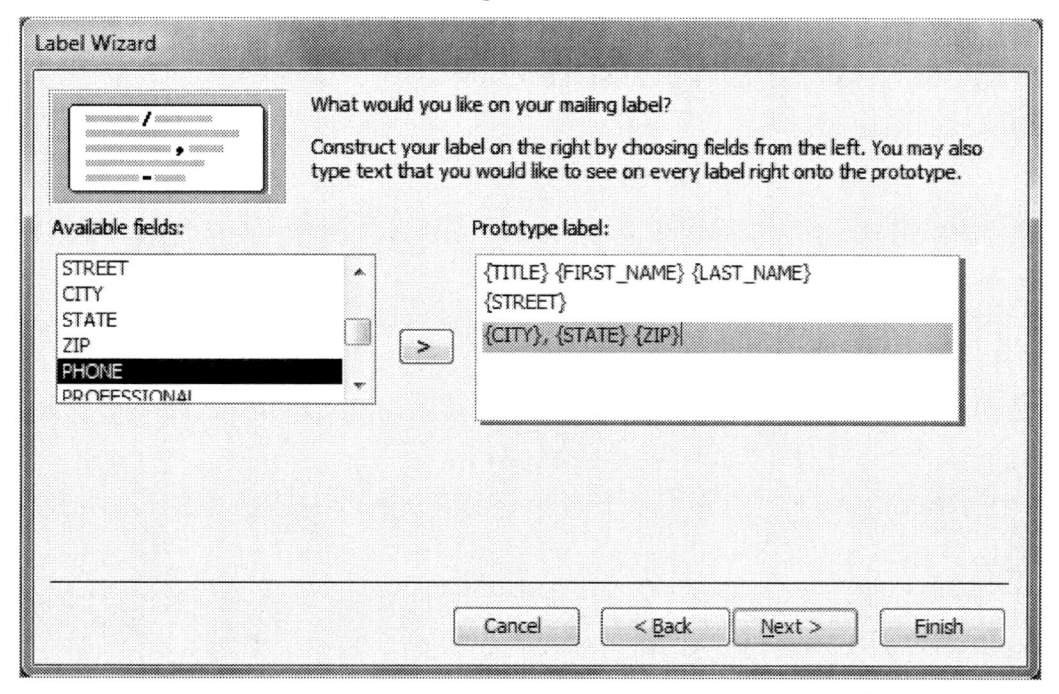

Database Case 7

Buryakov Respiratory Therapy

Problem:	Develop a payroll system
Management Skill:	Control
Access skills:	Select Queries (calculated fields) Append Queries Reports (wizards)
Data Tables:	BURYAKOV BURYAKOV_JANUARY BURYAKOV_FEBRUARY BURYAKOV_MARCH

After working for a Respiratory Clinic for eight years, Dr. Anton Buryakov started his own Respiratory Therapy practice, Buryakov Respiratory Therapy, in 2002. For a start-up practice, Buryakov had done extremely well. In 2012, the company showed gross revenues of $26 million and a net profit of $1,440,000.

Before starting his own practice, Dr. Buryakov had gained a sound understanding of respiratory therapy working under a renowned pulmonologist who had developed the latest protocols for treating patients with breathing and other cardiopulmonary disorders in Omaha, Nebraska. He developed a network of contacts among local government officials, educators, hospitals, and local practitioners. Fortunately, the local economy grew very rapidly as major corporations relocated and government agencies expanded. The related population influx created a boom market for healthcare.

The key to Buryakov's success has been in keeping permanent employee numbers low, relying on sub-contractors, and keeping his capital costs down by renting or leasing heavy equipment.

About 70% of Dr. Buryakov's practice is treating previously diagnosed asthma patients. Buryakov Respiratory Therapy also responds to local School Board requests for asthma educators to work with teachers and students, teaching them how to recognize symptoms and respond to emergencies.

Payroll, Human Resources, and other office administrative tasks are somewhat chaotic. There are only 6 full-time employees (Dr. Buryakov, three respiratory therapists, and two office staff). However, about 40 respiratory therapists, asthma educators, and asthma specialists work as independent contractors for the practice during a typical monthly payroll period in response to specific requests from schools and air transport companies in need of an in-flight specialists as part of their transport teams. More than 100 individuals will work for the firm in a year.

Currently, one of the office staff spends 75% of his time keeping track of the firm's part-time and full-time employees. Originally, Dr. Buryakov had considered outsourcing his payroll, but this proved far too expensive an option. Dr. Buryakov is convinced the answer lies in building a simple in-house personnel system to handle employee wages and related payroll information.

Last year, the situation became serious when the Internal Revenue Service (IRS) audited the firm's books. The IRS wondered why Dr. Buryakov had more than 100 employees but showed very low tax withholdings. Dr. Buryakov explained that most of the employees were short-term, part-time workers and/or independent contractors. In recent times, the IRS has taken a dim view of employees being declared "contract workers" because federal tax is not withheld for contract workers and the IRS has trouble collecting taxes from them later.

While Dr. Buryakov's contract workers appeared legitimate, examination of the records found a number of errors in withholding statements for regular employees who were part-time workers. For 21 part-time workers, no withholding was deducted or submitted to the IRS because of clerical errors. The IRS has given Dr. Buryakov one year to straighten out the records.

Dr. Buryakov has decided that an Access database system would be ideal for a small payroll. He wants you to design such a system for a sample quarter. Employees are paid monthly.

A sample of the employee database showing the ID number, name, and address can be seen in the BURYAKOV table in the SOLVEIT_CH5 database. Create a new Access database and import this table now. A monthly file has been created for each monthly payroll period. Three hand-calculated files for the first quarter have been built for you in Access: BURYAKOV_JANUARY, BURYAKOV_FEBRUARY, and BURYAKOV_MARCH. Import them into the new database too.

Tasks

There are five tasks in this case:

1. Combine the three individual monthly reports (i.e.: BURYAKOV_JANUARY, BURYAKOV_FEBRUARY, BURYAKOV_MARCH) into a single data table representing the First Quarter.

> **Hint:** Use an append action query to do this. You should end up with 90 records in a single, new data table.

2. Develop a query that will calculate the gross, pay, federal and state withholdings, FICA, and resulting net pay for all employees in the first quarter. Set federal withholdings at 20.4% of gross, FICA at 7.65% of gross, and state withholding at 8.25% of gross, and then calculate net pay as gross pay minus all deductions.

3. Use this query to create a report that shows the gross pay, all deductions, and net pay for all employees for the quarter, sorted by last name. Provide subtotals for each employee and a grand total for the firm.

4. Develop a payroll report that shows only the firm's totals for each month for gross pay, all the deductions, and net pay and grand totals for the quarter.

5. Produce a report for the IRS for the first quarter that shows the employees' name, address, gross pay, all deductions, and net pay for each month and totaled for the quarter.

Time Estimates
Expert: 1.5 hours
Intermediate: 2.5 hours
Novice: 4+ hours

Tutorial for Database Case 7 Using Access 2010

Copying and Pasting Table Structures

Using the Access Copy and Paste commands, you can create an empty copy of an existing table (i.e.: field structure only) as a first step in merging records from a number of different tables to a single table. Let's practice this by creating an empty copy of the FRIENDS table:

1. Open the SOLVEIT_CH5 database. In the Navigation Pane, select the FRIENDS table.

2. Right-click the FRIENDS table and on the shortcut menu, select *Copy*.

3. Right-click the FRIENDS table again and select *Paste*.

4. In the Paste Tables As dialog box, give the table the name *Tute7CopyTable*.

5. In the Paste Options section, select the *Structure Only* option button and click OK. Access creates an empty table with an identical field structure to the FRIENDS table.

Action Queries

When you create a new query with the Simple Query Wizard or in Design View, Access generates a Select query by default. Select queries retrieve and display data from tables according to specified criteria. We have used Select queries for *Solve it!* Database Cases 1 through 6. In contrast, *Action* queries, which are constructed starting with the Select query window, actually alter data in tables. Action queries can be used to add, delete, or change data and to create new tables from existing records. For example, a Delete action query is used to delete obsolete records from a table. Access uses four types of action queries. A brief description of each type appears in Figure 5-35, and the icons that identify them in the database appear on the Query Tools: Design tab (Query Type group) shown in Figure 5-36. In this tutorial, we will concentrate on *Append* queries. Other Action query types will be covered in later tutorials.

Append Queries

Append queries copy some or all records from one table and add them to the bottom of another existing table. This is especially useful if you use separate tables to manage certain data (e.g. you keep payroll data on a month-by-month basis and need to merge it every financial quarter).

Figure 5-35

Access Query Types

Select Queries	**Select query** Select a group of records from one or more tables.
Action Queries Action queries change the data in your tables:	**Make-table query** Create a new table from all or parts of other tables. **Delete query:** Delete records from one or more tables. **Append query:** Add a group of records to a table. **Update queries:** Make changes to data in a group of records.

Figure 5-36

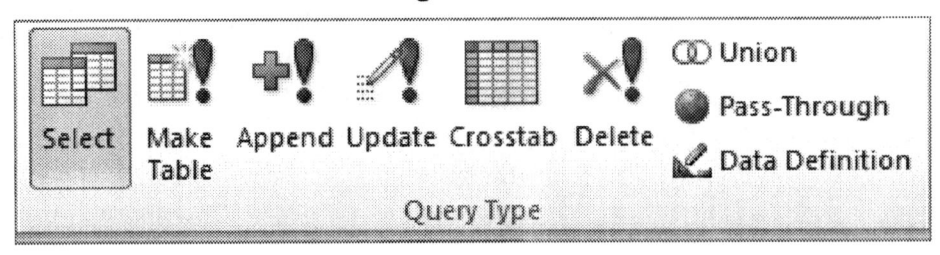

Append queries are also handy for storing historical data. For example, in an Orders table, completed orders could be separated from active, incomplete orders to prevent the Orders table from becoming too large, as well as to provide a backup for future reference.

When data is appended, the tables involved in the query need not have the same structure, but the data types of the appended fields **must** be compatible. The source table must have fields with data types that are compatible with the destination fields. Text fields can be appended to fields with most other data types, but a Number field cannot be appended to a Text field. Number fields are only compatible with other Number fields. When records are appended to a table, the records in the original table remain intact. Access does not delete the original records.

> **Note:** If two tables involved in an Append query have identical field structures, the * in the table field list can be used instead of the individual field names in the Field row of the design grid.

Let's use the FRIENDS table and the empty copy of the FRIENDS table, (Tute7CopyTable) we created earlier in this tutorial to generate an Append action query.

1. On the Create tab, click *Query Design* to create a new query in Design View. Add the FRIENDS field list using the Show Table dialog box.

2. On the Query Tools: Design tab, click the *Append* button to change the Select query into an Append query. The Append dialog box opens.

3. In the Append dialog box, click the down arrow button on the *Table Name* list box, select *Tute7CopyTable,* and click *OK*. This means we will append records from the FRIENDS table to Tute7CopyTable. An *Append To:* row is added to the design grid below the Sort row.

4. In the Append query design window, select and drag the all fields symbol (*) in the FRIENDS field list down to the first cell in the Field row in the design grid. This tells Access two things: that all FRIENDS fields should be included in the query, and that the field structure of Tute7CopyTable is identical to FRIENDS. Access immediately adds notation to this effect in the *Append to* cell.

5. Test the Append query before committing to its execution. One of the things to note about any Action query is that it **changes** table data in some way. For this reason, it is a good practice to test the query before running it. Testing also allows you to check for errors in the query design.

6. To test your Append query, switch to Datasheet View to view the resulting dataset. The dataset should display all the records in the FRIENDS table. Return to Query Design View and run the query. Access should append all FRIENDS table records to Tute7CopyTable. A warning dialog box will advise you that you are about to append the number of rows selected by the query and that the action will be irreversible. Click *Yes* to append the records to Tute7CopyTable.

7. Save your query as *Tute7AppendQuery* and close it. Double-click *Tute7CopyTable* in the Navigation Pane to open it and check the contents.

Database Case 8

Pocatello Auto Rentals

Problem:	Develop a transaction and fee checking system
Management skills:	Control
	Decide
Access Skills:	Forms
	Action Queries
	Macros
Data Table:	POCATELLOAUTO

Claire Davis punched the buttons on her hand-held calculator. Three months ago, Pocatello Auto Rentals had been an independent rental car dealer based in Pocatello, Idaho. Idaho Discount Rentals, a medium-sized operator, then offered a sizeable sum for majority ownership of Pocatello Auto. Idaho Discount recognized that the recent boom in the Pocatello area, and in the state of Idaho, was the beginning of a period of sustained growth. Idaho Discount also realized that the three existing rental agencies (two of them franchises of national dealerships) would provide intense competition for any start-up enterprise in the area, so it decided to approach the single independent dealer with a partnership offer.

Davis was surprised and relieved when the Idaho Discount offer arrived. Her 20-year-old dealership was straining under the pressure from the newly established national franchises that could offer some cut-price deals, one-way rentals, and arrangements with frequent-flyer schemes that she could not match. Idaho Discount had a cooperative deal with one of the key domestic airlines, and Davis realized that when rental dealers' prices were very similar, customers made decisions based on issues such as frequent-flyer points. Idaho Discount could also assist during temporary price wars. Faced with deciding between hard times as an independent dealer and receiving cash for losing control, Davis accepted Idaho Discount's offer.

Davis soon realized that the extra security offered by Idaho Discount came with additional obligations, such as monthly reporting duties. These reports involved the calculations she was currently performing manually on her calculator. Robinson already had a computerized reservation and charging system, a necessity in the industry; however, her system could not provide the required reports. Although Idaho Discounts was willing to supply its own software, Davis was happy with her system. She knew that it could write the details of transactions to an exportable file. With this knowledge, Davis asked Idaho Discount to send one of its system programmers. Idaho Discount obliged by dispatching David Chavez.

Chavez examined a typical file on Davis' system and found that it could be readily imported into any common database management system. Although not ideal, this solution would certainly prevent the need for Davis to calculate her reports manually. Chavez advised her to purchase a Windows-based database package and use it to meet Idaho Discount's monthly reporting requirements.

The senior managers at Idaho Discount need quarterly information to make informed decisions. They require the total revenue derived from each of the car model sizes over each month. Each transaction record contains certain information: a sequential code generated by the computer, date of transaction, model code (S=Small, M=Medium, L=Large, H=High Occupancy (min-van, van, SUV),or F=Fuel-efficient & hybrid), car registration, miles traveled, number of rental days, rental fee, and a logical field signifying whether or not the rental was "limited miles." The customer can usually choose unlimited miles or a limit of 100 free miles with a lower base rate. For a limited-mile transaction, each mile above 100 miles incurs a per mile cost.

The POCATELLOAUTO table supplied in the SOLVEIT_CH5 database contains a partial list of transactions downloaded from the Pocatello Auto Rentals reservation system.

Tasks

There are three tasks in this case:

1. Claire Davis wants Chavez to develop a simple solution for her so she can check the accuracy of the transactions in the sample list against the paper records she has in her office. She wants the solution to include an entry screen where the user can enter the transaction code (e.g. T24155). The procedure will then display the record corresponding to the code if it is valid. If the code is not valid, the user should be informed that the entry is invalid and be required to re-enter the code. The user also should be able to exit the system easily. The entry screen should have ample instructions for the user to use the system.

Solve it!

> **Hint:** Create two forms with command buttons to complete this task.

2. To meet her reporting commitments, Davis must currently manually calculate the revenue from each transaction. Thus, she wants Chavez to develop a procedure to calculate the fee for each transaction and place the result in the RENTALS table. The charges for each model type appear in the table below:

	Small (S)	Medium (M)	Large (L)	High Occupancy (H)	Fuel-Efficiency (F)
Limited Rate ($)	$36.19	$43.99	$50.99	$71.99	$87.99
Additional cost per mile ($)	$0.59	$0.69	$0.79	$0.89	$0.90
Unlimited Rate ($)	$45.99	$54.99	$62.99	$59.99	$80.99
Depreciation Rate (%)	8.9%	8.2%	8.1%	8.6%	6.5%
Purchase Price ($)	$16,699	$20,199	$28,999	$30,899	$24,499

> **Hint:** First create a table to store the rate information for each car model type from the first three rows in the table above. Then create three update queries to complete this task. The first query will calculate the charge for customers who choose the Unlimited rate. The second query will calculate the charge for customers who choose the Limited rate and do not go over the allotted 100 miles. The third query will calculate the charge for customers who choose the Limited rate and exceed the 100 free miles. The last expression will multiply the limited rate by the number of days and add to that the total miles driven minus the free 100 miles multiplied by the additional cost per mile. Enclose the parts of an expression that must be performed first (i.e. addition and subtraction to override the order of operations) in parentheses. Each calculation will update to the CHARGE field in the RENTALS table.

3.* Idaho Discounts is becoming more demanding in its reporting requirements, adding to Davis' workload. The company wants to know the depreciation of any car in Pocatello Auto's yard. The method for calculating depreciation in the car rental industry is dictated by the Internal Revenue Service. The depreciation amount for each vehicle depends on the total distance traveled (read from the odometer), the rate of depreciation for the model type (i.e. small, medium, large, high-occupancy, fuel-efficiency), and the purchase price of the vehicle. The IRS says the depreciation amount is defined as a fixed percentage (i.e. the depreciation rate) of the purchase price for every 7,500 miles the vehicle has traveled. Develop a procedure to calculate the amount of depreciation for each car based on the depreciation rates and purchase prices appearing in the table above. Enable the user to enter the registration of a particular vehicle and then calculate the depreciation on that car.

> **Hint:** First create a table to store the depreciation and purchase price information for each car model type from the bottom two rows of the table above. Set the Format property for the depreciation rate field to Percent and the Field Size property to Single. Then create a Parameter query to complete this task. You must first create a calculated field to compute the depreciation. The expression will divide the depreciation rate by 100 and multiply the result by the purchase price multiplied by the odometer reading divided by 7,500. You must enclose parts of an expression that must be performed first (i.e. dividing the depreciation rate by 100) in parentheses. The parameter query will prompt the user to enter the car registration number.

Time Estimates (excluding tasks marked with *):
Expert: 1.5 hour
Intermediate: 2.5 hours
Novice: 4 hours

Tutorial for Database Case 8 Using Access 2010

Creating Forms in Access

Forms are used to view, enter, or edit data into a database and often serve as the most convenient way of performing these operations. Forms can be based on tables or queries, and they can display data on a record-by-record basis. As with reports, forms can be created using a wizard. A series of dialog boxes enables the user to customize the way data will be organized and displayed. With one mouse click, you can switch from Form to Datasheet View, which is a tabular view of the same set of records.

An Access form, just like a report, is constructed from any number of controls: text boxes for entering and editing data; label controls to identify the text boxes; and other controls, list boxes, or combo boxes from which a user can select a value, and toggle buttons, option buttons, or check boxes for *Yes/No* fields. You can modify forms in various ways, including using colors to highlight important data, inserting graphics, and displaying messages to indicate when an incorrect value has been entered. You can also set up your form so that Access automatically inserts data for you, prints data on the click of a command button, and/or displays the results of calculations. Let's use the FRIENDS table to create a simple form.

Forms

1. Open the SOLVEIT_CH5 database and select the FRIENDS table in the Navigation Pane.

2. Open the Create tab on the Ribbon and click *Form* in the Forms group. Access automatically generates and opens a new form for the selected table that includes all of the fields in the table in one or more columns. The form shows the first record in your table (see Figure 5-37). Notice that three Form Layout Tools tabs, Design, Arrange, and Format, appear on the Ribbon.

3. Click *Save* on the Quick Access toolbar. Name your form SHOWFRIENDS and save it. In a matter of minutes, you have created a simple form that can be used for viewing, editing, adding, and deleting records in the FRIENDS table.

Access offers a number of different types of forms you can create using the commands in the Forms group on the Create tab on the Ribbon:

- **Simple form** (Form): This form displays one record with fields in one or two columns.

- **Datasheet forms** (More Forms>Datasheet): Displays fields in datasheet (table) format

- **Tabular forms** (More Forms>Multiple Items): Displays each record as a row of fields

- **PivotTable forms** (More Forms>PivotTable): Creates a form with a Microsoft Excel pivot table, a feature that enables analysis and summarization of data in lists and tables

- **PivotChart forms** (More Forms>PivotChart): Creates a form to display PivotCharts.

- **Split forms** (More Forms>Split Form): Displays the current record as a simple form and additional records as a datasheet form.

- **Modal dialog** (More Forms>Modal Dialog): Based on asking the user a question as part of an automated process; used with VBA scripting.

- **Blank form** (Blank Form or Form Design): Creates a blank layout to which you add all form fields and formatting. Blank Form opens the empty form palette in Layout View, while Form Design opens in Design View with the gridlines and section bars visible.

You can also use the **Form Wizard** (Form Wizard) which will assist you in selecting the table, fields, and layout (Columnar, Tabular, Datasheet, or Justified), for a form.

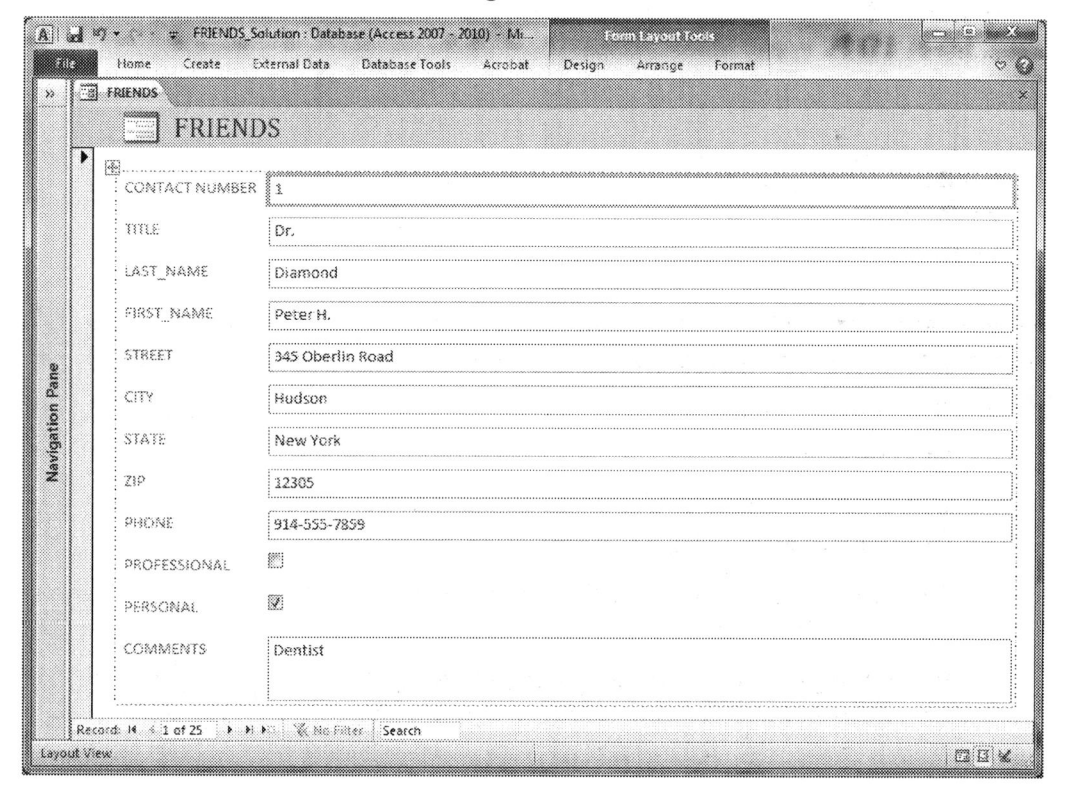

Figure 5-37

Four Ways to View a Form

Access offers four quick and easy ways to view a form. You will use each of these when designing and using forms. To switch views, simply click the bottom half of the View button and select the view. You can also view forms as either pivot tables or pivot charts.

- *Design View:* Use in conjunction with Layout View to customize the appearance or change the structure of forms and to add and modify controls. In Design view, a larger selection of controls is available, you can enter the control source directly into a text box, resize form sections (header, footer, and detail section), and change properties that cannot be changed in Layout View.

- *Layout View:* Use in conjunction with Design View to make design changes to a form. Layout View is more user-friendly for certain design tasks, particularly resizing controls, because you can view the data entered in the controls.

- *Form View:* Use to view, enter, and edit record data.

- *Datasheet View:* Displays the underlying table or query dynaset on which the form is based.

You can also use the Print Preview button to see how a form will look when printed.

Creating a Form in Design View

As the name suggests, you start with a blank form and use the commands in the Controls group on the Form Layout Tools: Design tab on the Ribbon to add controls in Form Design View. You use the buttons in the Controls group to add all of the text boxes, labels, combo boxes, list boxes, check boxes, and other controls required for your form. For this reason, blank forms often have no initial connection to an underlying query or table.

> **Hint:** You must create a form in Design View by adding unbound controls to a blank form for Task 1 of Case 8.

To create a blank form:

1. On the Create tab on the Ribbon, click *Form Design* to open a blank form in Design View. The initial form contains only a Detail section. Forms use the same type of sectioning as reports. Review the Access tutorial for Case 2 for an explanation of report sections.

Let's create a simple customized form using the FRIENDS table. The form is designed to look up and display specific FRIENDS records based on their ID numbers.

> **Hint:** The criteria used could just as easily be product numbers or transaction codes.

2. To add a form header and footer section to your form, right-click the form and select *Form Header/Footer*. On the Form Design Tools: Design tab, click the *Label* button and use the label pointer to click in the form header section of the form. Type a heading for the form, *Friends Lookup*. Change the label size, font, font size, and font color as you see fit. If necessary, increase the size of the form header by positioning the pointer over the top edge of the Detail section bar and dragging downward with the horizontal split-bar pointer.

3. Click the *Text Box* button and then click in the *Detail* section of the form to create an unbound text box and label for the form. Right-click the label and select *Properties* on the shortcut menu. On the Format tab in the property sheet, change the *Caption* property to *Search for a Friend*. Resize the label (and reposition the text box) so that the label box displays all of the text.

4. Select the unbound text box. On the property sheet, select the Data tab. Locate the *Validation Rule* property, click in the settings box, and type the following expression (right-click and select *Zoom* if you need more room to type):

    >= 1 And <=200

> **Note:** The ID numbers in the FRIENDS table must be greater than or equal to 1 and less than or equal to 200. This will allow you to enter up to 200 names in the table and will catch typing errors that include letters, negative values, or numbers greater than 200. It creates a valid ID number range.

5. Press the down arrow key on the keyboard to move to the *Validation Text* property settings box. Enter the following message to display in an error dialog box if a user enters invalid data: *You must enter values between 1 and 200. Click OK and re-enter.*

6. Click the *Other* tab. Change the *Name* property for the text box to *FriendID*. In the *Status Bar Text* property settings box, type *Enter an ID number*.

7. Save your form as *FRIENDSLOOKUP*.

Next, we will create three *command buttons*: One that links FRIENDSLOOKUP through an event procedure to the FRIENDSSHOW form and displays the relevant record, one that exits FRIENDSSHOW so that FRIENDSLOOKUP displays, and one to exit FRIENDSLOOKUP.

Using Control Wizards in Forms

The Access Control Wizards will help you to create complex controls for your forms by taking you step-by-step through the creation process. Control Wizards are available for creating option groups, list boxes, combo boxes, and command buttons. Command buttons can be created to start many different types of actions or sets of actions. These are referred to by programmers as *event procedures*. An *event* is a particular action that triggers a procedure, such as clicking a command button in a form or report. A *procedure* is a unit of programming code designed to accomplish a specific task.

You will not be directly required to do any programming because the Command Button Wizard will write either the Visual Basic for Applications (VBA) code or an Access macro for you. You can create command buttons that will automate many frequently-used activities associated with forms and reports, such as opening and closing objects, linking fields between objects, printing individual records, going to specific records, or updating data.

1. Let's create the first of our command buttons. First, make sure that the FRIENDSLOOKUP form is open in Design View. Select the *Use Control Wizards* command in the list box in the Controls group on the Form Design Tools: Design tab so that it is highlighted, if necessary.

2. Click the *Button* button on the Ribbon and then click in an empty section of the *Detail* section on the FRIENDSLOOKUP form.

3. The first of several Command Button Wizard dialog boxes opens. Make these choices as you proceed through the dialog boxes:

    a. In the Categories box, select *Form Operations*. In the Actions box, select *Open Form*. Click *Next*.

    b. Select SHOWFRIENDS as the form to open. Click *Next*.

    c. Choose to *Open the form and find specific data to display*. Click *Next*.

    d. In the FRIENDSLOOKUP box, select *FriendID*. In the SHOWFRIENDS box, select CONTACT NUMBER. Click *Next*.

    e. Select the *Text* option button and type *Show Record* as the text to display on the button. Click *Next*.

Database Management Software Cases 217

    f. Type *ShowRecord* to name the button. Click *Finish* to generate the command button.

> **Hint:** If you have any problems creating this button, you can follow the steps in Step 5 to open the Code window for the button and type the appropriate code for the button as seen in Figure 5-38.

4. Save the changes to the FRIENDSLOOKUP form.

5. Right-click the *Show Record* button and select *Properties*. Click the Event tab. In the *On Click* property, notice that Access has added *[Embedded Macro]*. Click in the *On Click* property settings box and then click the ... *(Build)* button. The Macro Tools: Design tab opens, displaying the code for the macro for the Show Record button (see Figure 5-38). Click the *Close* button at the top right of the On Click macro window to close it and return to Design View.

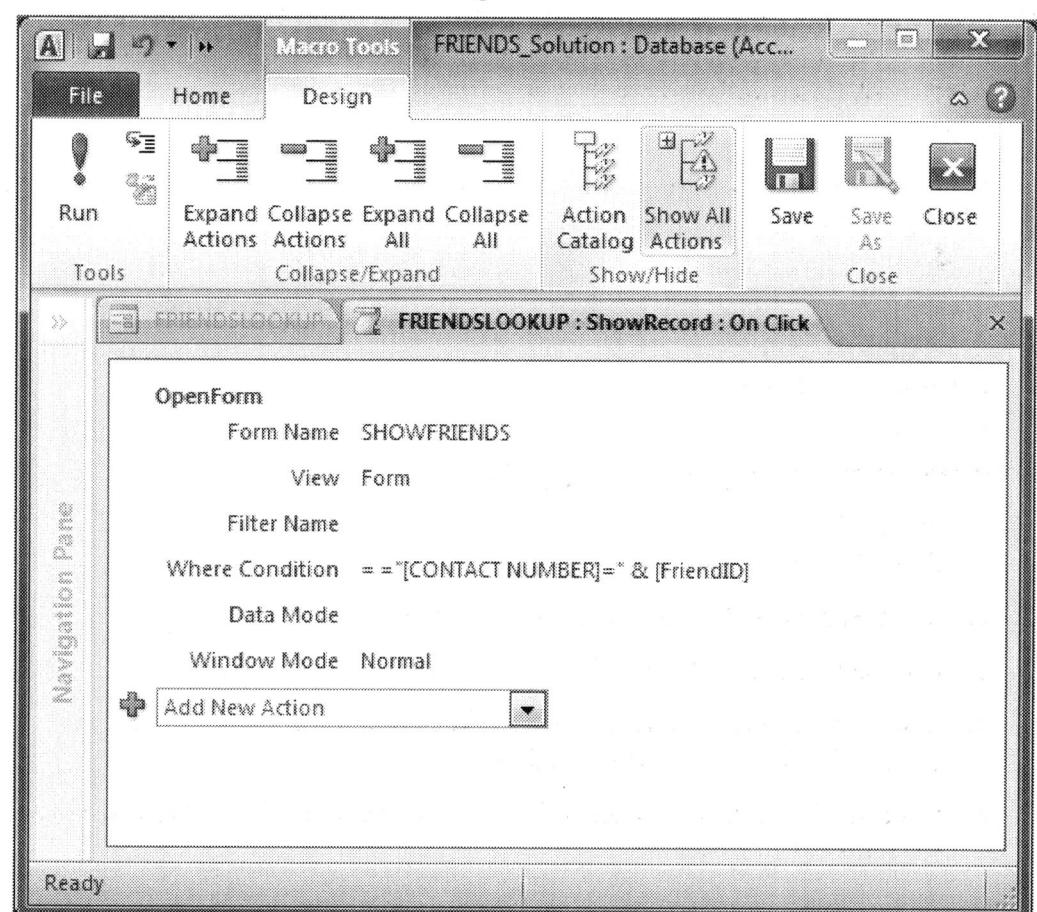

Figure 5-38

```
OpenForm
    Form Name       SHOWFRIENDS
    View            Form
    Filter Name
    Where Condition = ="[CONTACT NUMBER]=" & [FriendID]
    Data Mode
    Window Mode     Normal
```

6. **Time to Test:** Close the property sheet and switch to Form view. Notice that the text you entered for the *Status Bar Text* property displays in the Status bar. Enter an ID number between 1 and 25 (or whatever the last record number is at present in your FRIENDS table), and click the *Show Record* button. The sequence works, but there is no easy or immediate way to run the procedure again or to exit from SHOWFRIENDS. You must add an *Exit* button to both the FRIENDSLOOKUP form and the SHOWFRIENDS form. Use the *Close* button to close SHOWFRIENDS.

7. Return to Design View in the FRIENDSLOOKUP form. Use the Command Button Wizard to create another command button in the *Detail* section to exit the form. Select the *Form Operations* category and the *Close Form* action. Use the Exit picture on the button, and name the button *Close Form*. Reposition the command button as necessary, save the changes, and close the form.

8. Open the SHOWFRIENDS form in Design View. Add a command button under the Comments field to close the form. Use the text *Close Form* on the button and name the button *CloseShowFriends*. Reposition the command button as necessary, save the changes, and close the form.

9. Open the FRIENDSLOOKUP form in Form view. Enter *10* in the *Search for a Friend* text box. Click *Show Record*. Click the *Close Form* button to close SHOWFRIENDS. Click the *Exit* button to close FRIENDSLOOKUP.

10. Reopen FRIENDSLOOKUP in Form view and test the procedure several times. Also, enter an ID not in the valid range to make sure the validation procedure is working. With two simple forms and three easy-to-generate command buttons, we have created a robust, easy-to-use FRIENDS lookup program.

Macros in Access

A *macro* in Access is a set of actions that automate common tasks, such as opening a table or printing a report. Macros help you to work smarter and save time without having to learn programming. Macros are simple to create, and Access offers a choice of approximately 50 different macro actions that include:

- Opening and closing tables, forms, and reports
- Opening a form and finding records related to another form

- Automatically printing reports upon opening a particular database
- Checking or improving data validity

The great thing about macros is that they can handle tasks that would often require extensive programming skills in other database packages. In other systems, a "macro" refers to a program written in VBA. Access macros use a modernized form of "declarative programming," which is code that describes the actions you want to do but not how the actions are to be accomplished. The compiler (program or set of programs that converts the source code into binary object code) figures out the intermediate steps. Macro actions often involve *arguments*. These are simply parameters that govern how an action is executed. If you have problems choosing macro actions or specifying arguments, press the [F1] key to open the Help file.

Let's create a simple macro that will open the SHOWFRIENDS form and display only records that contain personal friends from Maryland before returning to the full FRIENDS table record set.

1. Open the Create tab on the Ribbon and click the *Macros* button in the Macros & Code group. The Macro Designer opens. The new Macro Designer has a text editor-like layout in which actions and conditional statements are entered and arguments display in a dialog box.

2. Click the list arrow on the Add New Action list box to display a list of all available Macro actions. Scroll down this list and select *OpenForm*. A panel with the Open Form action at the top opens.

3. In the *Form Name* list box, click the list arrow and select the SHOWFRIENDS form.

4. In the *View* list box, you can choose to open the form in Form View, Design View, Datasheet View, Print Preview, Pivot Table or Pivot Chart View, or Layout View. Select Datasheet.

5. In the *Filter Name* text box, enter: *Personal Friends*.

6. In the *Where Condition text* box, type the following:

    [FRIENDS]![PERSONAL] =YES

7. In the *Data Mode* list box, you can choose to allow users to add new records, edit existing records, or only view the records. Select *Read Only*.

220   *Solve it!*

Figure 5-39

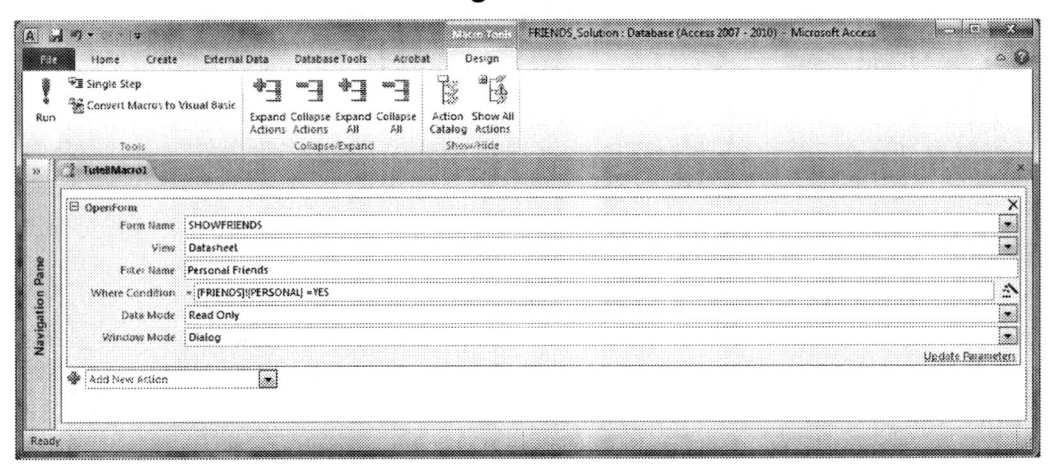

8. In the *Window Mode* list box, you can choose to open the form as dictated by the form properties (Normal), to hide the form (Hidden), to display the form minimized at the bottom of the screen as a small Title bar (Icon), or as a free-floating window/dialog box (the Modal and Pop-up properties are set to Yes). Select *Dialog (Figure 5-39)*.

9. Click the Save button on the Quick Access toolbar and name the macro *Tute8Macro1*. Run the macro. Only personal friends should display in a pop-up window. Close the window.

10. In the *Where Condition text* box (see Figure 5-40) add the following:

    AND [FRIENDS]![STATE]="Maryland".

11. In the *Control Name* text box, enter: Personal Friends AND MD.

> **Note:** Additional records were added to the FRIENDS table in the Tutorial for Case 4. If you did not do this tutorial, you must add the 5 new records to the FRIENDS table shown in Figure 5-21.

12. Save the macro and run it. There should be two personal friends who live in Maryland.

Use Macros When: You are performing tasks, such as opening and closing tables or forms or running reports. Your application involves custom menus and

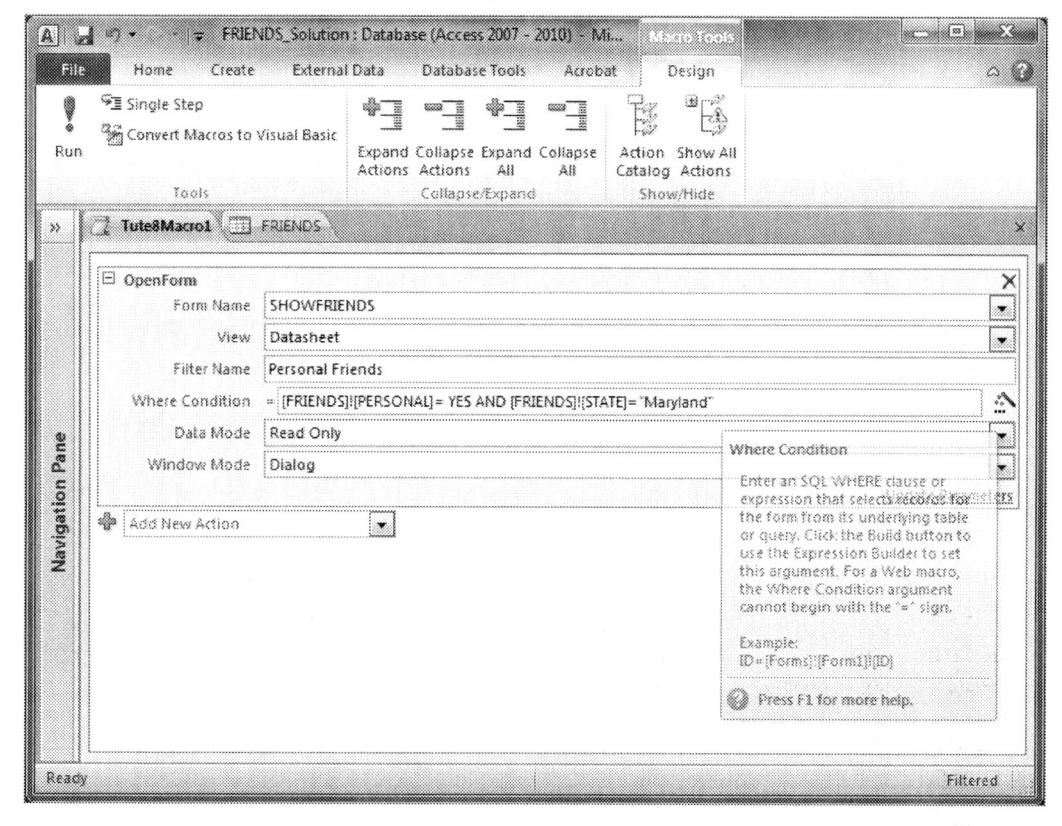

Figure 5-40

submenus for forms. Your application is basically simple and uncomplicated, and does not require debugging procedures.

Update Queries in Access

Update queries are action queries that modify data according to specific criteria, such as increasing **all** car rental rates or certain product prices by 15%. Update queries are created in much the same way as other queries, except that a new value is specified for a particular field. Like all other types of action queries, update queries save time and effort, but they must be used carefully because they actually change the data in the underlying table. Let's use the sample data table COSMETICS to create a simple update query.

1. Open the COSMETICS database you created in the Tutorial for Case 2. If you did not create this database, create a new empty database and import the COSMETICS table provided in the SOLVEIT_CH5 database. Open the

222　Solve it!

COSMETICS table and browse the records, specifically noting the data in the UnitCost field (see Figure 5-41).

2. Create a new query in Design View using the Item and UnitCost fields from the COSMETICS table. Select *Update* on the Query Tools: Design tab (Query Tools group) to turn the Select query into an Update query. This will add an *Update To:* line to the design grid.

3. In the *Update To* cell for the UnitCost field, enter the expression *[Unitcost]*1.15*. This expression will multiply the current value in the UnitCost field by 115%, thereby increasing the prices of all items in the COSMETICS table by 15%.

4. In the *Criteria* cell for the Item field, type *Blush*. This tells Access to limit the update of the UnitCost field to only those records that exactly match the

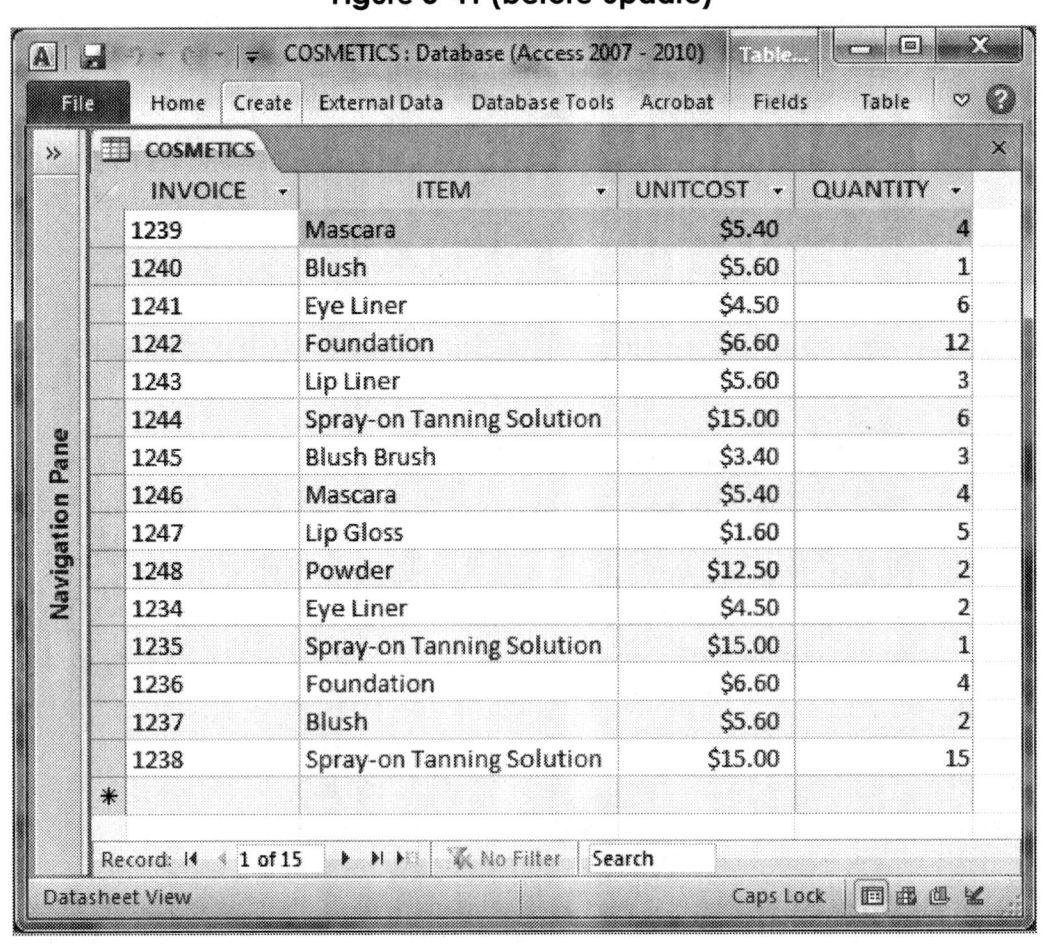

Figure 5-41 (before update)

INVOICE	ITEM	UNITCOST	QUANTITY
1239	Mascara	$5.40	4
1240	Blush	$5.60	1
1241	Eye Liner	$4.50	6
1242	Foundation	$6.60	12
1243	Lip Liner	$5.60	3
1244	Spray-on Tanning Solution	$15.00	6
1245	Blush Brush	$3.40	3
1246	Mascara	$5.40	4
1247	Lip Gloss	$1.60	5
1248	Powder	$12.50	2
1234	Eye Liner	$4.50	2
1235	Spray-on Tanning Solution	$15.00	1
1236	Foundation	$6.60	4
1237	Blush	$5.60	2
1238	Spray-on Tanning Solution	$15.00	15

word *Blush* in the Item field. If you wanted to update all records that contained the word Blush followed by any other string of characters, for example, the Blush Brush, you would include an asterisk (*) after Blush (Blush *). Also called a wildcard character, the asterisk represents any string of characters. It instructs Access to select all items that contain the specified text string with any string of characters following it.

5. Click the *Datasheet View* button to make sure that only invoices for blush are being selected for updating. If you entered Blush *

6. Return to Design View and save the query as *Tute8Query1*. Run the query. Click *Yes* to update the two rows containing the unit cost for blush. Close the query. Open the COSMETICS table and notice the changes made to the UnitCost field (see Figure 5-42). All invoices for blush have been increased by 15%. Close the table.

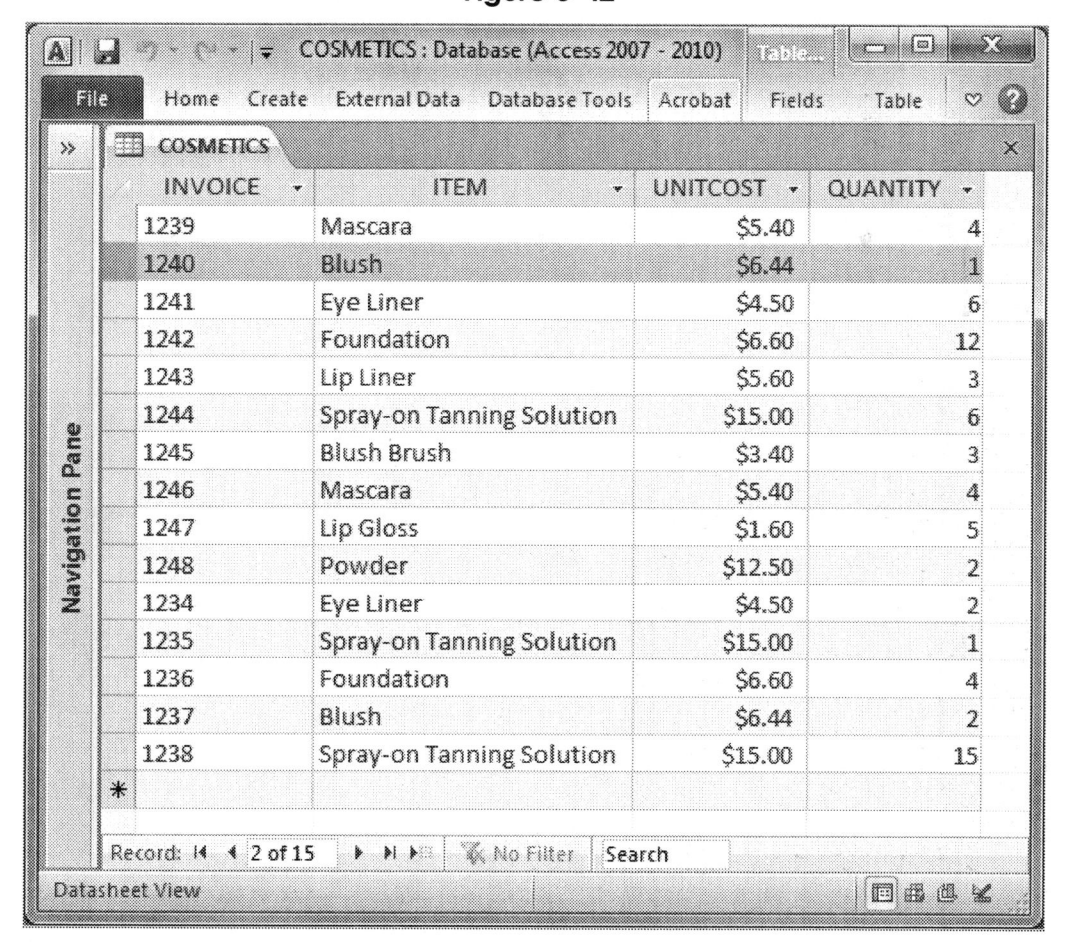

Figure 5-42

INVOICE	ITEM	UNITCOST	QUANTITY
1239	Mascara	$5.40	4
1240	Blush	$6.44	1
1241	Eye Liner	$4.50	6
1242	Foundation	$6.60	12
1243	Lip Liner	$5.60	3
1244	Spray-on Tanning Solution	$15.00	6
1245	Blush Brush	$3.40	3
1246	Mascara	$5.40	4
1247	Lip Gloss	$1.60	5
1248	Powder	$12.50	2
1234	Eye Liner	$4.50	2
1235	Spray-on Tanning Solution	$15.00	1
1236	Foundation	$6.60	4
1237	Blush	$6.44	2
1238	Spray-on Tanning Solution	$15.00	15

224　Solve it!

Parameter Queries

You can also create a parameter query that will prompt the user to enter criteria each time the query is run. For example, instead of entering *Blush* as the criterion in the Item field, you could enter *[Enter an Item]*. When the query is run, the Enter Parameter Value dialog box will open prompting the user to "Enter an Item" (see Figure 5-43). The text that will serve as the prompt is enclosed in square brackets in the criterion expression. This way, the query can be saved and rerun each time

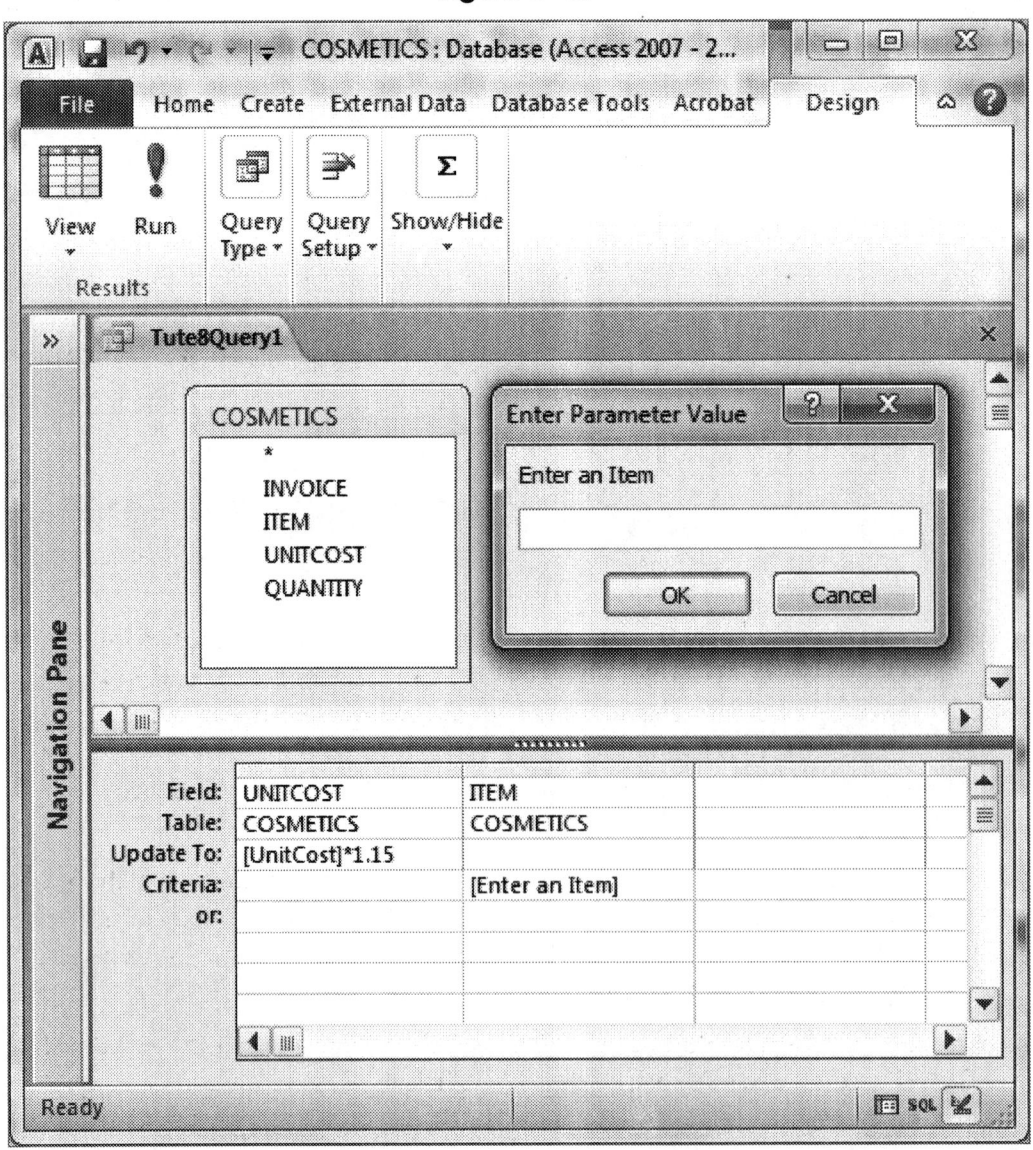

Figure 5-43

a price increase occurs. As is, the query will increase the price of any product entered by the user by 15%, but the expression can be modified to accommodate larger or smaller percentage increases. Parameter statements can be used with all types of queries - select and action.

More about Forms: Main/Subform

A *subform* is a form embedded inside another form (known as the main form). Main forms and subforms are used to generate and display data from any two tables or queries that have a one-to-many relationship. The main form will be based on the table that is on the "one" side of the relationship, and the subform on the "many" side of the relationship (e.g. one hotel guest might have many reservations).

The relationship between the two tables **must exist before** attempting to create the subform. In addition, the main form (the table on the "one side") should have a primary key, while the subform (the table on the "many side") must contain a field with the same name and data type as that primary key. Primary keys are usually unique identifiers. You may have to recreate primary key fields and relationships after importing tables to a new database. Review the section *Creating Relationships Between Tables* at the end of Chapter 4 if you are unsure how to do this.

To create a Main/Subform:

1. Create a new empty database named AKKERMANFURNITURE and import the Customers, Products, Orders, and Order_Details tables from the SOLVEIT_CH5 database into it.

2. Open the Relationships window and add the 4 tables to the window. If necessary, recreate the relationships. Select the CustomerID field in the field list for the Customers table and drag it to the CustomerID field in the Orders table. Click the *Enforce Referential Integrity* check box and then the *Create* button to create the one-to-many relationship between the two tables.

3. Select the ProductID field in the field list for the Products table and drag it to the ProductID field in the Order Details table. Click the *Enforce Referential Integrity* check box and then the *Create* button to create the one-to-many relationship between the two tables.

4. Select the OrderID field in the field list for the Orders table and drag it to the OrderID field in the OrderDetails table. Click the *Enforce Referential Integrity*

check box and then the *Create* button to create the one-to-many relationship between the two tables. The Relationships window is shown in Figure 5-44. Close the Relationships window, saving the changes to the layout of the window when prompted.

5. Select the Customers table in the Navigation pane. Open the Create tab on the Ribbon. Click the *Form* button in the Forms group. A form is automatically generated with the Customers data in the main form and the Orders data in a datasheet subform. The Order details can be viewed by clicking the expand button.

6. Switch to Layout view. Adjust the overall height, width, column width, and font size of the ORDERS subform. Save the changes and return to Form view. You can now view all orders placed by a particular customer in the subform. New orders can be entered in the subform.

7. Use Design and Layout View to make any other changes as you see fit to the sizes or positions of the controls on the form. Save the form as Customers/Orders and close it. The form/subform is shown in Figure 5-45.

Make-Table Queries

A make-table query is a simple action query that creates a new table. It is different from other queries in that there is no query results set to view. Instead, the data is inserted into a new table which can be saved in either the same database or a different database. Begin by creating a select query with the necessary criteria. Then test the results. When you are sure that you have designed the query correctly, convert it to a make-table query by clicking the Make-Table button in the Query Type group on the Query Tools: Design tab. A Make Table dialog box

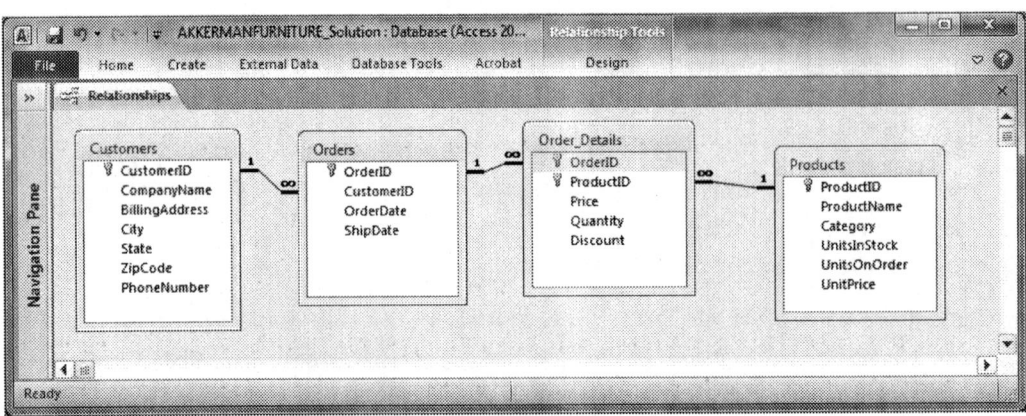

Figure 5-44

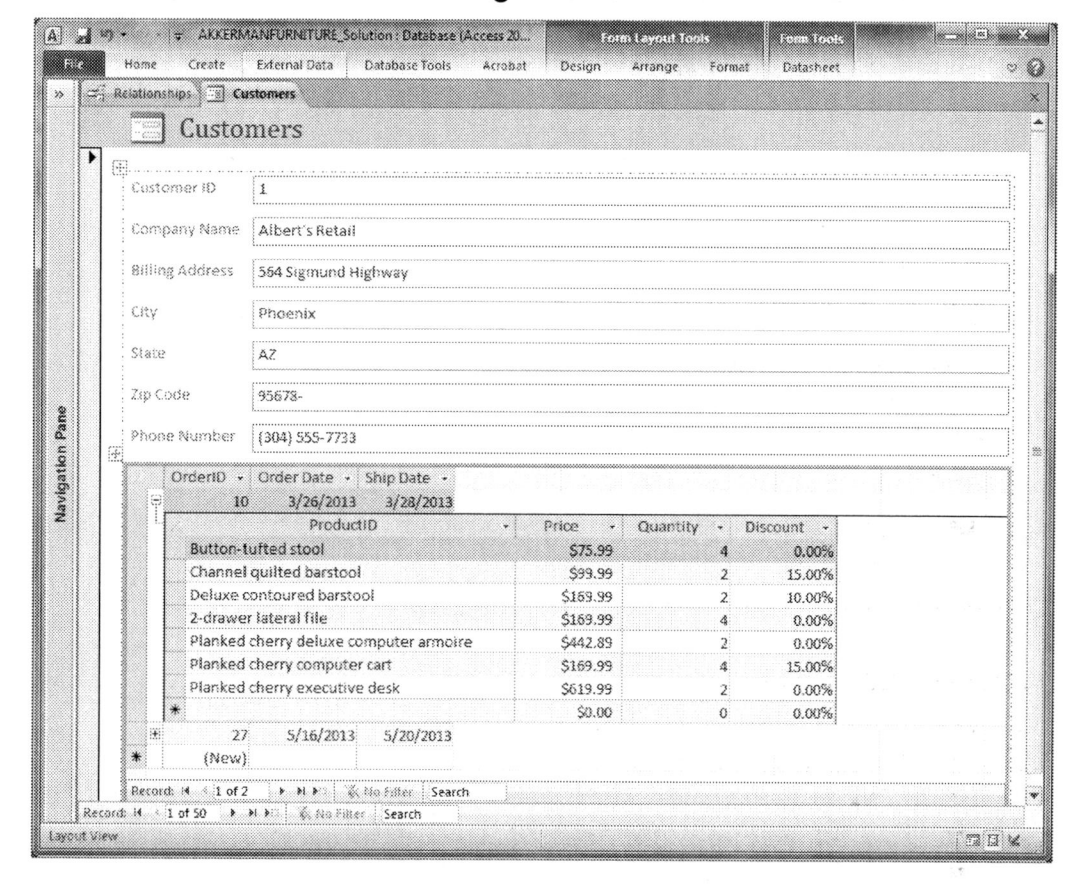

Figure 5-45

prompts you to name the new table and specify the database in which to save it. Make-table queries are used to isolate records for export to other databases and to create history tables to store old records. They are also used to create time-specific record sources for reports.

Delete Queries

Delete queries are action queries that remove records from a table according to some specified search criteria. Delete queries are created in the same way as other action queries. Begin by creating a select query, which contains field criteria, such as parameter statements for isolating the records targeted for deletion. **Warning:** *A delete query always deletes **entire** records, not just the contents of specific fields.*

On the Query Tools: Design tab, in the Query Type group, click the *Delete* button to turn the select query into a delete query. This adds a *Delete*: row to the design grid. Test the query without committing to execution by using the Datasheet View button to preview the targeted records. Execute the query by clicking the *Run* button on the Ribbon. **Warning**: *Delete queries cannot be undone, so test thoroughly before committing to Run.*

1. In the AKKERMANFURNITURE database, open the Create tab and click *Query Design*. Add the Orders and Order_Details tables to the Query Design window and close the Show Table dialog box.

2. Drag the * (all fields) symbol for the Order_Details table to the design grid.

3. Drag the CustomerID field from the Orders table to the second column in the design grid.

4. Drag the ShipDate field from the Orders table to the third column in the design grid.

5. Type *11* in the *Criteria* cell for the CustomerID field. This is the ID for a customer that has gone out of business.

6. Type *Is Null* in the *Criteria* cell for the Ship Date field. This command will delete all unshipped orders (those with a blank ship date).

7. Click the *Datasheet View* button to check that the correct records will be deleted. There is only one order with two products (Order_ID 24) for CustomerID 11 that has not yet shipped (see Figure 5-46).

8. Return to Design View and select *Delete* in the Query Type group on the Ribbon. The Sort and Show rows are replaced by the Delete row. Orders will be deleted **from** the Orders table **where** the CustomerID is 11 AND **where** the ShipDate field contains a null value, as shown in Figure 5-47. Run the query. A warning message asks you to confirm the deletion of two rows. Click *Yes*. Close the query. Save it as DeleteOrderQuery. Close the database.

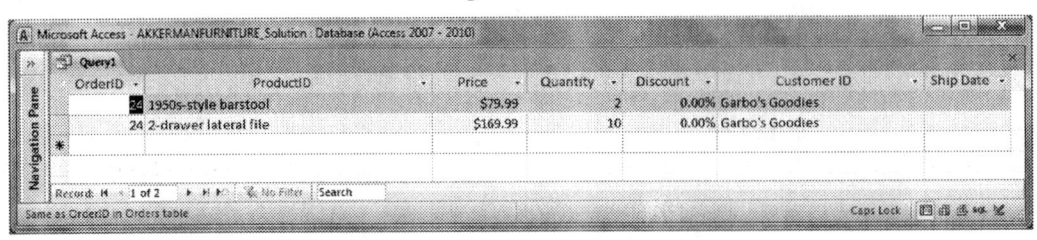

Figure 5-46

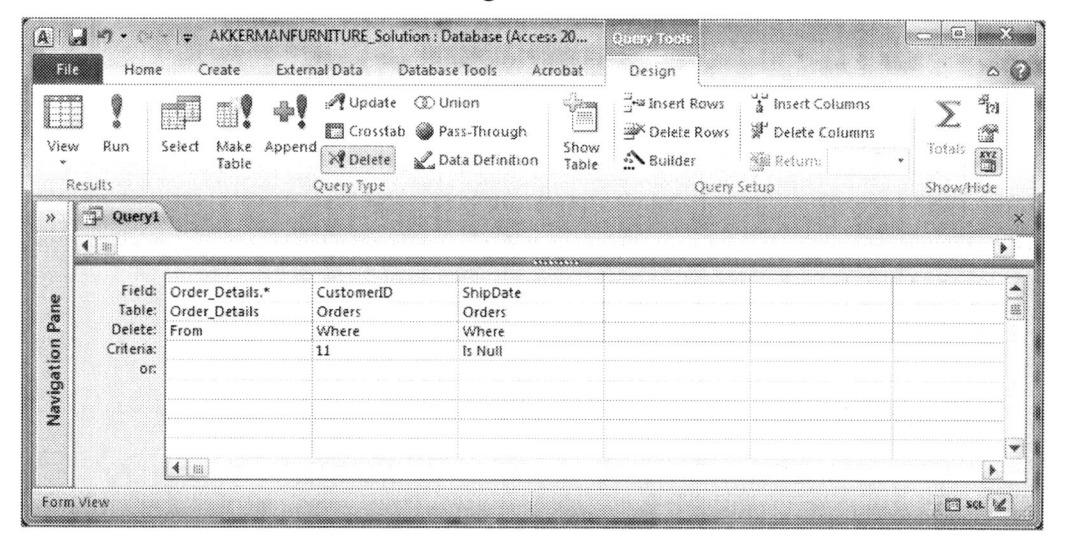

Figure 5-47

Functions in Access

A *function* in Access performs some sort of calculation on data and returns the result of that calculation. There are over 130 different functions available in Access. Functions can be used in macros or modules, in query expressions, or in calculated controls in forms or reports.

DateDiff

The *DateDiff* function is used to determine how many time intervals (e.g.: days, weeks, years) exist between two dates. In the following example, the DateDiff function is used to calculate the number of days between an Entry and Exit date

Type of Function	Name of Function	Calculation Performed
Date/Time	DateDiff	Number of time intervals between dates
Domain Aggregate	DLookup	Finds/Looks Up and displays a Value

at a parking garage. The result of this calculation is then multiplied by the Daily Parking Rate to give a total amount owed by the driver. Required syntax is exactly as shown.

The syntax is: DateDiff ("interval", date1, date2).

> DateDiff("d",[Entry_Date],[Exit_Date]*[Daily_Parking_Rate]

Or you could first create a field to store the days elapsed and enter the total charge in a separate field.

> Days Elapsed: DateDiff("d", ",[Entry_Date],[Exit_Date]
>
> Total Bill: [Days Elapsed]*[Daily_Parking_Rate]

The interval can be expressed in years (yyyy), quarters (q), months (m), weeks (ww), weekdays (w), days (d), hours (h), minutes (n), or seconds (s). This is the interval of time used to calculate the difference.

The DateDiff function can be used in an Update action query, first to determine an interval of, for example, a number of weeks, and then to multiply a charge per week by the number of weeks to calculate the appropriate bill.

DLookup

DLookup returns a field value from a domain (a specific set of records as defined by a table or query). The syntax is: DLookup (expr, domain, [criteria]).The three items are enclosed in parentheses. They are: the field you want to look up (expression), the table or query in which that field resides (domain), and the conditions under which the field should be looked up. This is the same as the WHERE clause in an SQL statement. Entering criteria is optional; it is used when you need to restrict the data returned by the DLookup function. Each of the arguments must be enclosed in quotation marks and separated by commas. As usual, square brackets must surround any field or table names that include spaces, start with a number, or contain any odd characters such as the number sign (#).

The following example looks up the LastName field in the Employees table where the Employee ID is 18

> =DLookup("[LastName]", "Employees", "[EmployeeID] = 18")

The following example first looks up the Tax Rate in a table called *Personnel* where data in the *Skill* field of a table called *Staff* matches data in the Skill field of the

Personnel table. The appropriate *Tax Rate* is then added to the Tax Rate field in the Personnel table. Required syntax is exactly as shown.

=DLookup ("[Tax Rate]", "Personnel", "[Skill]![Staff]=[Skill]![Personnel]")

More about Macros

Macro Action	What It Does
CloseWindow	Closes the current active window
Echo	Hides or shows the result of a macro while it runs
MessageBox	Displays a message box with informational or warning text
OpenForm	Opens a specified Form object
OpenQuery	Opens a select query and/or runs an action query
BrowseTo	Replaces an existing subform control with the object designated in the action arguments. You enter the type of replacement control in the Object Type argument, the name of the object in the Object Name argument, and the path to the subform control in the Path To Subform Control argument. There must be a period between the name of the main form and the name of the subform.
OpenReport	Opens a specified Report object
Set Value	Sets the value for a control field or property on a form or report Note: Make sure the Show All Actions button in the Show/Hide group on the Macro Tools: Design Ribbon is selected.
Set Warnings	Turns off all system messages such as warnings while a macro is running. Note: Make sure the Show All Actions button in the Show/Hide group on the Macro Tools: Design Ribbon is selected.

Database Case 9
SoundSpeed Audio II

Problem:	Create a complete system
Management skill:	Control Organize
Access Skills:	Forms Macros Advanced Queries (Union)
Data Tables:	SOUNDSPEED_A SOUNDSPEED_B SOUNDSPEED_C

This case is a continuation of Solve it! Database Case 6. Refer to this case for background information. We recommend that you make a copy of the Case 6 files and save them as Case 9 before starting this case.

Alessandra was feeling very pleased with herself as she gazed out of her office window at the busy Hoboken street. She had just finished her perusal of SoundSpeed Audio Arcanum's financial performance figures for the 2011-2012 year. Her mail order music company had performed stunningly last year, with sales improving by nearly 25%. Alessandra had also noticed that the costs associated with postage and packaging of her mail order catalogs, as well as the maintenance of her mailing list, had dropped significantly.

Alessandra believed that these results were largely due to the ability of the PC-based database mailing system her company had developed to provide carefully targeted mail-outs for her various customer segments. Previously, Alessandra had relied on blanket mail-outs to all of the customers on her mailing list whenever she wanted to advertise new product offerings. Thanks to her new mailing system, her company is now able to tailor its mailings so that catalogs are sent out only to customers with interests in the music areas relevant to her new products.

Alessandra now wants to complete the development of her new system by adding some enhancements and new features. She has jotted down her main requirements.

    a. A system that is easy to use

The new system has worked well, but it requires a thorough understanding of the database package in which it had been created to operate effectively. Alessandra is the only one who knows how the system works and what it does, and she currently maintains the system herself. She does not regard this as a productive way to spend her time, and now she wants to pass over the operation and day-to-day maintenance of the system to her clerical staff.

As it stands, Alessandra must remember which query did what and which report gave her the result formats she wanted. The system is efficient, but it is not the kind of product she wants in the hands of untrained people. What she needs is a more user-friendly version of the system.

Alessandra's objective is to produce a self-contained mailing system that can be operated by someone with little or no database knowledge. The system must be menu-driven and modular in design. The menu should also execute automatically when the user opens the database that contains the system (i.e.: the .ACCDB file). When a task option is selected from the menu, the menu will open the required object and then execute that option. Each option should contain a facility to exit back to the menu.

b. Integrate the SoundSpeed Audio Arcanum mailing list with that of SoundSpeed Audio Lab

Alessandra suspects that at least 25% of the customers on her mailing list are also customers who regularly purchase from SoundSpeed Audio Lab, her sister's side of the business (refer back to Case 6). While the marketing side of Audio Lab has been handled by a PC-based database package for some time, the system is not menu-driven and requires someone with a good understanding of databases to operate it. Alessandra and her sister Valentina would like to combine their mailing lists under one menu-based system. They have agreed that while information unique to each of the businesses will be maintained separately, the names and addresses will be shared. Although the two divisions do business with many of the same organizations, SoundSpeed Arcanum's customer contact names may often be different than the ones used by SoundSpeed Audio Lab.

Alessandra D'Argenio would like to test how well this procedure will work. Valentina has provided her with a sample listing of Audio Lab' customer names. This is provided on the *Solve It!* data table SOUNDSPEED_C. Alessandra wants to combine this file with her own listing (SOUNDSPEED_A). The result of this procedure should show no duplicate records. The combined listings will then be incorporated into a menu option on the new system.

234 Solve it!

Alessandra needs your help. She does not have the time or expertise needed to create the menu-driven mailing system required, and she would like you to develop a prototype. Part of the job was completed in *Solve It!* database Case 6, and you will need to use the database used in that previous case to complete Case 10.

Tasks

There are six tasks in this case.

1. Create a Main Menu form (that you will call MAIN MENU) and appropriate command buttons, which allow the user the following executable options:

   a. Add a new customer

   b. Add a new company

   c. Produce a complete mailing list

   d. Exit the system

   > **Hint:** Insert command buttons without the Control Wizards activated on the Main Menu form for the first three options. These options will not initially be active. Use the Command Button Wizard to set up an active Exit procedure for option four.

2. Create data entry forms for command buttons 1 and 2. Include Exit and Add New Record command buttons and test them thoroughly. Call these forms ADD CUSTOMER and ADD COMPANY.

3. Devise a procedure that will automatically execute the Main Menu whenever the database is opened.

4. Create a procedure that will combine the customer name tables of SoundSpeed Audio Arcanum (SOUNDSPEED_A) and SoundSpeed Audio Lab (SOUNDSPEED_C). There are a number of names that appear in both tables. Your goal is to produce a listing that contains no duplicate records.

   > **Hint:** Use a Union query to complete this task.

The combined file should then be joined to the SOUNDSPEED_B table to give a full listing of the customers and their organizational details. This task can be accomplished with a Select query.

5. Create a report to display results for Task 4. The report should be sorted first by organization, and then by last name. Incorporate this report as Option 3 on the Main Menu form.

> **Hint:** Use the existing report created for Tasks 2 and 3 of Case 6 (Marketing Report), and simply change the record source for the report to the TASK4B query. Also, change the title and the name for the report to Full Mailing List (both the Caption property for the report and the Caption property for the title label.) Save the report with the new name: Full Mailing List.

6.* Extend the system even further to include the sales and number of sound recordings sold to each customer. Add the necessary fields and some sample data to the appropriate table. Then add a new option to the menu that will calculate and display the total sales for SoundSpeed Audio Arcanum and the average price per recording.

Time Estimates (excluding tasks marked with *):
Expert: 2 hours
Intermediate: 3 hours
Novice: 5 hours

Tutorial for Database Case 9 Using Access 2010

Advanced Queries: The SQL-Specific Query

SQL (Structured Query Language) is a simple programming language used for querying, updating, and managing relational databases. When you create a select query or action query, Access automatically generates the equivalent SQL statement in the background. You can view or edit the SQL statement by choosing *SQL View* on the *View* button menu.

Other Access query types included in the Query Type group on the Query Tools: Design tab on the Ribbon include:

- *Union:* Queries that combine fields from two or more tables or queries
- *Pass-Through:* Queries that send commands directly to a database server

- *Data-Definition:* Queries used to create or alter database tables in the current database

A **subquery** is an SQL SELECT statement nested inside another SQL statement. The main SQL statement can be a select or action query. SQL statements refer to expressions that define SQL commands, such as a SELECT, UPDATE, DELETE, INSERT...INTO (Append) or SELECT...INTO (Make-Table) statement. They can include clauses, such as WHERE, GROUP BY, HAVING, and ORDER BY. SQL statements are used to construct queries and aggregate functions. Subqueries are used to limit the amount of data returned by a query, often by nesting the subquery in either the WHERE or HAVING clause.

The Union Query

You must use the Union SQL-Specific query type as part of the requirement for completing Task 4 of Case 9. You can use Union queries to combine the result sets of two or more Select queries into a single result set. You can also create Union queries that combine rows in two tables.

Using simple *SELECT ... FROM* SQL statements, *Union queries* enable you to combine fields from two or more tables into one listing. In contrast, *Select queries*, which are based on a join, create a dynaset only from those records whose related fields meet a specified condition. Commands and clauses commonly used in the creation of Union queries include:

- **SELECT** fieldlist
- **FROM** tablenames **IN** database name
- **WHERE** search conditions
- **GROUP** BY fieldlist
- **HAVING** search conditions
- **ORDER** BY fieldlist

Creating a Union Query

1. Create a new empty database named LAWNENFORCEMENT and import the LandscapingCustomers, Landscaping Orders, LandscapingOrderDetails, LandscapingServices, LandscapingServicesCategories and Landscaping Suppliers tables from the SOLVEIT_CH5 database into it.

2. Open the Create tab and click *Query Design* to open the Query Design View window, but do not add any field lists to the design grid. Union queries do not use the query design grid for their construction. Close the Show Table dialog box.

3. Click *Union* on the Query Tools: Design tab in the Query Type group. Access displays the Union Query window into which you type the appropriate SQL SELECT *statements* needed for your Union query.

   For this query, you will create a simple Union query that will combine rows from two tables. The SQL statement will select the records of all customers and suppliers who live in the state of Texas. Type the following (See Figure 5-48):

   SELECT LastName, Street, City, State, Zip, PhoneNumber, CustomerID

   FROM LandscapingCustomers

   WHERE State ="TX"

   UNION SELECT CompanyName, Address, City, State, Zip, Phone, Supplier_ID

   FROM LandscapingSuppliers

   WHERE State ="TX"

Figure 5-48

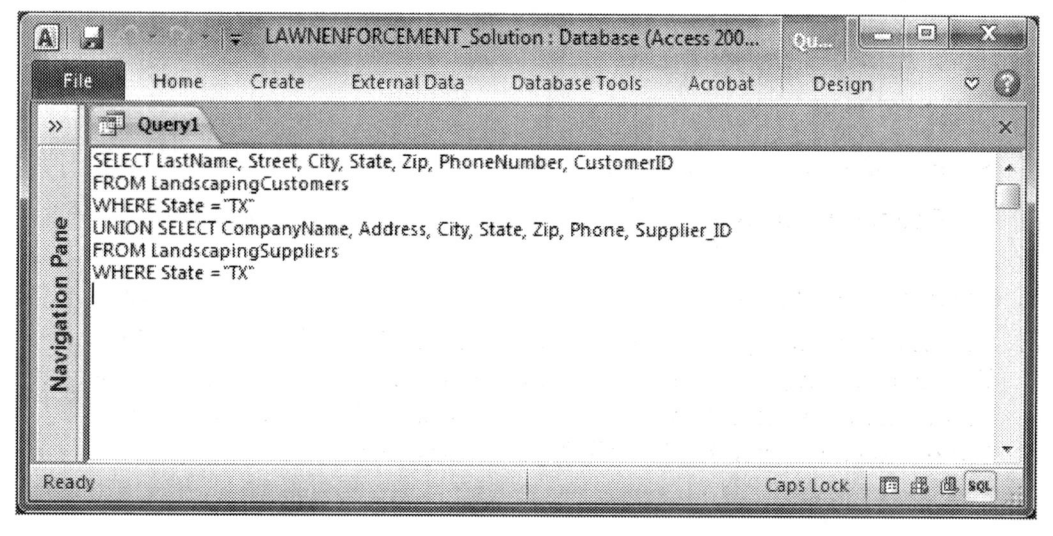

4. Click the *Run* button. The query result set is shown in Figure 5-49. Save the query as *Tute9UnionQuery* and close it. Close the database.

The number of fields in the field list of each Select and Union Select query must be the same. You will receive an error message if the number of fields differs.

The sequence of the field names in each field list must also correspond to the similar entity in the other field list. You will not receive an error message, but the result set may be incoherent.

Commas are used to separate members of lists of parameters, such as multiple field names as in the example.

Square brackets are required only around field names that include a space or other symbols, including punctuation. Field names that use an underscore to create a space between words do not require a square bracket. If fields from more than one table are included in a query, a period must separate the table name and the field name (e.g. Suppliers.[Company Name]).

Here are some other examples of SQL statements:

To retrieve the names and cities of suppliers and customers from the Suppliers and Customers tables:

> SELECT [Supplier Name], [City]
>
> FROM Suppliers
>
> UNION SELECT [Customer Name], [City]
>
> FROM Customers;

Figure 5-49

LastName	Street	City	State	Zip	PhoneNumber	CustomerID
Collins	449 Roaring Brook Blvd.	Arlington	TX	76001-1234	(214) 555-3928	33
Pardman	364 E.56th St.	Arlington	TX	76001-2378	(214) 555-4065	71
PlantDelight	2678 Investment Loop	Hutto	TX	78634-0000	(512) 759-6830	5
Rodriguez	56 Laurel Rd.	Hutto	TX	78634-0000	(512) 555-4912	25
Sellingham	122 7th Ave.	Austin	TX	73344-1122	(512) 555-5609	69
Vukovich	108 Smith Ave.	Hutto	TX	78634-0000	(512) 555-8410	44
Zamore	1062 Bowery	Austin	TX	73344-112	(512) 555-4907	95

To retrieve the names and cities of suppliers and customers located in Brazil, sorted by the City field:

```
SELECT [Supplier Name], [City]
FROM Suppliers
WHERE [Country] = "Brazil"
UNION SELECT [Customer Name], [City]
FROM Customers
WHERE [Country] = "Brazil"
ORDER BY [City]
```

> **Note:** Unless you specify otherwise, a Union query automatically removes duplicate records from the result set. If you want to show all records, including duplicates, add the word ALL after the word UNION in your statement. For example:

To retrieve the names and cities of suppliers and customers from the Suppliers and Customers tables, and show all records including duplicates:

```
SELECT [Supplier Name], [City]
FROM Suppliers
UNION ALL SELECT [Customer Name], [City]
FROM Customers
```

Task 1 of Case 9 requires you to create a merged file of the customer records of SoundSpeed Audio Arcanum and SoundSpeed Audio Lab. Contrast the difference between omitting and including ALL in the Union query you create to complete this task.

> **Warning:** Do not convert an SQL-specific query to another type of query, such as a Select query. If you do, you'll lose the SQL statement that you entered. You can, however, use an SQL-specific query as part of a Select query.

Creating an AutoExec Macro

You can create a special macro that automatically runs whenever you open a Microsoft Access database. For example, you may wish to open certain tables and forms every time you open a database.

To create a macro that runs whenever you open a database:

1. Create a macro.
2. Add the actions that you want this macro to perform.
3. Save the macro. **Its name must be AutoExec**.

AutoExec macros can be used to create a custom workspace, import data from other databases, or execute tasks that you want to perform every time the database is opened. To prevent the AutoExec macro from running, hold down the *Shift* key while opening the database.

Setting Startup Options

You can easily control many aspects of how an Access database looks and behaves when it opens without writing a macro or any Visual Basic code. You can set startup options to give your database a title and/or to program Access to open a particular form first when a user opens the database. Click the File tab and click *Options* to open the Access Options window. Select *Current Database* in the left pane to open the options for the current database. Type the name you want for your application in the *Application Title* text box. Click the list arrow on the Display Form list box and select the form you want to open first.

Other startup options include using a custom application icon and choosing whether or not to display the Status bar. You can also decide if you want full menus to display in the database and whether or not you want users to be able to make changes to the menus or toolbars. Make sure that any actions in an AutoExec macro do not change the effect of the startup option settings.

Database Case 10

Rio Rancho Trading Co.

Problem:	Develop a comprehensive database for use with an e-commerce website
Management Skill:	Plan Coordinate Control Organize
Access Skills:	Creating a Database Creating tables Creating relationships Creating and running queries
Data Source:	RIORANCHO.xlsx

Jessica Moore is facing one of the biggest decisions in company history: whether to take her successful trading post business, Rio Rancho Trading Co., online. Moore knows from others in the trading post business that success locally does not automatically mean success online. In fact, a few of her competitors lost significant amounts of money in their online ventures and had to declare bankruptcy. Moore wants to explore the issue fully before committing significant resources.

Rio Rancho Trading Co. was founded in 1990 by Jessica's father, Wesley Moore, in Rio Rancho, New Mexico. The company started by selling high quality handcrafted jewelry. It has since grown to offering a wide range of Native American crafts including baskets, pottery, beadwork, sand paintings, fetish carvings, and kachina dolls. The company takes pride in the fact that it still offers high quality traditional hand-crafted goods at affordable prices and has established a loyal customer base that produces more than 1 million orders annually. Jessica Moore has recently taken over the company after her father's retirement and is reviewing the company's operations and financial position.

Rio Rancho Trading sends out catalogs to customers quarterly and occasionally mails out a special sale catalog when higher-than-normal levels of inventory warrant it. The time between selecting items for the catalog, producing the publication, and printing it, and the time when customers actually receive it is four to six months; this requires significant planning throughout the entire company to ensure that proper inventory levels are maintained during the period in which the catalog is active.

Moore has been considering an online e-commerce presence for the company for more than a year. She decided to start with an informational site to assess the level of interest a Rio Rancho Trading site would generate. To date, the site has received a great deal of positive feedback, but site visitors are becoming increasingly frustrated that it does not support online ordering.

A well-designed and executed e-commerce site could save the company money in the long run through the automated processes (ordering, inventory control, and shipping) that would be embedded in the site. However, there would be a substantial initial investment for the site: hardware and software to host and maintain it, design and maintenance of the site itself, training for staff on the new processes, and advertising to draw traffic to the site. Moore wants to know if this investment will pay off and how it will impact the company.

Moore has met with the heads of the marketing, sales, customer service, product development, inventory control, human resources, and shipping departments to discuss how they currently process information. She has discovered that the data entry process in each department is mostly manual in nature. Employees enter information into Excel spreadsheets designed specifically for that department. There is significant redundancy in the data entry process across the company. For example, the product development department establishes the product ID number and product description for an item when they finalize it for the catalog. They create a spreadsheet with all this information. The customer service department must enter all of the product ID numbers and descriptions into their spreadsheet to correspond to orders they have taken. Moore wants to eliminate this redundancy.

Last week, Moore met with Naalnish Montoya, a web developer who runs his own company, Los Alamos Tech. Montoya's specialty is e-commerce sites with database back ends, which means he designs websites that allow the information gathered on the site to be merged into a database. Montoya also designs the databases that support his sites. This is an extremely efficient way to process information from a website because the data only has to be entered through a form on the site once by the customer, and then it can be accessed and queried in a variety of different ways by the company. Montoya has designed a prototype website for Rio Rancho Trading that includes an online catalog and shopping basket so that users of the site can purchase items online. Users will submit their orders through a form on the site and the information from those orders will be merged into an Access database Montoya will design for the company.

Montoya has asked Moore to provide him with representative data from each of the departments involved so he can design the database. Moore's assistant, David Ferrer, has compiled this information into one Excel spreadsheet and has given it to Moore for this meeting. Moore would like to see the following before she decides how extensive the shopping cart portion of the site will be:

- How the database will be divided into tables
- How the database will reduce or eliminate redundancy of order entry

Tasks

There are three tasks in this case:

1. The employee, product, customer, and sales data that Ferrer has gathered is provided for you in RIORANCHO.xlsx. Determine how the data should be divided into tables to create the least amount of redundancy possible. Create a database named RIO_RANCHO and import the tables (name the tables after the function represented (orders, employees, products, customers, for example). Save this database.

2. Establish the relationships between the tables so that you can easily create queries from the tables.

3. Moore wants to do a test query to see how the data can be manipulated. She wants to know how often the 8 inch x 6 inch beaded purse (product ID # 20010) is ordered. Create a query that determines this information. Save this query as Case10Query1.

Time Estimates:

Expert: 1.5 hours
Intermediate: 2 hour
Novice: 2.5 hours

Tutorial for Case 10 Using Access 2010

There is no tutorial for Case 10. It draws upon the knowledge and skills you have acquired in previous cases and tutorials. The following lists the required skills for this case and the tutorials in which they were covered:

Creating Databases	Chapter 4
Creating Tables	Chapter 4, Chapter 5 (Case 1)
Joining Tables/Relationships	Chapter 5 (Case 6)
Creating and Running a Query	Chapter 5 (Case 1, Case 3)

Database Case 11
Rio Rancho Trading Co. II

Problem:	Obtain information from the completed database created in Database Case 10.
Management Skill:	Plan Coordinate Control
Access Skills:	Creating and printing reports Creating and utilizing forms Creating and running macros
Database:	RIORANCHO.accdb

This case is a continuation of Solve it! Database Case 10. Refer to this case for background information relating to Case 11. You will be using the database you created in Case 10 for this case.

Nine months ago, Jessica Moore made the decision to create an online e-commerce presence for her company, Rio Rancho Trading Co. The new website has received positive reviews from users and seems to be attracting new customers. Moore decided to spend extra money on the database back end for the site so that data entry would be more efficient. She feels it is working, but knows that it can be more efficient and provide more information than the original design is supplying.

Moore initially met with the heads of the departments that would be affected by the implementation of the website: Hector Moreno from Sales, Ryan Asennase from Product Development, Olivia Cross River from Customer Service, Susan McBride from Order Fulfillment, and Noah Solomon from Human Resources. They each gave Moore an outline of the data they collect and the ways in which they use it. Naalnish Montoya then designed the website and database to solicit the information from customers when they ordered.

The transition from the manual system Rio Rancho Trading had been using to the new automated system was not easy. It took hours of work to create the database that holds all of the information. Employees had to be trained in the new processes and systems. There were numerous test orders entered into the website to make sure all pertinent data was collected, and then queries, forms, and reports were created to make sure all departments' data needs were met.

Moore is now ready to test the new website with a system-wide evaluation. The following tasks will help her do so:

Tasks

There are six tasks in this case:

1. Design and create a report that details the total number and dollar amount of orders taken by each employee.

2. Noah Solomon from Human Resources wants to evaluate how employees hired after 2009 are doing in terms of productivity. Produce and print a report for him that details orders taken by employees hired after the year 2009. Note: Date values must be surrounded with the # character so that Access can distinguish between date values and text strings.

3. Ryan Asennase would like a form his employees can use to enter new products into the system. Design and create a form that will allow Product Development employees to enter Product ID, Product Name, Product Description, Cost, and Selling Price easily and efficiently. Name the form PRODUCTS.

4. Asennase would also like anyone in the company to be able to quickly locate information about products. Design and create a form using command buttons that allows employees to look up products individually by Product ID number. Label the button *Find Product*. Include an Exit button.

5. Hector Moreno would like to target customers who have bought specific products when sales of the same or related products are offered. Create a form with a subform that lists Product ID number, Product Name, and Product Description in the main form and Customer ID, Last Name, First Name, and Date Ordered in the subform.

6. Jessica Moore has requested that she receive an annual report that details orders by zip code. Susan McBride would like to automate this report so that she can run it very quickly each month. Design and create a macro that will open a report that lists and sums orders by zip code for each month. Hint: You can use the BETWEEN…AND operator to run the report each month. For example, BETWEEN #12/31/2011# AND #1/30/2012# will filter out the records for the month of January 2012. To create a parameter query that

prompts the user for two dates to define a range, enter BETWEEN [Enter the beginning date] AND [Enter the ending date] in the Criteria cell for the date field.

Tutorial for Case 11 Using Access 2010

There is no tutorial for Case 11. It draws upon the knowledge and skills you have acquired in previous cases and tutorials. The following lists the skills required for this case and the tutorials in which they were covered:

Creating and Printing Reports	Chapter 5 (Case 2, Case 4)
Creating Forms	Chapter 5 (Case 8, Case 9)
Creating and Running Macros	Chapter 5 (Case 8)

6

Internet Cases

Web Case 1
JumpSpot.com Web Portal

Problem:	Prepare a report on Web portal technology
	Calculate the return on investment for a portal project.
Management skills:	Planning
	Deciding
Web skills:	Business research
File:	JUMPSPOT_Q.xlsx

JumpSpot.com started as a simple search engine in 1996. Today it provides a wide range of travel, entertainment, and financial services, as well as in-depth content on sports, medical issues, and news in an effort to find a wider audience and keep visitors at its site for longer periods of time. The longer visitors can be induced to stay at the site, the greater the revenue potential for JumpSpot. Companies and individuals now use JumpSpot to find low-cost airline fares, discounted hotel rates, rental car deals, and related travel information. Individuals often use the site to research entertainment packages at popular tourist destinations and find financial information about companies for stock picks. Using JumpSpot's unique reservation system, registered site users can make airline reservations and purchase tickets, rent hotel rooms, reserve cars, buy entertainment packages, and make other travel arrangements all in one Web site visit.

Since JumpSpot has grown from fifteen employees providing a simple search service to a Web portal with 450 employees providing many services, the management team has become overwhelmed with information. The small management team must keep track of various Web activities at its site, including the number of visitors, sales for each of its services, and results of promotional campaigns, as well as weekly and monthly cost reports.

And although they are a Web services company, managers are overloaded with paper-based reports. Different managers need different types of reports, and each report requires data that the IT Department must provide on a routine basis. With so many employees, there is a growing demand for information on training, pensions, and benefits. As the customer base has expanded, it has become increasingly difficult to respond to customers seeking help with JumpSpot's various service offerings or deal with customer complaints.

As a result, the costs of managing the firm have skyrocketed despite a long-term effort to keep the management head-count down.

CEO Charles Alonso wants to move the firm toward a more uniform information management environment, one that would be more efficient, provide better service to customers, impart employees with more information on company activities and programs, and offer managers a coherent online information environment. He is considering the development of an internal Web portal as a tool for organizing and accessing the company's critical management information.

A corporate portal is an internal Web site running on a corporate intranet that organizes and distributes important management information for decision-makers, as well as general corporate information required by all employees. Portals provide a single point of access and a delivery vehicle for important corporate information. Users can customize and personalize the content they see to focus on just those pieces of information they require to do their jobs. Portals can also be configured to call information from a variety of back-office legacy systems and present it to users in an easy-to-use Web environment.

Although the JumpSpot technical development team could build such a corporate portal, this is not one of their core competencies, and Alonso does not want to pull the technical team off more valuable Web site development work. Therefore Alonso is planning to purchase an off-the-shelf Web portal service from a firm that specializes in this technology.

Alonso has given the job of designing and developing a successful corporate portal project to CIO Erika Landers. Landers supports the idea of purchasing a corporate portal from an outside firm that has experience with this technology rather than building it in-house. She needs some help identifying vendors in this area and acquiring background information on costs and benefits. As Landers' executive assistant, your first assignment is to use the Web to research corporate portal vendors and develop a report for the portal project.

Tasks

There are three tasks in this case.

1. Use a search engine such as Google.com or Yahoo.com to find three Web sites of companies that sell corporate portal technology. Prepare a short report (3-5 pages) or PowerPoint presentation (5-7 slides) describing the features of corporate portals, their benefits, and costs. Many sites will include case studies of "success" stories. Be sure to include at least one successful case in your report. Include a section in your report or presentation that describes some of the potential risks and pitfalls of using this technology.

2. Landers has provided you with some initial estimates of the costs and benefits of the new portal for the next three years. These estimates are provided in the accompanying spreadsheet JUMPSPOT_Q.xlsx. He would like your help in analyzing the results.

    Calculate the following:

    a. Total projected costs for each year, and the total costs for all years

    b. Total projected benefits for each year, and the total benefits for all years

    c. Depreciation: Assume a straight line depreciation over three years.

    d. Annual net benefits (nominal) for each year (benefits-costs for each year)

    e. Cumulative payback (nominal)

    f. The accounting rate of return for the next three years; the accounting rate of return (ARR) is defined as:

    $$ARR = \frac{(\text{total benefits} - \text{total costs} - \text{depreciation})/\text{useful life}}{\text{total costs}}$$

    We will assume in this problem that the useful life of the portal is three years, the depreciation is equal for each year, and at the end of the period, the portal has no salvage value (the value is zero after three years).

g. Prepare a brief statement arguing for or against this investment by the firm.

3. Calculate the net present value of the investment in the portal technology. Assume a prime interest rate of 5%. You must calculate the present value of the annual net benefits.

> **Hint:** Use Excel's NPV function to do this. The net present value is defined as the present value of annual net benefits minus the total investment cost.

4. On the basis of your results, do you recommend this investment? Write a paragraph describing the benefit of this investment for the firm.

Tutorial for Web Case 1

Search Engines on the Web

Search engines are software programs that help people find information stored in computer systems, including the Web. Users enter a word or phrase or other argument (such as a telephone number or zip code) into the search engine, and it returns to the user a list of references to the location of content which meets the search criteria. The list is typically sorted by relevance and/or popularity, which can be determined by the use of software algorithms or human editors, or some combination of these. From the list of references users can navigate to the actual content which is typically in the form of documents. The most common search engines are those which are used to search the public Web, but the same software can be used to search your own computer, or a corporation's library of documents stored on a private intranet. Though there are hundreds of search engines available for use on the Web, most of them free, the search sites listed below account for more than 95% of U.S. search activity (source: ComScore.com, 2012).

Continuing search technology improvements as well as industry consolidation and shared indexing technologies among the search sites make it difficult to predict which the "best" or "most comprehensive" search site is at any particular time. Different search engines produce some differences in results, especially for very specialized search topics. Researchers have found, for instance, that there is about a 60% overlap among search engines. Nevertheless, this also suggests that 40% of the pages found on one search engine will not be found on another search engine even when using the same search argument. Repeating a search on multiple

Top Three Search Sites

Google	www.google.com
Yahoo	yahoo.com
Bing (Microsoft)	www.bing.com

Other Popular Search Sites

Ask.com	www.ask.com
AOL	www.aol.com

Multi-Site Search Engines

Excite	www.excite.com
Web Crawler	www.webcrawler.com
DogPile	www.dogpile.com

sites is not only a good technique, but will also provide ideas for refining your search.

Search engines typically produce very large lists of search results. Therefore, be careful to narrow your search arguments. For instance, if searching for information on security alarms, narrow your search by specifying "home," "business," "boat," or "automobile." What type of security alarm are you really looking for? If you are really looking for a wireless car alarm that will sound an audible alarm and then send a radio signal to your beeper, your search argument on a keyword search engine should be something like "security alarm and automobile and wireless." A good search approach is to enter the minimum number of words which uniquely refer to information you want, then—if necessary—add additional words to further limit the search.

The most widely used search engine is Google which at one point claimed to index over 6 billion Web pages. Google uses a combination of techniques, including Web crawlers and proprietary relevancy algorithms. As of late 2006, Google stopped publishing a claimed number of pages indexed, stating that freshness and relevance were of more importance to searchers. In any case, pages-indexed claims must be viewed skeptically because of the impact of duplicate pages, link-only pages, and other Web anomalies.

Understanding the Financial Value of Information Systems

Businesses invest in information technology applications for a variety of reasons. In some cases, the investment is undertaken to achieve growth in market share, in other cases, it is simply as a requirement for staying in business, and in still other cases, it is undertaken to achieve a return on invested capital. Sometimes all three motivations are important. Whatever the reason for investment, most businesses will perform a financial returns analysis. The two most common financial return calculations are the accounting rate of return (ROI) and net present value analysis.

Accounting Rate of Return

The accounting rate of return is defined as:

$$ARR = \frac{(\text{total benefits} - \text{total costs} - \text{depreciation})/\text{useful life}}{\text{total costs}}$$

For instance, in the example below, the total benefits of an investment over four years are $450,000, total costs are $100,000, and depreciation of the investment is $50,000. The useful life is four years in this example. Using the formula above, the accounting rate of return is 75% over the life of the project.

Total benefits	$ 450,000
Total costs	$ 100,000
Depreciation	$ 50,000
Useful life	4 years
ROI=	75%

Net Present Value Analysis

The accounting rate of return does not take into account the time value of money, and the fact that the benefits you receive in future years will be worth less than their nominal or face value because of the opportunity cost of money and inflation. For instance, if I promise to pay you back $15 one year from now in return for a $10 loan from you to me today, you would have to take into account at least two facts: (1) you will lose the $10 you loan me for one year and give up the interest you could have earned in a bank, and (2) inflation will erode the value of money, so the $15 I pay you next year will be worth less because of inflation.

In net present value (NPV) analysis, you must first understand the value in today's dollars of a future set of payments (this value is called "the present value"). In net present value analysis, both the opportunity cost of an investment and the inflation factor are summed up and taken into account by the use of a "prime rate" or other bank rate to deflate the value of future payments.

The net present value is defined as:

NPV = Present value of total annual benefits − total investment cost

In Excel, you use the net present value function (NPV) to calculate the present value of total future annual benefits. Unfortunately, the Excel NPV function is misnamed and does not give you a true net present value, but in fact returns the present value of a set of payments in the future. To calculate the net present value, take the present value of future payments and subtract the total initial investment (usually made in today's dollars).

In the spreadsheet below, there are future benefits of $100, $150, and $300 in the next three years. The initial investment is $300 made in the first year, and the interest rate is 6%. Is the investment worth it?

Year 1 benefits	$100
Year 2 benefits	$150
Year 3 benefits	$300
Total benefits	$550
Cost	$300
Interest rate	6.00%
Present value	$480
Net present value	$180

This investment is "worth it" because in today's dollars it has a net present value of greater than $0 and will return, in fact, $180 today's dollars in the future.

You can use the Function Wizard to calculate the Excel NPV function. Follow these steps:

1. Click on the cell in the spreadsheet where you want the NPV calculation to appear.
2. On the Formulas tab on the Ribbon, click the *Insert Function* button in the Function Library group or click the *Fx* button on the formula bar to open the Insert Function dialog box.
3. Select Financial functions.
4. Select the NPV function.
5. Fill in the wizard information for the interest rate and the values of the annual payments. You can also enter cell references for these values if you think they might change.
6. Click *OK*.

Web Case 2

PeoplePower.com

Problem:	Analyze the online job posting industry
Management skills:	Planning
	Deciding
Web skills:	Competitive intelligence
File:	PEOPLEPOWER_Q.xlsx

PeoplePower.com is a start-up venture founded by a group of human resources professionals who have decided they would rather be entrepreneurs than employees. CEO Christina Monteiro and CFO Greg Nguyen—the two main founders—have approached a West Coast venture-capital firm, Canopus Ventures, to provide start-up capital for the Web site. Canopus Ventures believes PeoplePower.com could be profitable if the financials worked out. Canopus is worried about the potential number of visitors, the competition from well-funded and established competitors, and potential operational costs.

The human resources officers who started PeoplePower.com have great track records in matching job candidates to open positions. Together the founding team of eight training instructors has a combined experience of more than 80 years in professional human resources. They feel confident they can leverage this knowledge into a successful online service business, and can differentiate it from its larger competitors by providing a cleaner and more targeted site and a more limited menu of service options than offered by the larger job posting sites. Despite this experienced management team, Canopus is cautious about investing in start-ups given the recent failures of so many dotcoms.

Canopus has requested that CEO Monteiro and CFO Nguyen do additional research on the financials of the online job posting business. Specifically, the investors want a better idea of the overall size of the online job posting market, and the principal competitors; the levels of traffic at the competing Web sites; and a better idea of what PeoplePower.com's budget would look like based on the experience of a similar firm. The management team at PeoplePower.com has asked you to develop the information requested by the investors.

258 Solve it!

Tasks

There are three tasks in this case.

1. Using a Web search engine, identify Web sites that have information about the leading firms in the online job posting industry. Build a spreadsheet of the top five most frequently visited Web sites. A sample spreadsheet has been started for you in PEOPLEPOWER_Q.xlsx. Sort the sites in terms of their unique visitors. In addition to visitors, find out how much revenue each of the top ten sites generates. Identify the major sources of revenue for online job posting sites, such as resume posting fees, advertising fees, and additional services. You may not be able to find this detailed information for all top five sites. Write a short report on your findings.

2. To understand the potential revenue and profit picture for the new company, the investors want you to look at a competitor's financial statements and calculate a series of standard financial ratios. Use Monster.com (Monster Worldwide, Inc.) as the competitor. As a public company, Monster is required by the 1934 Securities Act to report its financial results and all other material developments at the company to the Securities and Exchange Commission (SEC).

   Calculate the following ratios for Monster Worldwide Inc.:

   - Gross Margin (Gross profit /Total revenues)
   - Cost of revenues/Total revenues
   - Net Margin (Net income (or Net loss) /Total Revenues)
   - Sales and Marketing Expense/Total revenues
   - General and Administrative Expense/Total revenues

   Express all ratios as percentages, and copy the formulas to previous years so that you end up with ratios for three years' worth of experience.

3. Canopus also wants you to create a pro forma profit and loss statement for the start-up company. A pro forma profit and loss statement is used to project the amount of money the business should allocate to various activities. Assume the new company will have first year revenues of $17 million. Using the five ratios you calculated in Task 2, calculate how much PeoplePower.com must spend for product development, for sales and marketing, and for general and administrative costs, assuming total revenues of $17 million.

Tutorial for Web Case 2

This case assumes the reader has already mastered the use of search engines.

Using the EDGAR Database

EDGAR is major research tool for business and stock analysts as well as ordinary investors. EDGAR provides a treasure trove of information that companies are required to reveal to the public to ensure efficient and honest capital markets. Only companies that sell stock to the public report to EDGAR. There are many different types of annual, quarterly, and event-driven filings.

To look up a public company, go to www.sec.gov and click the *Search EDGAR for Company Filings* button. In the *Company or Fund Name* text box enter the company name *Monster Worldwide* and click the *Find Companies* button. Scroll down the list of search results and click the *Documents* button beside the most recent 10-K listing. On the list of documents that is displayed, click the *FORM 10-K* link.

Once you have the html version of the 10-K filing on screen, read the Introduction and Strategy sections of the report. Then locate the table labeled *STATEMENTS OF OPERATIONS*. This summary is also called the Income Statement.

Select with your mouse the entire table, from the heading *Monster Worldwide, Inc.* to the last line, *See accompanying notes*. Copy the data to the Clipboard (or use CTRL+C). Open Excel and paste the data into an Excel spreadsheet.

You will notice that the data you pasted spreads haphazardly across the worksheet and must be formatted for readability. In the worksheet, delete extra columns and rows as needed to format your categories and data in related groupings and create an attractive format. Delete extraneous formatting symbols and unneeded text. Delete columns containing previous years of data—you are interested only in the latest year's data. You may need to widen the columns, change font sizes and styling, to display all the information properly and legibly.

Select just the financial data and format it with the *Currency Style* button on the Ribbon (Home tab, Number group). Also in the Number group, use the *Decrease Decimal* button to delete the two decimal places. Save the workbook.

Display all financial ratios as percentages. In this case, you are only interested in the most recent year's data, so you can eliminate the information from earlier years.

Pro Forma Profit/Loss Statements (Income Statements)

A profit and loss statement (P&L) describes the total revenue and operating expenses of a firm. These statements are also called "Income statements." A "pro forma" P&L is a forecast based on best management judgment either for a new business or for a future year. Generally, a profit and loss statement has the following categories of revenue and expenditures (the starred items are calculated by the user and are not usually a part of the 10-K statement). Companies may present these categories using different terminology, and may combine or split out some categories; interpretation may be required to place the data into appropriate categories, especially when you are comparing the performance of multiple companies.

Category	Description
Revenue	
Net sales	Gross sales revenue minus any returns
Cost of sales	The cost of physical products or services
Gross profit	Sales revenue minus cost of goods
Gross Profit Margin	Gross profit divided by net sales (%)
Operating expenses	
Marketing and fulfillment	Marketing and advertising costs
Technology and content	Research and development costs
General and administrative	Administrative costs, mostly labor
Stock-based compensation	Options programs for employees
Amortization of goodwill and other intangibles	Costs associated with purchases of other companies for prices higher than their book value
Total operating expenses	Total operating costs
Gain/Loss from operations	Gross profit minus cost of operations
Net Margin	Gain/loss from operations divided by gross profit
Other Income/Expenses	
Interest income	Income from interest bearing accounts
Interest expense	Expenses for short term loans
Other income (expense), net	Miscellaneous income
Net Gain/Loss	Gross profit minus operating expenses and other incomes/losses

Web Case 3

Health Management Partners

Problem:	Research Internet security and privacy
Management skills:	Research analysis
	Decision-making
Web skills:	Business research

Health Management Partners (HMP) is a regional firm in Parkersburg, West Virginia, that administers health insurance and retirement plans for the employees of small to midsize businesses. HMP does not provide the services, but acts as an agent between businesses and healthcare providers and investment services.

HMP has achieved moderate success in its twenty-year history. The founders of the company believed that many businesses would prefer to outsource the legwork of researching and maintaining health and retirement plans rather than devote human resources personnel to this work. Their theory was correct. However, the growth of the Internet has allowed HMP to re-examine its services with an eye toward making the company even more successful.

Jodi Coronado, Director of Customer Service for HMP, has worked with the IT Department for several years to make the company's Web site as helpful to customers as it can be. However, until now, that is all the Web site has been: a source of information. In the near future, HMP will launch a new Web site that will allow customers to interact with their accounts online. Some of the new services will include enabling health insurance customers to submit requests for changing their primary care physician or for obtaining referrals. Retirement plan customers will be able to submit requests for changing their contribution amount or for adjusting the allocation of their investment to different funds.

Coronado realizes that this new venture carries a great deal of responsibility for the company. To make such transactions possible, customers will have to submit personal information, such as name, address, phone number, policy or account number, and Social Security number. For the new services to be successful, customers must feel secure in HMP's ability to protect their personal information. They also must trust that their personal information will not be used for undesirable purposes. Furthermore, HMP must consider their legal obligations regarding privacy as they pertain to the Internet.

Coronado has determined that she can use the Web to investigate the current state of federal legislation concerning Internet privacy. She will compile details about relevant active legislation in an Access database so that the company can use it as a guideline for designing the new site and setting policy. She will also expand her research on privacy, and prepare a report for the company's CIO that summarizes the advantages and disadvantages of existing and pending legislation to both the company and the consumer. The report will include legal proposals and the main trends in Internet privacy. Ultimately, Coronado will make a recommendation regarding the company's official response to the issue of Internet privacy.

Tasks

There are five tasks in this case:

1. Visit www.house.gov (The United States House of Representatives) and http://epic.org (Electronic Privacy Information Center) to find active bills on Internet privacy. The House site contains Bills & Reports search form, which allows you to search for bills by keywords or bill numbers. The EPIC site features news and events regarding current topics in privacy issues, such as body scanners at airports and the effects of cloud computing.

2. Use Microsoft Access to create a database of existing and pending legislation that is relevant to Internet privacy. The database fields you should use are law (or bill) number, law (or bill) name, proposing legislator (sponsor), and a brief summary of the law or bill. The summary field should use the Memo data type. Save the table.

3. Enter the relevant legislation data you have found on the Web in the database table.

   > **Note:** If you prefer, you may skip ahead to Task 4 and create the form first so you can use it to enter the data.

4. Once you have created the initial database table that organizes the data, create a form to facilitate entering additional data and a report for printing the data. Use all of the fields from the table in the form and in the report.

5. Prepare a report or presentation for the Chief Information Officer that summarizes the advantages and disadvantages of various privacy laws to both the company and the consumer. Also, include recent trends in privacy legislation and its application. Present the views of a pro-privacy organization that you find on the Web. Finally, conclude your report or presentation by making a recommendation about how the company should approach the issue of privacy in creating its new Web site.

Tutorial for Web Case 3

This case requires you to use the Web to conduct business research. The table below lists URLs that will help you complete the research tasks.

URL	Description
www.house.gov	United States House of Representatives
www.senate.gov	United States Senate
epic.org	Electronic Privacy Information Center
epic.org/privacy	EPIC Privacy page
www.cdt.org/privacy	Center for Democracy & Technology
thomas.loc.gov/home/c107query.html#keyword	Library of Congress bill search

Previous tutorials you may find useful for this case:
- Database Case 1
- Database Case 2
- Database Case 8

In this case, you are required to place data found on Web pages in an Access database table. You can transfer data by manually keying it into the table or using copy and paste techniques. To copy and paste data from a Web page into a database table, use the mouse to drag over the piece of data, such as a bill number or description, on the Web page. Once the piece of data is selected (highlighted in blue), use the Copy command on the Edit menu in the browser to copy the selection to the Clipboard. You can also use [Ctrl]+[C] to execute the copy command. Then switch to Access, click in the appropriate field, and use the Paste command on the Home tab of the Ribbon in Access, or [Ctrl]+[V] to paste the copied data.

Web Case 4
Blackmore Investments

Problem:	Prepare a financial analysis of two publicly held companies based on data from Web sources
Management skills:	Planning Deciding
Web skills:	Financial analysis

Blackmore Investments is a financial advising firm in Provo, Utah. Blackmore encourages clients to invest for long-term capital gains. Clients may call, visit, or use Blackmore's Web site to get advice about stocks they want to buy. Elaine Thao, who owns Thao Consulting, a firm that provides consulting services to restaurants, wants to invest in a specialty beverage company that provides exotic coffees and teas to specialty restaurants and coffee houses. Thao believes that the long-term market for restaurants that offer brand name specialty drinks such as coffee and tea is increasing, and that patrons will come to expect such items on the menus of restaurants around the nation.

But Thao knows very little about how to analyze potential specialty drink investments. She has retained Blackmore to do some financial research for her on two of the leading specialty drink companies in the United States: Starbucks Corporation and Green Mountain Coffee, Inc. Thao would like to invest in one of these companies, but she does not know which one is the better investment.

- **Green Mountain Coffee, Inc.** is a major player in the specialty coffee industry. The Company offers more than 100 coffee products such as single-origins, estates, certified organics, FairTrade, proprietary blends, and flavored coffees that it sells under the Green Mountain Coffee Roasters® brand. Green Mountain's major revenue source is their wholesale operation serving supermarkets, convenience stores, offices, and other retail locations. They also sell via direct mail and online. The Company went public in September, 1993, and is listed on the NASDAQ (stock symbol GMCR).
- **Starbucks Corporation** is the world's #1 specialty coffee retailer. It operates, licenses, and franchises more than 17,000 retail stores in more than

55 countries. The shops offer a variety of coffee drinks, along with food items and other beverages. The outlets also sell whole bean coffee and branded coffee accessories. In addition to its shops, the company sells beans through grocery stores and licenses its brand for other food and beverage products. It also trades on the NASDAQ.

To make sound recommendations to Thao, Blackmore's analysts will examine two key financial documents of the two companies: the income statement and the balance sheet, which were first introduced in Spreadsheet Case 2. From that case, recall the following types of financial statements:

- *Income statements* (also called operating statements) summarize the income, expenses, and profits (or losses) of businesses for a period, usually a year, quarter, or month.

- *Balance sheets* identify the assets, liabilities, and shareholders' equity of a firm at a particular point in time. The difference between assets and liabilities is net worth or equity (literally what the organization is worth net of all other factors).

As you did in Spreadsheet Case 2, you must calculate a number of financial ratios based on the financial statements of these two companies. Before doing this case, review the descriptions and formulas that appear in Spreadsheet Case 2 for the following ratios:

- Current Ratio
- Quick Ratio (or "Acid Test")
- Total Assets Utilization
- Debt Ratio
- Return on Total Assets (ROA)
- Return on Equity (ROE)
- Profit Margin
- Price/Earnings Ratio

Tasks

There are two tasks in this case:

1. Obtain the financial statements of the two companies, Green Mountain Coffee and Starbucks, and import the statements to an Excel spreadsheet. Go

to the Security and Exchange Commission's Web site (www.sec.gov) and obtain the data from each company's latest 10-K filing. Follow the directions for capturing the data at EDGAR and pasting into an Excel spreadsheet given in the Tasks section for Web Case 2.

Copy and paste the income statement and balance sheet, one at a time, for the first company— Green Mountain Coffee, Inc.—onto a blank Excel worksheet. Copy the income statement first, and the consolidated balance sheet second. Place the balance sheet below the income statement in your spreadsheet. Immediately save the worksheet with an appropriate file name (e.g., WebCase4 Green Mountain.xlsx).

Repeat these steps for Starbucks. Create a new spreadsheet file WebCase4 Starbucks.xlsx.

2. Below the bottom of the financial statements, calculate the first seven financial ratios outlined above for each company. Look up the most current price/earnings ratio on the Web for both companies and manually enter it into the spreadsheet.

In a few paragraphs, write an analysis of both companies. Based on the information provided in this case, which firm has the strongest set of ratios? Which would make the better investment? Review the financial statements of both companies for any items that might help explain their financial condition. Include a table of your financial ratios for both companies as supporting evidence.

You may also use financial content Web sites such as finance.yahoo.com, Bigcharts.com, Hoovers.com, Smartmoney.com, etc. to find additional information on these companies. The 10-K statement also contains very insightful sections on firm strategy, operations, and future prospects.

Tutorial for Web Case 4

Web Case 4 requires skills for obtaining financial data from the SEC EDGAR database that are covered in the Tutorial for Web Case 2. The new skill in this case is learning how to read a typical consolidated balance sheet that is a part of the 10-K statement.

Consolidated Balance Sheets

A balance sheet describes the assets and liabilities (debts) of a firm. Because the assets must equal the liabilities, the statement is called a "balance" sheet. Generally, an SEC 10-K balance sheet contains the following types of information:

Summary Balance Sheet Data

Assets

Cash and cash equivalents	Cash or immediately available funds
Marketable securities	Usually stock in other companies
Other assets	Real estate and office equipment
Total assets	

Liabilities

Current liabilities (short term debt)	Payments required in the current year
Long-term debt	Usually long term bonds
Stockholders' equity	Shares issued to stock holders

Along with information on the SEC 10-K income statement, you can calculate the ratios required in this case.

Web Case 5
CommChoice

Problem:	Analyze the communications market
Management skills:	Data analysis
	Developing strategy
Web skills:	Market research

CommChoice is a regional communications company serving eight states. CommChoice provides a number of communications services, the main ones being local and long distance telephone service, cellular phone service, and cable television. The company has known for some time that it has the infrastructure in place to add Internet service to its stable of services. Until now, it has resisted this move due to a saturated market. However, a number of local and regional Internet service providers have gone out of business in the last two years, leaving a gap in the marketplace.

CommChoice's CEO, Myriam Lydell, wants to cautiously approach an entrance into the Internet service market. CommChoice' Marketing Director, Pete Tsang, knows he must consult hard statistics to make the proper recommendations to the CEO.

Tsang's first goal is to determine whether CommChoice should even consider expanding its services in the first place. For this, he intends to research the growth of Internet usage since it became a common tool for both business and home users. He wants to know if Internet usage will continue to increase or if it will plateau in the near future.

Next, Tsang must devise a marketing strategy, assuming that CommChoice will choose to introduce an Internet service brand. He has already given the task some thought, and he has determined that CommChoice should begin by targeting its existing customers. Since CommChoice phone service users and cable subscribers are already familiar with the company, they would likely trust CommChoice as their first Internet service provider or as an alternative to their current provider. Targeting existing customers would initially allow CommChoice to quickly build a customer base for its Internet brand at a lower cost than if the company tried to target the general public. Including all of its services, CommChoice already has a database of 5 million customers. Acquiring a database of new prospect names that large is an expense the company would prefer to avoid at the stage of the venture.

Going further, Tsang would like to determine which segment of CommChoice's existing customer base should be most aggressively targeted with promotional material for a new Internet service. He has already narrowed down the choices to cellular customers and cable subscribers, who are more technically savvy. He has found no data indicating a significant growth in landline telephone use, and people who have only landline telephone service are far less likely than cell phone users to want Internet service. Tsang's approach will be to target the segments of CommChoice's customer base which are showing the most growth in recent years. He believes that if people are already embracing technology products or services, they are more likely to continue spending money on technology.

The result of Tsang's research will be a full-scale report to CEO Lydell that includes an outline, statement of goal, presentation of the facts, and concluding statements. Hard statistics will be introduced in written arguments and illustrated with spreadsheets and charts.

Tasks

There are seven tasks in this case:

1. Go to relevant government Web sites to find statistics on Internet usage. Be certain you can answer these questions: Has the number of Internet users increased consistently over the past few years? Has the number of people using the Internet at work increased during that time? Has the number of people using the Internet at home also increased? What are the statistics regarding "intensity of use" or hours using the Internet?

2. Transfer the statistical data you have found into a spreadsheet file either by copying and pasting it from a Web page or by manually keying it in. Some online resources will also allow you to download data tables directly into an Excel file. If you wish to cut and paste data from online sources into an Excel spreadsheet, consult the instructions in Web Case 2 first.

3. Display the Internet growth data you have found in the form of a chart in the spreadsheet file.

4. Go to relevant government Web sites to find statistics that track the number of cellular phone subscribers and the number of cable television subscribers over the last several years. Be certain you can determine which is the more promising market based on Tsang's criteria.

5. Transfer the subscriber comparison data you have found into a separate worksheet in the same spreadsheet file you used for the Internet growth data. Display the subscriber data in the form of a chart.

6. Search the Web for companies or services that sell mailing lists. Determine what the approximate cost would be to acquire a list of potential customer names equal to the number of customers CommChoice already has (5 million). Decide whether you can use this figure to fortify the position of targeting existing customers first.

7. Write a report for the CEO as described above (include an outline, statement of goal, presentation of facts, including your spreadsheets and charts, and concluding statements). Do not forget to cite your statistical sources.

Tutorial for Web Case 5

A great source for statistics such as those required for this case is the U.S. Census. The Census web site is located at www.census.gov. From the Census home page, you can access the Statistical Abstract of the United States www.census.gov/compendia/statab/. From the Statistical Abstract home page, pay particular attention to the USA Statistics in Brief link in the section titled *Summary Statistics* and the *Browse Sections* section, which provides tables of statistics for major market sectors. Also, the Pew Foundation Internet and American Life Project conduct regular surveys on Internet usage (www.pewinternet.org).

Use of the suggested sources is not mandatory, but they are stable sources that provide accurate, user-friendly data. As a whole, U.S. government sites are very useful for this type of research. Another source you may want to consider is the U.S. Department of Commerce's National Telecommunications & Information Administration report entitled "Falling Through the Net: Defining the Digital Divide." The document and accompanying charts are located at http://www.ntia.doc.gov/report/1999/falling-through-net-defining-digital-divide.

Previous tutorials you may find useful for this case:
- Spreadsheet Case 1
- Spreadsheet Case 5

Web Case 6
Uber Audio Lab

Problem:	Research competing patents
Management skills:	Data analysis
Web skills:	Research

You were introduced to Uber Audio Lab in Database Cases 6 and 10.

Dennis Uber wants to expand Uber Audio Lab to include soundproofing material for music studios. Many of his customers who purchase the custom-built sound systems, the famous Uber Amp valve amplifier, and high performance ribbon speakers want to incorporate this technology into their recording studios, and they need soundproofing material to ensure high quality recorded sound. Soundproofing is integral to a recording studio as it eliminates noise from outside of the studio and makes sounds within the area more true. Dennis has been developing acoustical foam for his own home-based studio and feels he has a product that would work better than similar products currently offered on the market. The soundproof acoustic foam material that Dennis has developed reduces echo and is made of a molded polymer material. Current products on the market are flat or egg-crate-shaped, but Ryan's foam is wavy, looking much like a piece of foam with rounded ridges in it.

Dennis would like to patent his acoustical foam invention, but he needs to make sure that a similar product is not already holding a patent. He must research all of the issued patents for acoustical foam material to assess whether his is unique. Dennis has asked you to develop a database of all the relevant patents so he can easily review them and determine which, if any, compete with his invention.

Tasks

There are 3 tasks in this case:

1. Determine all patents that appear to be relevant to Dennis's search. Go to www.uspto.gov and perform a patent search for acoustical foam or soundproofing foam or similar terms. Search the Abstract portion of the document to determine the patent's relevancy.

2. Once you have determined the relevant patents, create a database that details the patent number, the title of the patent, the inventor(s) name, the date the patent was filed, and a brief description of the patent.

3. Create a lookup form with command buttons so Ryan can easily look up patents by the patent number.

Tutorial for Web Case 6

The United States Patent and Trademark Office (USPTO) has a website that allows visitors to search for issued patents and trademarks. Patents dating back to 1976 can be searched online using the database at the site. Searching the database is relatively easy and uses the skills you learned for performing BOOLEAN searches on search engines. Patent and Trademark searching is found at patft.uspto.gov.

The USPTO site has two methods for searching its database without knowing the document number of the patent: Quick and Advanced. The Quick search allows you to input two terms and choose which field of the patent to search. The Advanced search allows you to make a query of the US Patent Full Text Database using command line search syntax. You are not limited in the number of terms when using the Advanced search, but you must write your query using specific language. The *Help* link on the Advanced search page assists you in writing your query using the correct syntax.

Previous tutorials you may find useful for this case:
- Database Case 1
- Database Case 8

Web Case 7
SeaTrade Consulting

Problem:	Evaluate export markets
Management skills:	Data analysis Developing strategies
Web skills:	Market research

SeaTrade Consulting, located in Portland, Maine, was founded by Matt Jahnke in 1986. Prior to starting the company, Jahnke worked in the fish products industry for many years in locations up and down the Eastern seaboard, including Nova Scotia. He accumulated significant knowledge about the fish products industry, including import and export patterns, and has leveraged this knowledge into a successful consulting business. SeaTrade Consulting advises clients inside and outside the fish products industry about the consumption patterns of countries around the globe and their import/export regulations.

SeaTrade has recently acquired a client, Halifax Fish, that is interested in exporting its frozen tuna to countries outside the United States. Halifax Fish is unsure which countries it should target for their export activities. Likely targets are those countries that already are major importers of tuna, or those whose market has yet to be developed. Halifax Tuna has requested that SeaTrade Consulting provides a detailed analysis of the export volume of the United States of all types of tuna—Bluefin, Skipjack, Bigeye, Albacore, and any other variety available in the data. SeaTrade must analyze the value, and destination of these exports before making its recommendations.

Tasks

There are five tasks in this case:

1. Obtain the data regarding the export of salmon from the USDA's Foreign Agricultural Service's Global Agricultural Trade System (GATS) database at http://www.fas.usda.gov/gats. Use the following criteria to perform your search using the Quick Query search feature:

    - For Product Type, select *Exports*.

- For Product Group, select *Tuna*.
- For Partner, select *World Total*.

Click *Submit*. The search results page will display an advanced search form, and below this, a Data table holding the current search results.

Click the + sign beside *Tuna* in the Product column of the Data Table to view world totals by type of tuna. To find country totals for the various types of frozen tuna (marked *FRZ*), click the + sign beside each relevant World Total in the Partner column.

You can also click the + sign beside *Salmon* (not canned) to view totals for the different types of salmon grouped under this category.

2. Once you have finished displaying the country totals for different varieties of frozen tuna, click *Create CSV spreadsheet file*. When you are prompted, save the file to your computer, and open it with Excel. Once opened, save the spreadsheet in the Excel format as SEATRADE.xlsx.

3. After creating the Excel spreadsheet, open Access and create a new database named *SEATRADE*. Import the data from the various sections of the Excel spreadsheets you created into new tables in this database. Delete all the records that pertain to category totals

4. SeaTrade would like a report that details the export dollar value of each type of tuna. Create a report that outlines the export dollar value of each type of tuna sorted by country with the results in ascending order.

5. Write a report that advises SeaTrade which countries Halifax Fish should target for the export activities. Should it target those countries already receiving exports or those whose trade is still developing and why?

Tutorial for Web Case 7

This case requires you to import data from an Excel spreadsheet to an Access database. Once you have created the Excel spreadsheet and a blank Access database, you can import data into your Access database. You will first need to review the Excel spreadsheet and remove rows of explanatory text and any totals columns, or columns with partial data or calculated data that re not a part of the raw export data.

1. Open the External Data tab on the Ribbon and in the Import & Link group, click the *Excel* button.

2. In the Get External Data dialog box, locate your Excel spreadsheet using the *Browse* button and select *Import the source data into a new table in the current database* option. Click *OK*.

3. The Import Spreadsheet wizard will appear, asking you which worksheets or ranges you would like to import. Choose the worksheet or range you would like to import as a table. Click *Next*.

4. If your spreadsheet has header columns, make sure the *First Row Contains Column Headings* checkbox is checked. If not, uncheck this box. Click *Next*.

5. To create a new table with this data, make sure the *In a New Table* option button is activated and then click *Next*.

6. The next part of the wizard allows you to specify the field names and data types of the fields. Select appropriate names and types for your fields. Make sure *No* is selected for *Indexing the fields* and click *Next*.

7. The wizard now allows you to choose a primary key for your data. You can allow the wizard to select one, you can select it, or you can pick *No Primary Key* and select one later in Design View. Click *Next*.

8. The last part of the wizard asks you the name of your table. If you do not change the default name, it will import with the name you have given the worksheet in Excel. Click *Finish*.

Previous tutorials you may find useful for this case:

- Database Case 1
- Database Case 2
- Database Case 3
- Database Case 6

Web Case 8
Tandem Trading

Problem:	Analyze the historical valuations of currency
Management skills:	Data analysis Developing strategy
Web skills:	Financial research

Tandem Trading is one of the top import/export firms in the Northeast. Run by Erinn Kaehler, its founder, it imports goods from around the world for sale in the United States, and exports products to countries throughout Asia, Central and South America, Europe, and Africa. Tandem's success is built on the good relationships it has with its vendors and suppliers as well as the competitive prices it offers in the marketplace. Tandem is able to offer such competitive prices because he tirelessly monitors currency rates throughout the world, waiting for the most advantageous time to buy or sell goods.

Toby Herschfeld, Tandem's Director of Import, has been approached by Arminda Sosbee of Toowomba Wines, a vintner in Queensland, Australia, to review a flight of Australian wines for possible inclusion in Tandem's sales in the United States. Herschfeld is intrigued by the possibility of adding wines to their list of goods because Tandem does not have a strong presence in the wine arena and Australian wines are becoming very popular in the United States.

Herschfeld must determine the stability of the Australian dollar to the U.S. dollar to evaluate whether Tandem can purchase Young's product at a profitable price. If there are large variations in the rate the currency trades, Tandem can either make or lose a great deal of money on its transactions with Sosbee. On the other hand, if the currency proves to be relatively stable, Tandem can feel fairly confident that their profit margin will remain constant.

Tasks

There are six tasks in this case:

1. Determine the historical exchange rates for the U.S. dollar and the Australian dollar for the two most recent full calendar years.

278   *Solve it!*

2. Transfer the statistical data you have found into a spreadsheet file by either copying and pasting it from a Web page, or keying it in manually. Some online resources will also allow you to download data tables directly into an Excel file. If you wish to cut and paste data from online sources into an Excel spreadsheet, consult the instructions in Web Case 2 first.

3. Display the exchange rate data you have found in the form of a chart in the spreadsheet file.

4. Go to relevant government Web sites to find statistics that track the volume of Australian wine exports to the United States. Herschfeld wants to know how much Australian wine has come into the United States over the past two years.

5. Transfer the import data you have found into a separate worksheet in the same spreadsheet file you used for the currency rate data. Display the import data in the form of a chart.

6. Herschfeld also wants to evaluate the volume of Australian wine exports to the United States to determine the level of competition Tandem would face. Write a report for Herschfeld outlining your recommendation regarding importing Toowomba wine. Your conclusion should factor in the historical stability of the currency and the amount of Australian wine imported into the United States. Do not forget to cite your statistical sources.

Tutorial for Web Case 8

Use of the suggested sources is not mandatory, but they are stable sources that provide accurate user-friendly data. As a whole, U.S. government sites are very useful for this type of research. The tutorial in Web Case 5 introduced you to a great source for statistics: the Census web site located at www.census.gov.

For statistics on import or export activity by commodity (for example, "wine"), go to www.fas.usda.gov/gats/. You will be able to search imports or exports, by FAS groups or 2-, 4-, 6-, or 10-digit "Harmonized Codes" (more digits = more precision). Harmonized Codes are simply commodity codes used mainly in import and export documents, and are used to aggregate trade statistics. FATUS (FAS) Codes are 211 trade codes which aggregate the Harmonized Codes into more general categories.

To find the figures on Australian wine imports into the United States:

- Go to www.fas.usda.gov/gats/default.aspx

- Under Product Type select *Imports - Consumption*.
- In the Product Group list box, select *Wine and Wine Prdcts*
- In the Partner list box, select *Australia*.
- Click *Submit*.

Numerous format options are available, and can best be understood by reading the site information and running test reports.

A comprehensive site for determining exchange rates is www.x-rates.com. There you can find current and historical exchange rates for a wide range of currencies.

Previous tutorials you may find useful for this case:

- Spreadsheet Case 1
- Spreadsheet Case 5

Web Case 9
ThermoTek

Problem:	Analyze the wages in a geographic region
Management skills:	Data analysis
Web skills:	Business research
File:	THERMOTEK_Q.xlsx

Louisa DiSalvo is the Human Resources Director at ThermoTek, a plastics casting company located in Scranton, Pennsylvania. ThermoTek makes a wide range of molded plastic parts, from computer tower cases to interior parts for automobiles, and employs more than 500 people in a wide range of positions. The turnover rate among employees is rather low for the industry, as ThermoTek prides itself on providing a working environment that values its employees and emphasizes longevity. The salary structure starts employees at the mid-range for their position, and then offers wage and salary increases on an annual basis based on job performance.

Each year, DiSalvo is responsible for presenting her recommendations for wage and salary increases to the CEO and CFO. She starts by reviewing the U.S. Department of Labor's Bureau of Labor Statistics report on the National Compensation Survey for ThermoTek's geographic region. This report details the hourly and salaried earnings of over 800 occupations based on the reporting of public and private companies (non-farm positions excluding the Federal government). This report, along with information about the competitors in ThermoTek's market, was used to establish the wage and salary structure for the company. DiSalvo wants to ensure that the company stays within these guidelines when administering its compensation program so that it can continue to remain competitive in the industry and attract qualified applicants.

Managers and supervisors are given a range (in the past three years, it has typically been six to eight percent) that they use to give wage and salary increases to their employees. This range is based on the Consumer Price Index (CPI), the financial health of the company, and information about other companies in their industry regarding their practices in terms of giving annual increases. This range coordinates with the performance review system and ensures that monetary increases are in line with the rating employees receive and are not subjective.

DiSalvo has asked you to assist her in analyzing the annual performance review, and the wage and salary increase period this year. She needs data to support her recommendations to senior management, which you will provide to him by performing the following tasks:

Tasks

There are five tasks in this case:

1. Open THERMOTEK_Q.xlsx. Column two of the spreadsheet shows the average salary for selected occupations in the New York metropolitan area. The third column shows the actual salary paid by ThermoTek for that position. Calculate the difference between the average metro salary and ThermoTek's compensation for each position. Express this as a percentage (either above or below the metro region average).

2. Find the mean hourly wage data for the following positions and include them with those already provided:

3. DiSalvo has decided that the range for increases will be 5% to 7%. She needs to obtain an estimate of the total cost of increases for this evaluation period. Use 6% to estimate what the new hourly wages will be, and then determine the total amount that will be paid in increases. Print these results.

4. DiSalvo would like to see what the total dollar figure would be if increases averaged 7%. Recalculate the increase percentage at 7% and print the results.

5. Find other sources for wage and salary data on the Internet and provide DiSalvo with a report listing those sources.

Position	Current Wage
Shipping/Receiving Clerk	13.90
Assembler	9.05
Order Clerk	19.85

Tutorial for Web Case 9

A great source for data like that required for this case is the U.S. Department of Labor: Bureau of Labor Statistics website (www.bls.gov). This site provides a wide range of information, from the Consumer Price Index to wage and salary data broken down by geographic regions to unemployment data. This data is used by companies to establish wage and salary guidelines, monitor the Consumer Price Index (CPI), and check unemployment rates. The CPI is important because it gives an indication of inflation, which contributes to the Cost of Living Adjustment (COLA) that many companies factor into the raises they give to employees.

Previous tutorials you may find useful for this case:
- Spreadsheet Case 1
- Spreadsheet Case 2